7 RULES OF SELF-RELIANCE

How to Stay Low, Keep Moving, Invest in Yourself and Own Your Future

MAHA ABOUELENEIN

HAY HOUSE

Carlsbad, California • New York City
London • Sydney • New Delhi

Published in the United Kingdom by:
Hay House UK Ltd, 1st Floor, Crawford Corner,
91–93 Baker Street, London W1U 6QQ
Tel: +44 (0)20 3927 7290; www.hayhouse.co.uk

Text © Maha Abouelenein, 2024

Indexer: J S Editorial, LLC
Cover design: Lillian Sotelo
Interior design: Joe Bernier

The moral rights of the authors have been asserted.

All rights reserved. No part of this book may be reproduced by any mechanical, photographic or electronic process, or in the form of a phonographic recording; nor may it be stored in a retrieval system, transmitted or otherwise be copied for public or private use, other than for 'fair use' as brief quotations embodied in articles and reviews, without prior written permission of the publisher.

The information given in this book should not be treated as a substitute for professional medical advice; always consult a medical practitioner. Any use of information in this book is at the reader's discretion and risk. Neither the authors nor the publisher can be held responsible for any loss, claim or damage arising out of the use, or misuse, of the suggestions made, the failure to take medical advice or for any material on third-party websites.

A catalogue record for this book is available from the British Library.

Tradepaper ISBN: 978-1-83782-478-6
E-book ISBN: 978-1-4019-7867-9
Audiobook ISBN: 978-1-4019-7868-6

10 9 8 7 6 5 4 3 2 1

This product uses responsibly sourced papers, including recycled materials and materials from other controlled sources. For more information, see www.hayhouse.co.uk

The authorized representative in the EU for product safety and compliance is Penguin Random House Ireland, Morrison Chambers, 32 Nassau Street, Dublin D02 YH68, Ireland. https://eu-contact.penguin.ie

Printed and bound by CPI Group (UK) Ltd, Croydon CR0 4YY

Praise for 7 Rules of Self-Reliance

Maha Abouelenein's *7 Rules of Self-Reliance is an absolute game changer for anyone hustling to build their dream, scale their business, or simply step up their game. In today's fast-paced world, waiting around for opportunities to come knocking will get you nowhere—Maha gets that. This book doesn't just talk theory; it walks you through the practical, gritty steps you need to invest in yourself and own your future.* 7 Rules of Self-Reliance *is your playbook for becoming unstoppable. Dive in and get ready to do the work!*

— **Gary Vaynerchuk**, 6-time *New York Times* best-selling author and chairman of VaynerX

Maha Abouelenein's *7 Rules of Self-Reliance is a profound exploration into the essence of creating one's destiny with conscious intention and deep self-awareness. Maha skillfully blends practical wisdom with spiritual insight, encouraging readers to harness their inner potential and navigate life's complexities with grace and courage.*

— **Deepak Chopra**, MD, FACP, FRCP and founder of the Chopra Foundation

In 7 Rules of Self-Reliance, *my friend Maha Abouelenein captures the singular spirit required to be a trailblazer in today's rapidly evolving world. Her book serves as a crucial manifesto for anyone looking to step into their power and chart their own course. Maha's approach to self-reliance marries practical wisdom with empowering strategies that resonate deeply—especially among those of us committed to advancing women's leadership. This book contains countless valuable insights that empower women to embrace risk, advocate for themselves, and redefine success on their own terms. This is more than a book; it's a definitive guide for finding self-reliance and making impactful decisions in both life and business.*

— **Shelley Zalis**, CEO and founder of The Female Quotient

The safest bets in life are the ones you place on yourself. And since the calvary is not coming, Maha teaches you how to hack into your own factory settings and master what brings out your best. This highly actionable book is an excuse killer and a dream maker.

— **Matt Higgins**, best-selling author of *Burn the Boats* and chairman of RSE Ventures

7 Rules of Self-Reliance *explores the indispensable need for self-reliance today, offering readers a practical and profound guide to harnessing their greatest asset—themselves.*

— **Cy Wakeman**, *New York Times* best-selling author and founder of Reality-Based Leadership

In a world that's overrun with bad advice, this is a fresh and relevant book that speaks to the huge opportunities looming in our changing world. This book speaks to both entrepreneurs and those aspiring to seize the opportunities that have emerged in today's fast-paced world of business. In this tell-all masterpiece, you will learn the personal and professional moves that helped Maha to be the force that she is today. Nobody teaches it better.

— **Charles Eide**, founder and CEO of EideCom

Maha Abouelenein's 7 Rules of Self-Reliance *is a powerful guide that mirrors the resilience and proactive mindset required in today's ever-evolving global landscape. This book doesn't just offer strategies; it serves as a crucial toolkit for anyone aiming to navigate the complexities of modern life and leadership. Maha's insights are particularly vital for those in dynamic sectors where decisiveness and self-assurance are paramount.*

— **Michael Goltzman**, SVP, Global Policy & Sustainability at The Coca-Cola Company

7 Rules of Self-Reliance *is an inspiring playbook in which Maha delivers a master class in empowerment and personal growth. Her personal stories and actionable insights will resonate deeply with anyone aspiring to lead a life of purpose. As someone who advocates for being authentic and embracing one's unique journey, I found the book refreshing, invigorating, and the perfect source for anyone who has ambition and wants to learn how to master the art of communications from one of the industry's most influential players.*

— **Karen Wazen**, Dubai entrepreneur & founder of Karen Wazen Eyewear

This book doesn't just teach you how to survive in our ever-changing world; it teaches you how to thrive, to make informed decisions, and to take control of your personal and professional destiny. Maha's blend of personal anecdotes with a global perspective makes this read not only engaging but deeply empowering.

— **Kevin McNulty**, president and CMO at Momentum Worldwide

Maha truly embodies the art of self-reliance and has mastered it in such a moving and empowering way that will inspire others to tap into their potential. As a parent of young adults, I am grateful for the opportunity they have to learn from their aunt and create the future they desire and deserve.

— **Amany Abouelenein**, vice president of International Innovation, Technology & Quality at General Mills

It's not often I would describe a book as "mentorship in printed form" but this book fits. For those looking to pivot, launch new businesses, or simply to push your life in an ever-evolving world, Maha gives you a fantastic start to your journey.

— **Jeffrey Nicholson**, CEO and co-founder at Tracer

I dedicate this book to my beloved mom and dad, whose presence is deeply missed but whose guidance is forever present because without them my story would have never been told.

And to Kenzie and Zane, I wrote this for you with hopes of inspiring you to *Stay Low, Keep Moving* throughout your journey.

CONTENTS

Introduction ix

CHAPTER 1   Self-Reliance 1

CHAPTER 2   Rule #1 Stay Low, Keep Moving 29

CHAPTER 3   Rule #2 Be a Value Creator 63

CHAPTER 4   Rule #3 Don't Be a Waiter 115

CHAPTER 5   Rule #4 Unlearn, Relearn, and Invest in Yourself 147

CHAPTER 6   Rule #5 Think of Your Reputation as Currency 177

CHAPTER 7   Rule #6 Be a Long-Term Player 229

CHAPTER 8   Rule #7 Live with No Regrets 259

Final Word 277

Join My Community 290

Index 291

Acknowledgments 297

About the Author 299

INTRODUCTION

People do not decide their futures. They decide their habits and their habits decide their futures.

— F. M. ALEXANDER

One of the most important things I learned from my dad was that your circumstances can dictate how you end up in the world, but you control what you do for yourself. He told me that self-reliance was crucial to succeed and that I had to build myself up as I moved forward in my life. He always said to me, "Put your head down and let your work and reputation speak for itself. Let that be what rises."

Although he shared this advice decades ago, it's more relevant today than ever. The importance of self-reliance is now and it's the future. As the world moves at lightning speed and technology accelerates at full throttle, everything is changing. And when I say everything, I mean everything—from how we approach and think about our businesses and manage our teams, to how we measure ourselves, our happiness, and our mental health.

So much about how we live today requires a new playbook and mindset. The environment we operate in today is complex. With the growing presence of AI, a trend of mass layoffs, and the potential for another pandemic—we can't afford to not be self-reliant. The most powerful tool in the world today is the Internet and because of the Internet, economic opportunity is at the fingertips of anyone willing to take advantage of it. Goldman Sachs estimates the creator economy will reach $480 billion by 2027—these are people creating content using social media and making money just by sharing their expertise or passions online—and that number sits at $250 billion today. In addition, more and more people are starting their own businesses, including the nearly 40 percent of Americans turning to side hustles as a means to boost their income and do something that is personally meaningful to them. The U.S. Census Bureau reported nearly 5.5 million businesses started in 2023, which is the highest year on record.

This is why celebrities and creators are launching their own brands and the market is big enough to take all of them. They have embraced the power of self-reliance—relying on themselves to be brands, to launch brands, and to create their own economic opportunities instead of waiting for a film, TV deal, or brand endorsement to come to them. They know it's about taking matters into your own hands in a big, big way. And you can do this too by learning the rules of self-reliance and putting them to work. Think abundance—there is so much abundance in the market that is available to us to take advantage of. And guess what? The good news is these tools are available for free.

Work-life balance has changed with remote and hybrid working. We're empowered to take more ownership for ourselves today. In fact, we must take more ownership, or we will be left behind. We have the power to create opportunities for ourselves and others. There are people making more money as content creators on the Internet and through social media than people who've had lifelong careers and postgraduate degrees. We're also juggling more in all aspects of life, focusing on our mental and physical health, caregiving, parenting, and living in the age of social media and an accelerating digital landscape,

INTRODUCTION

in a profoundly new way. And these inevitable changes are happening ten times more quickly than at any other period in history. It's a fact that in today's world you need to be nimble and rely on yourself. You need to be prepared. But this doesn't have to be intimidating or scary. Think of self-reliance as making yourself uber "resourceful" and wouldn't you want to have access to tapping into those resources when you need them most!

Hustle culture is out, value culture is in. Everyone is done with being always on and grinding. What we want to do is focus on the quality of life and do work that is of value, that brings value and makes us feel fulfilled. That is where self-reliance comes in as a playbook to go from the live-to-work era to the creating value era by deploying your most valuable asset—you!

Hustle culture promotes being constantly busy as a virtue. The idea is that the more you work and the busier you are, the closer you are to achieving success. Value culture promotes intention as a virtue. The idea is that delivering with intentions based solely on what someone values will not only help you achieve your ultimate goals but will also help you build stronger relationships and connections with others. So often we go into a business relationship focused on our own outcomes—and my idea is to lead by focusing on what they value first.

Both can coexist and both have to do with working hard, but my point is that bringing value to other people is something we need to put on a pedestal. When you create value for other people, you ultimately create value for yourself because you learn immensely from those encounters and experiences.

The tools of self-reliance that are laid out in this book will help you navigate this new era and provide a blueprint for successfully operating in today's environment. This book shows you the power of relying on yourself and removes the pressure of being reliant on others. My friend Brandon Trup said it best, "When you are not reliant on somebody else to say yes to you in order for you to be happy, successful or make money, all pressure is removed and an energy shift takes place and you start to attract opportunities that you want. You will literally be able to pick and choose what you want to do and who you want to do it with." This book takes that statement to heart and shows you how to bring it to life.

7 Rules of Self-Reliance embodies a mix of personal and professional principles based on how we actually live our lives. We do not compartmentalize. *7 Rules of Self Reliance* is for anyone with ambition who is curious about what it takes to elevate themselves and their passions. This book will help entrepreneurs, professionals seeking career advancement, recent graduates, and students, those thinking about a side hustle or second-act career, and anyone inspired to take control of their lives. If you are curious about current events, the Middle East, the internet, pop culture, and newsmakers you will get a front row seat to those experiences and my personal stories. These seven rules will teach you to bring value to how you approach your life. Want to attract new clients? Don't make it about you. Make it about them and how you can contribute fresh and meaningful value to their business. Too intimidated to talk to someone at an event? *7 Rules of Self-Reliance* will give you the tools to walk into any room with confidence and walk out with every contact you want. Debating whether you should quit your job and start your own venture? This book is for you. These are just three examples, and your goals may be different, but the point is this: these rules teach you how to use

INTRODUCTION

your personal strengths to get what you need and want out of life. These seven rules will lead you to self-reliance. And these rules work; I live by them and fail-test them daily. Self-reliance may not be something you're born with, but it is something you certainly can master: these seven rules show you how. I am living proof.

I know this because I definitely wasn't born with the ability to rely on myself. It's a skill you have to learn and a muscle you have to build. I didn't come from privilege. I didn't come from money. I grew up a brown girl in Minnesota and ended up moving to a country I was "from" but where I could barely speak the language, didn't have any friends, and didn't know my extended family who lived there. So I had to learn how to make it and rely on myself in completely new environments. For more than a decade, I had to navigate the lives of two gravely ill parents who were diagnosed with serious neurological diseases, one suffering from Lou Gehrig's disease (ALS) and the other multiple sclerosis (MS). I was their primary caretaker at the same time that I was trying to build a career. I've had a lot of serious challenges on my journey and could regret them, but that idea has never crossed my mind. Those obstacles gave me the character I needed to push through, rely on myself, and do what I didn't know I was capable of achieving. They gave me the tools for self-reliance. Not only did I survive, but I am proud to report that I am thriving.

Let me explain how I define self-reliance and what it means to me. To make it simple: self reliance = self confidence + self worth + believing in yourself + equipping yourself with tools to be your own power. Self reliance is not about going it alone and shutting the world out; in fact, it's the opposite. It's about leveraging the power of yourself and others to own your future. This is not a book preaching independence. This book is a manifesto to upskilling yourself to be valuable to your employer or your own business if you are an entrepreneur.

Think about the struggles in your own life. Didn't some of them become your strengths? Aren't you glad some of them happened to you? That's the inspiration. That's the story. You can create your own opportunities. The playbook to self-reliance doesn't involve luck. And it doesn't need to. For me, the struggles I went through became the catalyst to my success. My career ebbed and flowed from an employee to a female founder of a business. I sat at the crossroads of technology, which later converged with communications, reputation, and media. I have created this career thanks to my identity and continue to do so in a way that is unique. I've been on the forefront of what's now and next in culture, from digital media to gaming and esports. I played an instrumental role in several pivotal moments in the Middle East, including the introduction of the Internet, mobile phones and social media. I joined Google the day the Arab Spring erupted, which meant I had to balance the duties and obligations of my job without compromising my personal security and values. I worked for one of Egypt's most famous billionaires and business tycoons and helped navigate the controversy behind the arrest of Bassem Yousef, known as the Jon Stewart of the Middle East. In 2020, I was nominated as one of the Forbes Power Women of the Middle East." When I moved back to the United States during the pandemic, I had a front row seat working to drive and shape the narratives around the Web3 tech revolution. I have advised heads of state, CEOs, and some of the largest tech companies in the world.

INTRODUCTION

I often find my way into high-profile events and influential rooms, networking with some of the world's most powerful people and brilliant minds—from Michelle Obama and Bono to Bill Gates and Jay-Z. And the only reason I am in those rooms is because I go there authentically seeking to bring value to others. That is the second biggest rule of self-reliance. Be a value creator. Any place I go, I leave with new relationships because I'm genuinely interested and focused on creating them. I am always a long-term player. Never short term. Ever. Whether it's my personal or professional life, I go above and beyond.

The goal of this book is to help you master self-reliance as your superpower. Although the specific details of my story and yours may differ, I want to share my experiences because the underlying themes and feelings are universal. As a result, lessons I've learned and insight I've gained can help you lean in to your strengths and rely on yourself. When you do that, you can achieve anything. Nothing is off limits.

By sharing the stories of others along with my own and detailing the seven key rules, you will understand the importance of self-reliance in your personal and professional life. As a result, you will carve the path you know you are meant to pave. You will no longer wait for opportunities to happen to you; you will create them and do so in ways that are bigger and better than you imagined were possible. If every time I lost a job—and I've lost several—you told me that the next one would be even better, I wouldn't have believed you. Yet that's what happened. Just when I thought my career was over, what came next was bigger and better than what I was upset about losing. Setbacks are par for the course in life, and especially for entrepreneurs. But everything is in our hands to create and solve. You just need to master self-reliance.

So why write a whole book with self-reliance as the center theme? Because I believe it's the single most important virtue that we need to learn that will have the most profound impact on the quality of our lives. When you are self-reliant, you are not let down by the expectations of others. When you are self-reliant, you're driving and in control of your life instead of waiting for others. We spend too much time waiting for validation of others. We spend too much time worrying about the judgment of others. We spend so much time wishing for things vs. taking action that we get paralyzed on how to start, when to start, what others will think. But if we all adopt a mindset that we control our futures and we know what's best for us and rely on ourselves to drive our futures, we become incredibly liberated, empowered, and powerful. And this leads to a great sense of satisfaction, happiness, well being, and balance.

I strongly believe that everybody will need to understand, practice, and master self-reliance—and not just because of AI. Self-reliance is the practice of having the ability to invest in yourself and own your future to achieve your goals. If you don't have the skills you need to stay sharp in an ever-changing world, you will be left behind.

We are no longer competing with people in only our markets. Thanks to virtual working environments, we are competing with talent around the world. And AI is not just coming, it's here. It's eliminating jobs and will create new ones, but don't let yourself get out-talented because you're not putting the effort into yourself.

Self-reliance is about pouring the work into yourself to give you a full deck of cards—these cards are skills,

INTRODUCTION

relationships, and experiences. It's also a mindset—to be a long-term player, to create value for others first, and to be a lifelong learner.

Because everybody has goals, but your goals don't work unless you do. Let's get started!

7 RULES OF SELF-RELIANCE

> self reliance
> = self confidence
> + self worth
> + believing in yourself
> + equipping yourself with tools to be your own power

1
SELF-RELIANCE

Beware of the little expenses.
A small leak will sink a great ship.
— BENJAMIN FRANKLIN

When I moved to Egypt from Minnesota in 1997, I didn't have any friends or a professional network around me. I had to build it all from scratch. This, coupled with the fact that at home I was taking care of my mother, who was fully disabled suffering from MS, meant that I had to work twice as hard to fit in, manage my time and build effective relationships. Then add that my Arabic was really weak and navigating the people, culture and nuances just magnified the learning curve of my new life on a whole new level. I was constantly looking for ways to be a part of the community and I learned about the AmCham (American Chamber of Commerce), which was a terrific way to meet other professionals, engage with the local business community to network and forge friendships. I joined AmCham and signed up to be on the Women in Business Committee, eventually becoming a long-standing active member of the organization for years. I loved being a part of AmCham Egypt.

In 2005, I signed up for a program they offered called the Doorknock Mission to the United States, which takes CEOs from Egypt to Washington D.C. There, you metaphorically knock on the doors of the U.S. administration, congressional members, and think tanks. The goal is to promote business in Egypt and strengthen bilateral ties between the two countries in core areas such as trade, investment, politics, and economic development. Egypt is the largest recipient of USAID (United States Agency for International Development) and has several bilateral agreements that are strategically important. When I heard they were looking for CEOs from Egypt to represent the mission, I signed up. It was something I'd never done before, and I didn't really know what I was getting into. However, getting to go to the White House, roam the halls of Congress and meet Cabinet level officials not only sounded interesting but would also offer me incredible access and learning.

Before we traveled to Washington D.C., the entire delegation of 35 people, which included only 5 women, went to meet with the different ministers in Egypt to get briefed on things like the country's economic, investment and tourism agendas. This way we'd have the latest and greatest information to share at the meetings that AmCham arranged in the United States. We met with Egypt's minister of investment, the minister of tourism, and the minister of international cooperation, among others. As part of the pre-travel briefing, our last stop was to meet the prime minister of Egypt. The prime minister reports to the president of the republic, and convenes and leads a Cabinet of 34 ministers that run the day-to-day operations of the Egyptian government. The Cabinet of Ministers, which the prime minister oversees, is in charge of setting up public policies, preparing draft laws and decrees, supervising the implementation laws, and managing the overall government budget. In other words, he is a big deal. He also happened to be the youngest serving prime minister in Egypt's history; he was progressive and was seen as a reformer.

I had never been to any official government office, and here I was in the office of the prime minister. In the United States we don't have prime ministers, so I had no idea what to expect.

The cars pulled up through a massive iron gate, and we walked up a grand marble staircase adorned with carpet and brass pillars. We entered the grand foyer where other prime ministers, heads of state, congressmen, and dignitaries arrived. There was a large photo of Egyptian President Hosni Mubarak framed in gold and tall gold stands with green marble tops holding ancient Egyptian granite vases. The hallway was lined with security and staffers ushering us in. They led us through the foyer into the conference room where the official cabinet meetings convened. There were 34 large leather yellow chairs, one for each minister—the head chair for the prime minister, and one to his left for the secretary general. There were smaller chairs—around the perimeter of the room for staffers of each minister to sit behind them. The stature and history of the room hits you the minute you walk in. It was grandiose and ornate, from the massive glistening chandeliers hanging from the ceiling to the details of the gold carved into seams of the massive wood conference table. I was in awe.

As I took my seat in one of those big leather chairs, I felt excited and nervous. *How did I get here? This is so cool*—I was going to be in a meeting with the prime minister **and** be briefed by him. I was excited to hear what he would tell us!

In front of each seat at the long table was a microphone, notepad, leather mat with the Egyptian presidential seal and a fancy pen. Sitting there, I felt both important and extremely grateful. When Prime Minister Nazif entered the hall, everybody stood. He asked us to be seated and briefed us in a very formal proceeding. He went over his vision for bilateral trade and investment between the United States and Egypt and his agenda to promote "Egypt is open for business" through economic reforms. He also asked us some questions, but you didn't speak unless you were called. *(I wasn't. Whew!)* The prime minister then stood up and shook everyone's hands and left the room. *(I got to shake his hand!)* After the prime minister left the room, we all sat down again. The secretary general of the Cabinet of Ministers, a role that's a bit similar to the chief of staff for a U.S. president, addressed us. He stood up to command the room and everyone's attention.

"Thank you for coming today. If you will all exit through these doors, security will lead the way to retrieve your phones and head to your cars. Everyone is free to go except for Maha Abouelenein. We need you to stay. Please go sit in the salon." I didn't even know the secretary-general and now he was saying my name. *Am I in trouble?* I thought, my heart racing. *Why is the secretary general telling me to stay here? This can't be good.* And I wasn't the only one who was concerned.

"Why do you have to stay behind? What did you do?" some of the others asked me. On top of this, my Arabic was not great. To say I was freaking out is an understatement. I watched everyone else in the delegation gather their belongings and leave one by one until I was left alone, and the secretary general walked over to me. My stomach started to turn, and my heart started racing. *Who am I going*

SELF-RELIANCE

to call for help if it's something bad? Would I be able to think on my feet and problem solve? I am just a member of a professional business network; what could they want with me anyways? I don't get sweaty palms, but suddenly I was feeling very anxious and I couldn't think straight. I took deep breaths and waited minutes, which felt like hours. And then I finally asked a question:

"How can I help?"

"The prime minister is going to Washington, D.C., and it's the first time that they're sending a prime minister, not the president," he said. "We understand that you've worked with Washington, you have a lot of experience, and you're American, so we'd like you to help him prepare for his trip." They knew I had done various consulting projects for the U.S. under secretary of state for public diplomacy and public affairs, and I knew my way around Washington generally.

"Of course. That sounds great." At least that's what I said; I was really thinking, *Why me? The ministry of foreign affairs is better equipped, no? And they have a whole embassy in Washington D.C.!* I felt that I didn't have what it took to do this for good reason; I never did it before! *What makes them think I am qualified to do this?* was playing on repeat in my head. *What if I fail? What if they don't like my work?* All I kept thinking was how to not get banned and to make sure I didn't mess up. I asked myself, *Would I get kicked out of the country? Will they take my passport?* I obsessively started to think of all the ways this could go sideways if I wasn't able to deliver. *Oh boy, Maha, what did you get yourself into. There is nobody who can get through this but you.* This was a real self-reliance moment.

"Come with me," said the secretary general. Then we walked into a conference room attached to his office, where the table was covered with binders. "These will help you," he said. Since the trip was less than a month away, I knew I had to get to work immediately.

"Great. I'll take these home," I said. I honestly had no idea what I was supposed to do and how I was going to do it. I was just trying to buy time so I could go home, study alone, and regroup. I had to gather my nerves off the floor. He shook his head.

"These are classified government documents. They can't leave this room," he said. "You need to work here." My heart sank. I was hoping I could just get out of there and regroup at home and burn the midnight oil without them seeing me sweat.

Although I had my own company to run, I returned every day that week, sat in the conference room by myself, and went through the papers. I put together a briefing document that included the who's who in Washington, some helpful lingo, and places the prime minister should speak, among other ideas. They also asked me to write the speech the prime minister would deliver in Washington.

You know that feeling when you decide you're going to clean out your closet? You start with a fervor and excitement, and then you can't see the end of the tunnel and want to stop because the piles are too big and you undid too much to put it back together. When they said write a speech for a prime minister I was not only immediately transported to that pile in the closet mid-project, I felt like I was buried under it and then asked to look and sound smart. I had to parse through papers, learn the back history and context, and create a well-crafted narrative that could capture, move, and influence an audience.

It was not lost on me that I'd never written a speech for a head of government and I don't write about public policy. Even more challenging, I had seen the prime minister from a

SELF-RELIANCE

distance but had barely spoken to him. Shaking his hand and saying "Hello, Your Excellency" when he was rounding the room didn't actually count. I didn't know his tone, tenor, language and style. Again, my first thought was, *Don't they have people who can do this better than me?* Sure, I had a moment of doubt about taking on something I'd never done before. But I still said yes. I figured if they thought I was capable, then why would I think I was *not* capable? I had to step up and own it. I spent a lot of time reading through those binders and trying to find words to put on a blank page. I admit that I was stumped. Then I had one breakthrough idea. It was the only thing I could come up with. And it saved me.

What would I want to hear if I was sitting in the audience?

As I put myself in the shoes of someone in the audience, the words started to flow. This was a big test for me, but I relied on my self-confidence to get me through. I kept saying to myself *If not me, then who?* to reassure myself.

The answer was me. I could do it.

The shift of visualizing myself in the audience was the unlock I didn't know I needed, and I want this idea to help you. When you think in terms of your audience instead of yourself, you are able to get out of your own way. You can also use this technique to remove your own mental roadblocks.

The speech was such a success that the secretary general called me from Washington.

"You did such a good job," he said. "So good that you need to write the prime minister's speech at the closing of the World Economic Forum in Jordan. That's when he'll announce that the Regional World Economic Forum meeting will be held in Sharm El-Sheikh, Egypt, next year." The World Economic Forum is a global meeting that takes place in Davos every year where world leaders and the private sector convene to address key global and regional challenges.

"Oh, okay, I'm actually traveling to the forum tomorrow," I said.

"Great. You need to meet the prime minister when he arrives and work on his speech."

All of a sudden it went from me going as a guest to attend a conference and network to going there to work. This meant I had to pay attention to things that would be relevant for his closing remarks, and I now had to turn around a speech on a dime. That was a new kind of pressure. Part of me was very happy and relieved that the Washington speech was a success because I was proud of what I overcame to deliver that speech. But could I do it again? I had more confidence this time so I was going to rely on that to carry me forward.

The next day, I flew to Jordan and went to the first two days of the event on my own. Then I got a message that I was to meet with the prime minister at two o'clock at the Four Seasons on the third and final day. When I got there, I was amazed to see what happens when a foreign official travels. Basically, they take over a whole floor or wing of a hotel and set up their own remote operations. In one hotel room, they had security people; a second hotel room had rows of TVs, printers, and computers; and a third hotel room was turned into a living room, which is where I waited.

After an hour, I was told the prime minister had arrived. (This was actually obvious without anyone saying a word because the change in energy and frenzy of activity made it clear he'd entered the building.) When the prime minister walked into the room, he came right over to me. He's tall—NBA player tall—so he towered over me. This,

SELF-RELIANCE

combined with the fact that he was a head of government, was intimidating. *I got lucky when I wrote the first speech for him,* I thought. *If I mess this up it could be bad.*

"So you're the person who's been writing my speeches," he said after glancing at my name tag and looking me up and down. It was clear that he wasn't expecting me to be so young. "You did a good job."

"Thank you."

"And this is the next speech you wrote for me?" he asked, waving a stack of papers.

"Yes."

"Let's go over it," he said. Then he just sat down next to me on the couch, telling me what he liked and didn't like.

"I want this in ten minutes," he said when we were done. Ten minutes? Sweating, I ran to my hotel room, which was on the other side of the resort, opened my laptop to make all the changes, and raced back to hand the new speech to the prime minister's staff on a jump drive for them to print and give to him. Two hours later, he went on stage and recited the words we had crafted together.

I was really proud of myself. That's two speeches I nailed, and I felt like I had won back-to-back championships. I felt bolstered and validated. I guess I am a speechwriter now! But here is another lesson. When you need to push beyond your perceived limits, you can look inward to find the answers. You'll find skills, strengths, and abilities you didn't know you even had. Imagine what you could uncover or discover if you bet on yourself and say yes to something you've never done before. I could have said no and insisted this wasn't for me. But instead, I just stayed low and kept moving. The answers presented themselves as my experience unfolded. Yes, I worked hard and applied myself, but I also trusted myself to find a solution. I practiced self-reliance, and it worked.

Although I was running my own company, after that trip I became a part of the prime minister's team and official delegation as a contractor, accompanying them on state visits as his international communications advisor. I was the only external consultant traveling with this head of government—the rest of the people worked for the government—so it gave me a really unique perspective. I learned all about protocol and what goes on behind the scenes between governments. It was fascinating and educational, and I had a front row seat to an incredible experience.

If you've ever watched *The West Wing*, the hit TV show starring Rob Lowe and Martin Sheen that takes place at the White House, or *Designated Survivor,* where Kiefer Sutherland becomes president after those in line before him are killed, you get a behind-the-scenes look at what happens in the hallways and boardrooms in government. I didn't realize how close those shows were to reality until I got my own sneak peek. There are staffers, security details, schedulers, and press teams that make things work and keep things moving round the clock. Each head of state has an "advance team," which is in charge of going to a location in advance of the principal (the head of state) to painstakingly plan and think through every detail so when the VIP arrives, it's all in place and runs smoothly. Where do cars pull up? Which door do we enter? Where is the exit and backstage? Where are the bathrooms and where can you set up a command center for on-site operations? Advance teams work on everything from emergency situations and evacuation procedures to who stands where in a receiving line and who sits where at a state dinner. (FYI: The guest always sits to the left of the host.)

SELF-RELIANCE

My tenure consulting for the Egyptian government—which you can see was something I just fell into—ended up being an extraordinary experience and a true privilege. I built so many groundbreaking firsts for them and myself. I never thought I would propose ideas that the Egyptian government would end up accepting and implementing. All I did was take pages out of the U.S. playbook and see if they would float. Most of them did and for that I am really proud.

My first suggestion was to create a government website for the prime minister's office where they could publish the minutes of the Cabinet meetings, cover news and events (complete with videos and photos), and demonstrate greater transparency in sharing policies and progress for the citizens of Egypt. Next, I suggested they institute having spokespeople across every single ministry and encouraged them to host and broadcast daily press briefings similar to those done by the U.S. State Department and White House. This proactive communication strategy would build trust with the public and raise awareness. They loved the idea and, as a result, hired and trained spokespeople at every ministry and created a briefing room in every office. I was floored that this was actually in motion. WOW. (I'm a news junkie and when I moved to Egypt, I was glued to MSNBC every day to see the press briefings live from Washington. Clearly, all that TV watching paid off.) Although I thought I was pushing boundaries, the Egyptian government was open to all of my suggestions, many of which they still implement today. And this all started by instinct: my idea to put myself in the consumer's shoes.

This story is a great example of self-reliance. I built a new spoke in my wheelhouse—a spoke that I didn't even know existed, that I didn't even know I was capable of, and that bolstered my sense of self-reliance and confidence. It also highlights something I'll talk about later (Rule #2) which is that by creating value for others, I actually created value for myself. The reason I share this story is that this scenario is something so many of you will face, personally and professionally. This is especially the case for entrepreneurs: you will be asked to do something you think you don't know how to do and need to find the answers. And guess what? When your back is up against the wall, you will find a way. That is if you practice self-reliance.

> **Self-reliance means not waiting for others to give you permission.**

What I Mean When I Say Self-Reliance

The bottom line is this: Entrepreneurs who aren't self-reliant are more likely to fail. They may not be able to make the tough decisions, solve problems, or take risks that are necessary to succeed. So what do I mean when I say "self-reliance"? First, let me tell you what I don't mean. Self-reliance is not about going it alone. A lot of people think, "If I'm self-reliant, I don't need anybody." But that's not what I mean. The difference is knowing when you need help and where to get it. What are you lacking? How and when can you leverage input, knowledge, and resources? Self-reliance is not about independence, individualism, or isolation. And it's certainly not about being selfish or arrogant. It isn't about adulting, either. Adulting is having the skills to live a grown-up life and taking responsibility for yourself.

SELF-RELIANCE

To me, self-reliance is a mindset where you first look inward to find answers and then go outward to get help, seek support, or build on your ideas. It's about upskilling yourself and being resourceful. And they go hand in hand—to be resourceful you must have skills and be valuable to others. It ultimately means you need to dig deep to use your personal strengths to create the life you want. When you're self-reliant, you don't wait for someone else to save or prepare you. It's motivating and empowering because you control your destiny. And once you know what you're capable of, you think bigger and bolder. Often, we expect others to remove roadblocks and solve problems for us; we expect them to support us when in fact we can support ourselves.

When I was hired to lead the communications department at Google in the Middle East, nobody handed me a blueprint. Initially I thought, *You're the employer. You're supposed to tell me what to do and how my career should look.* But working at Google was the ultimate masterclass in expecting you to step up. Nobody hands it to you. Just like they do with all their employees, they said, "That's not how it works here. We give you tools, resources, empowerment, and OKRs (objectives and key results), but you drive your career. You tell us what you want and how you want to spend your time." Googlers are expected to ask for lateral moves, promotions, and more responsibility and to initiate projects or campaigns they want to be a part of. I had to reach out to schedule one-on-one meetings with other people to learn about their jobs. Also, Google has a policy called 20 percent time where you can spend 20 percent of your time there working on something you're passionate about. They want employees to tell them who they are and what they want. I've adopted something similar in my own business. When we talk about setting their priorities, I tell my employees, "You drive your career and your day-to-day work based on what our big goals are. You are accountable for your time and your results. You are empowered to set your priorities and share with your manager for input and support to help you prioritize."

Having the confidence to rely on yourself to figure things out is a crucial part of self-reliance. When I first started my own business, I was asked to help train public affairs officers (PAOs) for U.S. embassies across the Middle East on modern communication tools. PAOs are the PR officials that every foreign embassy puts in place to handle communications and public affairs. One night I was at dinner with a really good friend. After explaining the project, I said, "I just don't know if I can do it." She looked at me quizzically.

"Go read your CV," she said. "You need to remember who you are and what you've done."

Go read your CV.

It was a simple piece of advice, but it was filled with insight. Many of us spend a lot of time thinking about what we haven't done and what we haven't achieved. And who can blame us with social media making us play the comparison game 24/7? But you're capable of doing many, many things. You just haven't been asked to do them yet. This is why it's so important to know your worth. Remind yourself that you are educated, can learn new skills, and can offer fresh insight and a unique perspective. Start focusing on what you have done! Now more than ever, we see the value of knowing more than one thing or doing more than one thing—it makes us valuable to others. Have multiple skills and interests gives you a competitive advantage too.

Last year, I was approached to lead the communications for a newly created event taking place at the annual Climate Change Conference (COP28) in Dubai hosted by the United Nations. The event was a Business and Philanthropy Climate Forum on the sidelines of COP28 designed to engage global CEOs, business leaders, and some of the biggest philanthropists on the planet. While I am generally aware of key issues facing the climate, it's not an industry I have ever worked in before. I have worked in consumer products, entertainment, tech, sports, food, and the automotive industries but never climate change. So when I was approached, I wondered whether this was something I could do. I wasn't sure but I approached it like I do most things; I seek to learn more and gain a better understanding. I trusted my ability to study and research to learn more. In the end, I leaned into it, wrote a proposal, and sent it to the potential client and he approved it.

This was a lesson I shared with my team. Someone else may know more than you, but that just means you're going to have to work harder—at least twice as hard—and focus to put yourself in a position to win. I put in the work to uncover another important finding: what don't I know. Once I understood that, I knew how to assemble a team around me to fill the gaps and deliver the work. Asking for help is not a sign of weakness; in fact, it's a sign of strength. I reminded myself that they came to me for a reason. It wasn't because I was a climate expert; it was because I was a communications expert. You also must have self-awareness to understand your intentions. My intentions were to serve the mission, not come off as a climate guru.

How are you using self-awareness to understand your intentions? Think about it. What are some of the things you want to do or achieve? What is the gap between what you want to do and what you are capable of doing? And are you willing to close the difference? Understanding your intentions will help you figure out what you need to rely on yourself for. Let me repeat that because it's that important: if you understand your intentions, you will know what you need to rely on yourself for. It helps you set goals.

Personally, I love challenging projects like the COP28. I wanted to write a book. I wanted to start my own company. Other people may want more independence, to manage a team, or to have more flexibility in their daily schedules. Understanding your intentions also helps you figure out what it's going to take to achieve those goals. Why? Because you are the driver and implementer.

You are the only one who can get things done for you. For example, if I set a goal to lose weight, I can't rely on anybody else to go to the gym and eat healthy foods. In order to achieve that goal, I have to rely on myself to move more, focus on nutrition, reduce stress and improve my sleep. This involves respecting yourself and keeping promises to yourself. If I'm trying to reduce stress, it's important for me to have a morning routine that includes meditating, journaling, and writing down what I'm grateful for. But this is easier said than done and requires that I keep that promise to myself. After all, no one is going to say, "Did you write in your gratitude journal today? Did you meditate?" As an entrepreneur, I've also made promises to myself that I won't work to promote specific industries like tobacco or alcohol. I also seek to support independent, small businesses as my suppliers and vendors. That's self-reliance. It's respecting what I care about and not compromising my values or needs.

SELF-RELIANCE

That said, although we can have goals and a plan to achieve them, the definition of self-reliance also needs to include the ability to adapt, evolve and build the resilience muscle. Five years ago, we could never have imagined what happened during the pandemic, being on lockdown and not being able to get our hair cut or go to the grocery store. We couldn't imagine holding meetings from home on our computer screens. But we survived. We learned to do things that seemed hard at the time, but we invested in ourselves. We evolved with time. In fact, we got better. It's like lifting weights. It doesn't get easier to lift those weights, but you get stronger. Even small things like learning how to change a tire or how to cook a meal for somebody is empowering. It seems so overwhelming before you do it, but the confidence that comes once you master it is unparalleled. And there is a snowball effect. Conquering one goal of self-reliance makes you feel better about yourself so then you master another and then another.

The more you do this, the more you get rid of the fear of failure that so many of us live with. For example, a lot of people want the freedom of being an entrepreneur and the ability to control what they do with their days. However, the number one reason why they don't start businesses is they are afraid to fail. They want the security of a regular paycheck and benefits because that feels safer than relying on themselves—even though they hate their day jobs. But if you trust yourself to create value for other people and understand your relationship with failure, you can take time to learn things.

We don't want to fail because we think that we don't have time to recover, to lose money, to embarrass ourselves in front of people. But you do have time to figure things out. In fact, you don't have time not to. When a friend of mine said she didn't have time to meditate, her meditation teacher told her that if you meditate—even for five or ten minutes—it actually opens up more time in your day because you're calmer and can think more clearly. As a result, you're more productive and creative, so the benefits of that five or ten minutes actually multiplies.

Years ago, we used to think that we should sleep less and work more. In the 1990s it was almost a badge of honor to talk about how little you slept. Executives and politicians bragged about getting just three or four hours of shut eye. But now there's a lot of science to say that this can be detrimental to our productivity, focus, brain power, and health. Studies have found that sleep deprivation can contribute to cardiovascular disease, obesity, poor mental health, dementia, and Alzheimer's, among other conditions. In fact, Margaret Thatcher, who had dementia, and Ronald Reagan, who had Alzheimer's disease, both boasted about how little sleep they got. Taking the time to snooze means the hours you're awake are so much more meaningful and fruitful.

So now that you know why self-reliance is so important, this book will show you how to master it.

Mastering self-reliance is related to two other important concepts: your self-confidence and self-worth. If you are self-confident and have a strong sense of self-worth, being self-reliant becomes easier to master and easier to practice. Because if we believe in ourselves and feel worthy, we trust ourselves more and that builds confidence.

If we are waiting for other people to validate us and accept us, we are giving our power, our futures, and our happiness to others. When we decide that we don't need to rely on others for anything we need, the pressure is automatically removed; and when the pressure is gone, you start to see opportunities everywhere and they have the chance to come in.

Modern life and social media have affected our ability, or lack thereof, to genuinely believe in ourselves. We live in a world where everyone is comparing themselves to others—even though everyone is on a different journey and path. Modern life is fast-paced and sometimes seems unrelenting in how much effort is required just to stay ahead.

This is why I am focusing on the concept of self-reliance. Slow down, build your skills, invest in yourself, and work on what you value most—not what others value. By leveraging your self-confidence, truly believing in yourself, and engaging in positive self-talk instead of negative self-talk, you will recognize your worth and the value you bring to others. This will help you trust and rely on yourself more.

How can you expect someone else to believe in you if you don't believe in yourself? I genuinely believe it's that simple. We often wait for permission from others when, in fact, it's already within us.

Five Characteristics That Are Inherent in Self-Reliance

I believe there are five major characteristics that define the backbone of self-reliant entrepreneurs.

1. Initiative and innovation. Entrepreneurs need to take the initiative to turn their ideas into reality. Being self-reliant enables you to identify opportunities, create solutions, and innovate without waiting for external validation or guidance. So much of how we operate stems from waiting for others to validate us or fearing judgment. When the going gets tough, a self-reliant entrepreneur thinks through alternative game plans. Sometimes we are forced to take initiatives to keep a business alive or moving.

With my own company, I discovered that our P&L wasn't healthy enough. It was time to tighten our belts.

First, I cut costs such as all non-billable travel and any expenses that tend to add up, like client dinners and subscriptions. Next, it was time to innovate. How could I boost revenue without increasing our prices, charging our existing clients more, or adding staff to our overhead and payroll? This is when I thought about how much my clients learn from my workshops. I love teaching my masterclasses on how to build your personal brand and how to communicate with confidence when speaking to the media. Some of the best feedback I've gotten is that my teaching style makes these concepts easy to understand and approachable. Why not offer these workshops to the public instead of just my clients? I could teach them online using existing materials. This meant no extra cost for me but big value for those who take them. So I spent a month tailoring my materials to this new audience, shooting additional videos, updating my website and promoting this offering on my social media. Once the courses went live—121 sessions over Zoom—they started to generate a fresh and steady stream of revenue each month. Finding a way to take initiative and innovate is a core self-reliant behavior.

2. Adaptability and agility. Taking initiative and innovating goes hand in hand with another key quality of self-reliant entrepreneurs: adaptability and agility. As an entrepreneur, challenges come your way and you have to rely on yourself to quickly figure out how to adapt, adjust and pivot.

A few years ago, we had a client who wasn't forthcoming when briefing us about their business. It was like pulling teeth to get the information that was critical to our storytelling. After all, how could we help them create a strategy to communicate better without this unique insight? This had never happened before, so my frustrated team and I brainstormed how we could get the data we required when they weren't being helpful. First, we had to make this a low-lift task for the client. Second, we had to adapt to their style. We created a questionnaire that they could share with the partners we needed to collect information from. All they had to do was pass it along. Not only did we get exactly what we needed, but we also received it from all the groups in the same format, which made our job easier. An adaptable and agile entrepreneur relies on data and insights to guide their decisions.

  3. Decision making. Owning your own business means you are constantly making decisions that impact the trajectory of your company, from hiring and people operations to supply chain and business-to-business relationships. Often leaders have to make high-stakes decisions that ultimately drive the strategic and financial direction of their success. Sometimes there is no time to consult anyone or get more information, so you need to make the tough calls. This is when it's a must to trust your instincts and listen to your gut—two things that take courage.

  The hardest decision I face is whether I should bring on new talent when I'm in the process of pitching new business. It's a chicken or egg dilemma that many entrepreneurs deal with. Should you hire people and have them sit on your payroll before you have the business to cover their costs? Or do you get the new business first and then add talent to your team? The problem with the latter is timing. What if I win an account and the client wants me to start ASAP but I don't have the right team in place? Because the recruiting process takes a long time, I am always looking for and talking to talent. That way, I know what skills are in the market that can add value to my needs and those of my clients. In the event that I win a piece of business, I am in a better position to move quickly, offer them a job, and onboard them. Being self-reliant allows entrepreneurs to trust their decisions based on their own judgment, instincts, and vision for their company.

4. **Leadership**. The entrepreneurial journey is often described as a roller coaster thanks to its ups and downs, twists and turns. It requires leadership sprinkled with grit and resilience because as a business owner you wear many hats. Entrepreneurs often lead small teams and manage everything from people to resources all while dealing with setbacks and challenges.

For example, I am the head of HR, the head of finance, the head of business development and the head of content for my brand. I also lead and manage my team and clients. I'll never forget the first day of work when I started my company in Cairo.

I was leading a company, and I had no idea how to do it. Was this imposter syndrome? Yes, but back in 2004 that wasn't even a mainstream term. I knew how to do communications, write strategies, and give counsel, but running a business was a whole different game that included managing people, finances, legal, administrative, tax reporting, labor laws! I didn't know what I didn't know until I was in the throes of it.

I sat at my desk for the first time and opened my laptop while my team worked outside my office. This overwhelming feeling rushed over me: I was the boss and they were going to come in, ask me questions and expect me to know the answers. I remember going to ask my boss questions when I needed help. Now I was the boss, and they were going to be coming in here to ask me questions. *What if I don't know the answers?* I was nervous. But it turned out that I actually knew the answers. And when I didn't, we solved them together through collaboration.

When you work across the business like this, self-reliance will give you confidence in your abilities; and this is essential for gaining the trust of clients, stakeholders, investors, partners, and your team. It's also crucial when you have to make tough calls internally, provide feedback to your team, inspire your employees and foster a proactive, problem-solving culture. The confidence that comes from self-reliance also helps you hire the right people. Over time, it became clear to me that once you find the right person, the winning formula centers around training and trust. Training is essential to get them to understand the rhythm of your business and excel on their own. Then you must trust them to find their way, bring their own experience, and shine. In other words, you are teaching them to be self-reliant, too.

5. Growth mindset. Lastly, it's crucial in today's world to continuously "sharpen your saw." Successful entrepreneurs embrace a growth mindset and constantly seek ways to learn and improve. They know that educating themselves is one of the best investments they can make. Self-reliance encourages them to take ownership of this learning and development and have an open mind about what they don't know, all of which drives long-term growth. As a big believer in lifelong learning, I am always assessing my progress and self-reflecting. For me, that is the key to growth. I like to celebrate wins, take note of where I've improved my ability to be self-reliant, and identify areas that still need improvement.

For example, I flew to London to take a course designed for Executives already in the workforce called "Finance for Non-Finance executives" that was offered at the London Business School. Why? Because I will celebrate 20 years of having my own company and I still don't feel I am financially literate. I want to be better at it and have more confidence with numbers. Nobody is going to teach me, and I don't have the patience to sit and watch YouTube videos. I need focused and applied learning. So, back to school I went! Be curious and open to learning new things. Are you willing to acquire new knowledge to keep you prepared for different situations? Having a growth mindset will get you there.

Cheat Sheet

Five characteristics that are inherent in self-reliance:

- Initiative and innovation
- Adaptability and agility
- Decision making
- Leadership
- Growth mindset

What Is Self-Reliance?

- Self reliance = self confidence + self worth + believing in yourself + equipping yourself with tools to be your own power
- It's about being resourceful
- Not about going it alone and shutting the world out; in fact, it's the opposite. It's about leveraging the power of yourself and others to own your future
- The act of not waiting for external validation to green light what's best for you; trusting yourself to know what's best and right for you
- A mindset where you first look inward to find answers and then go outward to get help and seek support
- Having the self-awareness to be honest about what you can and can't do or where you can and can't grow
- Digging in deep to use your personal strengths to create the life you want
- Not waiting for someone else to save or prepare you; you control your destiny
- Having the self-confidence to rely on yourself to figure things out
- Knowing your worth
- Trusting yourself to create value for others
- Understanding your intentions and setting goals to achieve them
- Respecting yourself and keeping promises to yourself
- Having the ability to adapt, evolve and build the resilience muscle
- Understanding your relationship with failure

What Self-Reliance Is Not

- Going it alone
- Independence, individualism or isolation
- Being selfish or arrogant
- Adulting

Reflection Exercises

1 Focus on learning one thing that you didn't know yesterday. This can be something simple like reading five articles about AI or learning to use a new app. Why not google the information about Gen Alpha and Gen Beta to learn what they are all about? Or take the first step to learn a new skill by researching classes on that topic.

2 Set up a meeting with someone and ask them how they rely on themselves. You will be surprised at what you can learn from others.

3 Ask yourself what your barriers are to self-reliance. What's missing? Is it knowledge? Time? Resources? Is it that you don't trust yourself? Are you afraid of the consequences? Are you unsure where to go to get the answers?

> Good things come over time by making small steps of progress and doing them consistently.

RULE # 1
STAY LOW,
KEEP MOVING

> *Success is often achieved by those who don't know that failure is inevitable.*
>
> — COCO CHANEL

I first heard the expression "Stay low, keep moving" from Mark Driscoll. I met Mark when I worked in sports marketing at General Mills and we hired his company, Momentum, to activate our engagement in the National Association for Stock Car Auto Racing (NASCAR). "Stay low, keep moving" is a term that I love and use to this day, but I didn't look up its meaning until I came to write this book. That's when I found a blog post where Mark wrote that he learned this expression from a friend who'd fought in the Vietnam War. It turns out that "stay low, keep moving" was used to remind soldiers to physically get down on the ground and army crawl their bodies forward, presumably so they wouldn't get shot by the enemy. They meant it literally, but I took it to be a metaphor for life. It became my mantra and guiding compass. It's how I signed e-mails to my team when I started my PR firm in Cairo in 2004.

The point is that we focus on what's in front of us and continue to move forward, despite the obstacles and roadblocks that come our way. That determination and focus is how we get through and succeed. I've stayed low and kept moving my whole life and that has helped me master self-reliance. It is the first rule because understanding it is the necessary foundation for the other six rules.

Later in this book, we will discuss the importance of building your personal brand; it's one of the core tenants of being self-reliant. Owning your narrative and how you show up in the world represents your biggest opportunity and asset enabling you to rely on yourself to create the life you want. So you may ask, "If I stay low, isn't that the opposite of building my personal brand and putting myself out there?" The answer is no. Staying low doesn't mean be low key. It means put in the effort, put your head down and apply yourself, do the hard work, and build so that your personal brand is strong, valuable, and meaningful.

Be the Office Manager

My dad was also a big proponent of "stay low, keep moving," and although he never said those exact words, his advice to do so changed the trajectory of my life.

In 1997, he was the dean of the business school at Mankato State University when he got a job offer to work for the emir of Sharjah to build the college of business at the American University of Sharjah in the United Arab Emirates. At this point, my parents had been living in the United States for 34 years. They'd always planned to go home to

RULE #1 STAY LOW, KEEP MOVING

Egypt, so this was an opportunity my dad couldn't pass up. But it was a big deal because it meant our tight-knit family of four—my mom, dad, sister, and me—was separating. My older sister, Amany, who was married and settled, would stay in Minnesota. My dad would go to the UAE for his new job, my mom and I would move to Cairo, which is where they wanted to eventually settle, and my dad would come visit us one weekend a month and on holidays. My mom had been living with MS for 13 years and at this point it had progressed to where she was completely disabled, unable to walk or speak. I had been her primary caretaker since I was 14 years old, so it was important that I go with them, and it was an obvious decision because I was single with no strings attached. At 27 years old, an age when a lot of people have already moved out of their parents' homes and are free to focus on themselves, I did the opposite. I went all in, I not only moved with them from the U.S. to Egypt, but I also moved *in* with them.

Although I saw this as my duty to parents who had given me an incredible childhood and done so much for me, it was still a struggle. I wasn't afraid of what I was going to; I was afraid of what I was leaving behind: my childhood and comfort zone. Everything I knew would change. I'd lived in America my entire life while Egypt was a place I'd only gone for holidays, and I had no connection to it. I also had no network, community, or support there. Typically, you have friends from grade school, high school, college, and the professional world, which is what I had in Minnesota in spades. In Egypt, I had none of those circles around me. The only people I knew were my cousins and the children of my dad's college friends who had moved back to Egypt after they graduated from the University of Michigan in Ann Arbor. But these were mere acquaintances, not people I called friends or found comfort in. To say I was walking into what seemed like a no-win situation is an understatement. To make matters worse, I also didn't have a job. At General Mills, I'd been working on engaging projects like the Olympics, NASCAR and the U.S. Tennis Association for of-the-moment brands like Wheaties, Yoplait, Betty Crocker and Pop Secret. But what would I do in Cairo? Would I even be able to get a job since I didn't speak the language? My Arabic was broken at best with a heavy American accent.

At the time, Americans living in Egypt either worked for global multinational companies that had offices in Egypt like Coca-Cola, Procter & Gamble or Unilever or one of the big family business conglomerates (and there were three of them): the Sewedy family, the Mansour family, and the Sawiris family. My dad did consulting work with the uncle of the Sawiris family and suggested I meet with the three brothers who ran the business. The Sawiris family is a dynasty of business tycoons in the Middle East. Their family who are valued at $11 billion, has been sitting at the top of the Forbes billionaires list for years. The first brother, Nassef Sawiris, was sharp, intimidating, and worked in construction, an industry I knew nothing about. The second brother, Samih Sawiris, had a consumer products company, worked in the tourism industry and owned a beautiful resort on the Red Sea. I liked him, and the fact that his business was consumer focused was right up my alley. We really hit it off, and I loved the lure of the business categories his company served. The third brother, Naguib Sawiris, the chairman of Orascom Technology Solutions, was decisive and direct.

"You don't want to work for them," he said. "Come work for me." Naguib's company had licenses to distribute

RULE # 1 STAY LOW, KEEP MOVING

tech products across the Middle East for U.S. brands like HP, Dell, and Cisco. He had just gotten the license to build the mobile network in Egypt and invested in their first Internet service provider, LINKdotNET. He was going to be the region's godfather of tech, and I loved the idea of joining his innovative company. That was until he said, "Come work as my office manager."

What? Office manager? I thought, feeling totally deflated. *Shouldn't an American education, master's degree and work experience at a Fortune 500 company get me more than a job answering phones, getting coffee, and filing papers? Do women only get certain jobs here? Am I the secretary in* Mad Men*? (Because they certainly smoke in offices here, too.)*

"I can't believe he asked me to be his office manager," I told my dad that night.

"Take it," my dad said.

"Take a job that I'm overqualified for?"

"Naguib is chairman of one of the most powerful companies and one of the biggest names in the Middle East. You just moved here and don't know anyone, so put your head down and learn," my dad said. "Work hard and prove that you're capable of doing more." I couldn't believe that he didn't agree with me.

"The office manager is a very powerful job in Egypt," my dad continued. "In order for people to connect with Naguib, they'll need to go through you, the gatekeeper. The contacts you'll make are priceless and ground zero for building your relationships and business acumen here. No better place to learn and grow if you ask me. Tell them you'll gladly accept it no matter what they pay."

I didn't have my dad's foresight, but much to my chagrin, I listened to him and took the job. And, yes, I sat outside Naguib's office, filing papers and scheduling meetings.

The good news was that I didn't have to make coffee because I soon learned that the most important person in any office in the Middle East is the "office boy." Not only does he make coffee and tea, but he also fetches cigarettes and sandwiches, makes copies, and picks up work-related deliveries. The "office boy" makes things run smoothly and he is not a boy but a man who is considered a key company asset. You treat him well and work hard to earn his respect.

Still, although I didn't have to make coffee, I wasn't thrilled to be an office manager. It can really be a struggle to accept something that you don't want to do. But it can turn out to be the exact lesson you need at the time; that is, if you're willing to stay low and keep moving. Becoming the office manager for a chairman of a company was the best learning ground for me. No, the job was not what I wanted so I asked myself, *How do I MAKE it what it needs to be*? I accepted the situation, looked inward and relied on myself. I realized that I was capable of turning it into something valuable if I put my head down and put in the work. In other words, I stayed low and kept moving. Over time, I got confident enough to offer small suggestions and share ideas with Naguib, adding a little nugget of value here and another there. I treaded lightly, careful not to overstep. Nearly two years later, my phone rang on a Saturday morning.

"Maha, I have a special mission for you." Naguib paused before lowering his voice to a whisper. "Go to the office and get a printer. Then head to the private jet terminal at the Imbaba Airport. My plane will bring you to El Gouna. Take-off is in an hour—don't be late!"

Naguib didn't tell me what the mission was, how long I would be out of town, or any other details. It was also a long holiday weekend, and I'd been really looking forward to the two extra days off from work. Still, I quickly put together an

RULE #1 STAY LOW, KEEP MOVING

overnight bag and scrambled to get my cousin to stay and take care of my mom. Then, I headed to the office, where I unplugged one of the printers and wrangled it into the largest suitcase I could find before rushing to the airport.

When I landed in El Gouna, the day was sunny and warm. There I was in a navy suit and heels pushing a trolley holding a printer past vacationers sipping colorful cocktails at the pool. Envy coursed through my veins because I was pretty sure that Naguib didn't fly me in to work on my tan. I continued through the main lobby of the hotel, then I lugged the printer up a flight of steps to a conference room on the mezzanine. When I opened the door, I found a dozen executives pouring over mounds of papers, oblivious to the gorgeous sun-kissed day outside. Not wanting to interrupt their work flow, I sat and waited until it was time to be briefed.

I felt like I entered the Matrix: hushed conversations on one side, another group of executives shuffling papers, others in the corner pouring over documents in boxes, a team at the end pounding on their calculators analyzing data. The room was lined with big whiteboards with various graphs, charts, and diagrams. I had no idea what was going on or why I was there.

It turned out that Naguib was negotiating to buy the largest African mobile telecom operator. His lawyers were doing due diligence and the papers were so confidential that they couldn't be sent to the hotel printer. That weekend, Orascom Telecom pulled off the largest corporate acquisition in the history of Egypt, taking a stake in 12 mobile licenses across Sub-Saharan Africa. This deal worth $213 million gave the company the largest footprint of mobile operations on the African continent. What I thought was a menial task and my boss ruining my holiday weekend turned out to be a critical mission that was a part of history. I was a part of history—all because I stayed low and kept moving.

After that, I went from office manager to having four different business cards: head of marketing, head of commercial, director of communications, and head of investor relations. I worked on the launch of almost all of Naguib's mobile networks and traveled all over Africa. Plus, I was one of two people he took on the global company IPO road show when Orascom Telecom went public. It was Naguib, the CFO, and me. What an experience! We gave the same presentation to institutional investors 108 times, from Wall Street to the West Coast, and throughout European financial districts. It was an experience of a lifetime! The company floated a dual stock listing on both the London Stock Exchange and the Egyptian Exchange. I mean, I had never even heard of a GDR before and now I was working on it! (A GDR is a global depository receipt, a fancy word for shares of a single foreign company.) I will never forget the day the company went public and the shares were listed. It was a massive accomplishment for any company to achieve, and the process is grueling and highly technical. I never would have gained that unique experience if I hadn't taken the job to be his office manager and what I learned on that journey has stayed with me through today. Being that close to the sun taught me how to operate in meetings, make decisions, handle people and manage a company.

I also learned about trust, humility, and putting aside ego. Naguib taught me about the importance of loyalty in business, how this matters above all else. He told me what matters is not what you are doing but *who you are doing it with*; those who believe in your mission and want to be a part of it will be loyal and support you along the journey.

> In your career you should either be learning or earning.

The lesson here is that an opportunity that you think you're overqualified for can end up being the best thing that ever happened to you. Look at the big picture. What will you learn? Who will you have access to? Where could you go from there? In your career you should either be learning or earning. Nothing is beneath you. This applies to all of us in life and business, but especially to entrepreneurs because you never know how one thing can lead to another.

Lives are not linear. Life ebbs and flows. Doors open and close. There are no wrong answers or choices; there are paths we build from one opportunity to the next. Learning is just as valuable as earning. Sometimes we make choices based on earning potential; and it is important to be paid what you're worth and to be valued based on your contributions and experience. We must value ourselves enough to earn what we deserve. But when you make choices based on learning, you are practicing a key rule of self-reliance and that is to be a long-term player. By placing value on learning, you understand that this experience and what you will gain from it will prepare for what comes next. Learning is so powerful and important that it cannot replace financial rewards. Because once you gain that learning and experience, you have made a significant deposit in your self-reliance toolbox. You invested in yourself and nobody can take that knowledge away from you.

Even now that I run my own business, I'm still the office manager and the girl wrangling the printer. I still stay low, keep moving. Say *yes* more often, and if it gives you an opportunity to learn, then make it a *hell yes*.

If it gives you an opportunity to learn, then make it a *hell yes*.

RULE # 1 STAY LOW, KEEP MOVING

Almost 20 years after I started working for Naguib, I still have a strong relationship with him. I was in Dubai at the grand opening of Atlantis The Royal, where they hosted a star-studded weekend at the resort, including a private performance by Beyoncé. I saw him at a private after-party where Jay-Z was impromptu DJing for the guests. We said hello, and then he grabbed my hand and said, "I need to introduce you to somebody." He brought me over to meet the CEO of a company valued at more than $1 billion in the United States. "This is the woman I was telling you about at dinner. You need to hire her," he said.

I put my heart and hustle into the work I did for him. I stayed low and kept moving. More than 20 years later, even though I don't work for him, I always make an effort to stay in touch, tell him how much he means to me, and share what he instilled in me. I will be forever grateful and indebted to him. He is still opening doors for me, and that means a lot to me.

I don't work for him anymore; he doesn't have to help me. But because I created value for him, he is creating value for me. This is what being a long-term player is about (see Chapter 7).

Look at the big picture.

Focus Relentlessly

When I say "stay low, keep moving," I mean put your head down and focus on what you care about in order to build your dream life. When you do, you are forced to rely on yourself and that's a good thing because you are the only person who can achieve your goals. By focusing on your needs and your world, you will win.

In 2015, I was having coffee with my friend Richard Fitzgerald at the cafe connected to my gym, Fit Republik in Dubai, after a workout. Richard had just moved to Dubai from Dublin, which is where he was born and raised. He had already acquired the license to bring Lovin Dublin—a website highlighting the best activities, food, news and more in the city—to the Middle East. His goal was to build the biggest media company in the region—starting with Lovin Dubai, with plans to expand to Lovin Cairo, Lovin Saudi, etc.—into the number one consumer platform for the hottest happenings in each city, focusing on culture, news, celebrity sightings and restaurant openings, among other things. He spoke with such conviction and confidence as he shared all of this with me. However, I was skeptical, not about his abilities, but because he had just moved to Dubai and didn't speak Arabic. His platform was about what's hot in culture, but he wasn't from the culture. And he was building it from scratch with no readers, listeners, or followers.

"How are you going to do it?" I asked.

"I'm just going to focus. There are a lot of distractions with people who want to go out for dinners, have meetings and network, but I'm going to say no to everything," he said. "I'm just going to put my head down. The harder you work today, the more you will be rewarded tomorrow." That was the first time I heard someone talk about the value of saying no to people, and it made me realize that it's not rude or standoffish; it's a way to focus relentlessly. It's a way to stay low and keep moving. (Warren Buffett was the king of focus and he used to say, "The difference between successful people and very successful people is that very successful people say, no to almost everything.")

RULE # 1 STAY LOW, KEEP MOVING

Richard is also a triathlete who uses what he's learned from his physical training to perform well in business. "I'm like a professional footballer for business. I don't take holidays. I train workwise," he says. "Business is the ultimate sport." Well, just a decade later, Richard learned how to speak Arabic—if you follow him on Instagram it's amazing to see this—and has built the hottest platform in the region. Not only Lovin Dubai, but also Lovin Saudi, Lovin Doha, Lovin Kuwait and 14 others. He's also built 10 Arabic content platforms including SmashiTV, Smashi Crypto and Smashi Gaming, the digital media company Augustus Media and two podcasts—all because he was relentlessly focused. Even 10 years later, Richard works six days a week; reads one day a week; and swims, bikes, and runs as part of his triathlon training seven days a week.

You can have that same relentless focus. You just have to make it a priority. In addition to the dinners, extra meetings and events Richard talked about as distractions, we have social media. We spend so much time mindlessly scrolling, which is terrible for your brain (making it mushy, but more on this later), and it sidetracks you as you're constantly comparing yourself to others and feeling like you're not doing enough/making enough/networking enough. Then you live with FOMO (fear of missing out) because you're convinced that everyone else is living his or her best life and you're not.

We all know this isn't true; it's just something social media has created. Social media is a snapshot; keep in mind that reality is sometimes edited. I am not talking about filters or the Kate Middleton Mother's Day photo editing drama. I am talking about real life vs. a 15-second clip of one's life.

Don't worry about what's happening in the outside world, focus on your inside world. Your goals, rules and life are not the same as anyone else's. Focus on yourself. If you feel like you need to learn new things, then put your head down and apply yourself to learn them. Doing this will also give you more confidence to keep going and help you achieve your goals, big and small. (We'll talk more about Unlearning, Relearning and Investing in Yourself in Chapter 4.)

Another personal example of this was when I managed two sick parents while building my career. Less than five years after my mom, dad, and I moved back to the Middle East, my dad was diagnosed with ALS. He was an athletic, muscular guy, so when he started falling, feeling weak, and losing his balance we knew something was wrong. After being misdiagnosed with a back problem and even having surgery for it, my dad flew from Egypt to the Mayo Clinic in Minnesota for extensive testing. This is where he was handed the sad diagnosis of ALS. My sister was with him when they called to tell me the news.

"Let's stay positive," I said. "We got this." But my words did not reflect the state of complete shock and helplessness that washed over me. *What are the chances that I'd have two parents with neurological diseases?* I thought. My life flashed before me, and I felt totally overwhelmed.

"ALS is a life sentence," my dad said angrily when I picked him up from the airport in Egypt. "I have a time limit now. I can't do everything I wanted to do." That comment sat with me because he was right. Although my mother's illness was debilitating, it was not life threatening with a time bomb attached to it. ALS is a crippling disease that has no cure. It starts in your feet, then moves up to your legs. Eventually, you can't control any of your muscles and you can't go to the bathroom, breathe, swallow, or talk. Your mind is intact, so you are cognitively aware, but your body shuts down. This happened very quickly with my dad, and it was devastating.

It's hard to lose control of your day-to-day functions, and for the head of the household and my idol, it was a slow and sad struggle. The days were hard but my job was to keep the vibes positive and energy up, and to find the bright side in every situation. I created a cozy environment with his favorite blankets, favorite music, comforting foods, and visitors. I had to dig deep and rely on myself to make him comfortable. My dad loved this pop song called *Leh Beydary Keda* by a famous Egyptian singer named Ruby. Ruby had a hit song and a viral music video in which she wore red (of course) and is dancing and singing while riding a stationary bike and pumping red dumbbells. If you lived in Egypt in 2004, you knew this video and this hit song. The music video was directed by Sherif Sabri, who I knew. I called in a favor and asked Sherif if Ruby could come over and visit my dad and cheer him up. And he delivered. I was so grateful he made it happen! Ruby showed up and sat bedside and chatted up my dad, who smiled from ear to ear. He was so surprised, and I was honored to be able to create a fleeting moment of happiness for him.

My dad had always been the life of the party because he was so outgoing and had so many interests, from cooking to sports to music. With his big presence and hearty laugh, you always knew when Gaber was in the room. His energy was so infectious that everyone loved to hang out with him, including all my friends, who called him Uncle Gaber. To watch this huge personality, this big man on campus, become a weak and diminished prisoner in his own body is something I can't put into words even decades later. For him, I imagine it was like observing life and not being able to participate in it. You understand everything and you feel everything, yet you're unable to function in it fully.

I'd been caring for my mother since I was 14 years old—bathing, feeding and dressing her—essentially acting as a parent at an age when I still needed to be parented. Now I was going to be caring for two parents who couldn't do anything for themselves.

You might think I sat there and surmised my future and thought about what this was going to do to my life, my future, my work life, my personal life, but honestly I was mostly consumed with what my parents were going through. The sadness and adversity. I couldn't think of anything else except conquering the next day, the next medical decision, the next thing to make them comfortable, the next doctor I needed to call, the next medicine I was going to have to search for. It was a series of never ending to-do lists and motions that caretakers go through. I reprogrammed myself and my priorities to do the right thing and to do it to the best of my ability.

Soon enough, we needed to replace the queen-size bed my parents slept in with a hospital bed. This way we could move my dad more easily and maneuver the foot and head of the mattress to make him more comfortable. He also needed 24-hour nursing. My mom couldn't sleep with his nurses going in and out all night and she needed her own care, so I put her in one of the two bedrooms in our apartment and my dad in the other. Then I shared a bedroom with my mom and slept next to her. I'm using the word *slept* loosely. The truth is, I hadn't slept through the night for years. Prior to getting help, I was waking up every two hours to move each one of my parents into different positions to prevent them from getting bedsores. Once I hired help, I went to sleep with a nurse in the room working the night shift caring for

RULE #1 STAY LOW, KEEP MOVING

my mom on the other side of the bed I was sleeping in. My dad also had a night-shift nurse. In fact, I had three eight-hour shifts a day of nurses for each of my parents.

I was running a makeshift medical startup at home, with 16 nurses, a cook, a maid, and a driver. That's how I thought about it; I had payroll and oversight of all the operations at home. I had to do supply management (medical equipment, food, medicine, supplies), get them uniforms, do regular check-ins with doctors and specialists, arrange physical therapy, and home doctor visits, and do research and keep an eye on any medical trials or drug studies. This was all while doing my full-time job as the family breadwinner, because who is supposed to pay for all of this? Me. Who is going to make all the medical decisions? Me. I had to rely on myself and I had no idea what I was doing or if I was doing the right thing; I just stayed low and kept moving to get through the next thing and the thing after. Looking back this seems crazy to think this was my life.

In addition to hiring and training the nurses (whom I found in the ER of a local hospital and lured away by doubling their salaries), I went to all my parents' doctors' appointments, read all the lab results, and made all the medical decisions. At one point, because I was at work all day, I created my own medical log books. I made a spreadsheet with the date, time, urine in/out, temperature and blood pressure, as well as what they ate. I printed 30 of these pages and brought it to the Egyptian equivalent of Kinkos to be bound into a book. I bought scrubs for the nurses and all the equipment we needed, like oxygen tanks, CPAP machines and monitors. Actually, because the electricity in Egypt would go out all the time, I bought two CPAP machines and a generator. This wasn't easy to do; after all, you can't just import your own medical equipment. I literally smuggled them in my luggage. (You gotta do what you gotta do!) Doctors would come over and say, "This is better than a hospital."

I also spent countless hours talking to doctors and doing research online so I could learn everything possible about reading charts, lab results, and medicines. I checked and double checked the doses that my parents were being given. I couldn't make a mistake. After all, I was dealing with life. Two lives, actually. I came to learn so much that more than one ER doctor asked me, "Where do you practice?" I joked with them that I was a visiting resident from the United States. Then I told them the truth: I was just an overzealous daughter and expert online researcher of medical info in order to educate myself. Since both of my parents had feeding tubes, they couldn't eat solid food, so I hired a cook to make and blend all their meals. Then I had a housekeeper to clean the two-bedroom apartment and a driver who would take me to work. Basically, I was running a small company with a staff of 19 people—at home.

When my parents got sick, a lot of people told me to put them in a nursing home. But that never crossed my mind. I just thought, *This is our journey. This is my story. We need to deal with it.* Today, when I share this very personal part of my story, people often say, "I don't know how you did it." And looking back, I'm not sure how I did it either, especially since I was only in my 20s and 30s and working a full-time job to pay the bills and have a career. How did I have the strength? The only answer is that I had relentless focus. Yes, looking back in its totality, it seems overwhelming. But I didn't have the luxury of being overwhelmed. I focused on keeping my parents comfortable every hour of every day. I threw myself into the deep end of the swimming pool and stayed low and kept moving, one stroke at a time. And I didn't sink. The goal was just to win the day and push through. In fact, one key quality of those who stay low and keep moving is that we understand that small things lead to big things.

Small Things Lead to Big Things

Change doesn't come in big waves. It comes from daily consistency and the regular chipping away at a goal. Journeys take time. You must have patience to travel through them and rack up experience, failures, and understanding. Daily habits become daily contributions. Outside forces can derail you or inspire you so learn the difference between getting sucked into hustle culture and putting in effort toward your goals. And don't be in a hurry. Good things come over time by making small steps of progress and doing them consistently. I never thought about my career until I stepped back and looked at how all the small things added up into big things. For example, when I saw the various assignments I did with government entities, I realized I racked up public policy experience.

My friend Richard knew his long-term goal—to have the biggest digital platform in the region—but what got him there was knowing that he needed to do a lot of little things. So, look at the small steps you can make in your journey as an entrepreneur. Build your brand and your name. Acquire your first client and keep your first client. Getting that momentum is really important. Don't underestimate the value of progress and that one small connection might lead to something that you don't expect.

Stay in Stealth Mode

Another key quality of those who stay low and keep moving is that they don't talk about their power and influence or seek attention for themselves. You can name drop and humble brag, but if you can't deliver the results, nobody really cares about who you know or what you did.

I talked about this earlier but it's an important point to repeat. Staying low = working hard and putting in effort, racking up experience. Being in stealth mode allows you to do the work without external pressure, expectations, or having to justify your work or actions to others.

I work with powerful and important people, but I don't disclose this information and all my employees know that confidentiality and discretion are a must. Integrity is everything. Why? First off, we sign non-disclosure agreements (NDA) with all our clients. But even if we didn't, the know-how we get from our unique access helps us create value for other clients and ourselves. And from that experience and knowledge, we also gain the confidence that we can get things done. Also, it's the doing, not the talking about it, that helps you keep clients, get future clients and master self-reliance. If you focus on your work rather than seek attention, it will speak volumes without you saying a word. Your efforts and contributions will rise to the top and show the world who you are and the impact you bring. You don't need to seek attention. You just need to create value for others and the attention will follow.

And by attention I don't mean—social media praise or media attention, I mean the recognition and barometer of success and KPI (Key Performance Indicator) that matters to your growth and development. For example, leading to bigger opportunities, gaining freedom, more financial

RULE #1 STAY LOW, KEEP MOVING

security, accomplishing a bucket list item. Only you should and can measure what has meaning for you.

I really care that the work my team and I put out into the world is recognized and respected. The operative word here is the *work*, not me. Because if the work we do is consistently good, people are going to say, "Who built that? Whose efforts are those? Whose contributions?" or "Who did that campaign or told that story?" By putting the work on the pedestal, and not me or my team, who did the work will be revealed in time. That will come naturally, for example, if some homes receive design awards from the industry on a consistent basis people will ask who was the architect or designer behind them. Instead of the designer saying "Hey look at me! I do award-winning work! Hire me!," the industry will draw customers to them because their work is outstanding.

I often get asked what it's like to do PR and communications for well-known figures and personalities. Time and again people say, "Does it bother you that you are helping other people look and sound good but you're behind the scenes? After all, you're the strategist and develop the messages and talking points for them." It doesn't bother me one bit! I love it. In fact, I thrive on being the person or team behind the scenes where I get to see my work come to life in public. Nothing is more rewarding and thrilling than drafting a story, crafting an ideal headline, and then seeing it on the news. If you want to be in PR, you have to be comfortable with being low profile so your clients can shine. This doesn't mean you shouldn't build your own brand or promote your work; it means you don't get in the photo with them, you take the photo. In fact, you stage the photo. I understand that it can be hard when you do something outstanding and don't get credit for it, especially if you put your blood, sweat and tears into it. But the recognition will come, even though it may not be in the time, place, or manner you're expecting it. What if the work you do only gets recognized years after you achieved it? Is it less worthy or important? I don't think so.

Staying Low vs. Being Low Profile

Somebody asked me how staying low helps women in the workforce who struggle to get noticed and earn recognition. What is the difference between staying low and being low profile?

"Stay low, keep moving" means you should put your head down and do the work—let the work speak for itself and gain recognition instead of going out of your way to get attention personally and seek validation from others. This is not the same as being low profile.

For women in the workforce who struggle to get noticed and earn recognition, they need to focus on a few things. First, build their personal brand and define what they want people to know about them. Have a plan and be intentional about it. Second, focus on communication—become very good at telling stories and connecting with others. Strong communication skills are essential for getting noticed and earning recognition. Next, build strong networks and relationships and invest heavily in them. All of these steps go a long way in demonstrating their value to others. Last but not least, put time and energy into delivering meaningful and valuable work and contributions. It's simple—do something worth getting noticed for. If you work hard and put in the effort, the work and your name will get the value and recognition they deserve.

Rewards Come to Those Who Don't Actively Seek Them

Stay under the radar—moving, operating, and crushing it because rewards come to those who don't actively seek them as motivation. For example, if you're an actor but your sole focus is receiving an Academy Award, you will overlook the day-to-day process. Ironically, you're so focused on the prize that you may not do the things that will help you achieve it: honing your craft, learning lines, going on auditions, etc. Being fixated on an outcome can lead to stress and disappointment. Do it for the work (the game), not the reward. Detach yourself from the outcome because most of the time when you try to control it, you're actually creating barriers.

Detaching yourself from the outcome is all about self-reliance. If you trust yourself to do the right thing and put in the effort you don't need to worry about the outcome—because you are gaining value from the process. This is so hard. We want the efforts we are doing to yield results not just "experience" and lessons learned. But the pressure of expectations can actually derail us from achieving the outcomes we want or cause us to misjudge what actually matters. For example, you're an entrepreneur and you need to acquire a database of leads and potential clients, but if you're worried about the number you're not able to appreciate the quality of the leads, or the potential of those leads and that matters more than the number.

Rewards come from two things: skills and applying those skills consistently. Nobody wants to work by spinning their wheels and end up short. But you will attract what you want to achieve if you are patient and are open to creating space for the unexpected.

For example, I've never been on the board of directors of a company. Then I got nominated along with several others to be on the global board of directors of the Associated Press, the gold standard for journalism, news, and media. It's certainly the most important industry board I could ever be on in my career. But I didn't seek it. It wasn't something I ever pursued. Getting nominated with other candidates and going through the interview process was just the culmination of all the work I did while I stayed low and kept moving. What's interesting is that the person who nominated me was someone I had met 10 years earlier at a business conference in Riyadh, Saudi Arabia. He knew the president of the Associated Press and they were looking for potential candidates. The lesson is make room for the rewards to come into your life without focusing on them as the driving force and motivation for your success. (P.S. I got appointed to the global board of directors of the Associated Press—a true honor and privilege and I couldn't have been more excited.)

Prepare to Pivot

Those who stay low and keep moving are builders and problem solvers. They are capable of shifting gears and adapting. They are willing to adjust plans and strategies as needed.

It was early 2001 and I was in Cairo looking to bring a global PR firm to the Middle East to open up a new region and market for them. I had convinced Naguib we could find a partner and build a business across the region. I had worked at Weber Shandwick in Minneapolis as an intern and worked my way up to become an account executive. My job duties were to support account managers with tasks they needed for clients and their campaigns. I was doing

RULE #1 STAY LOW, KEEP MOVING

everything from clipping newspaper stories and creating reports, to planning logistics for events. It was grunt work, let's be honest. I was attending meetings and supporting accounts, but I wasn't creating campaigns, pitching the media, or dealing with the press.

I was in an entry level position, so I worked across various projects in a contributor role, but I wasn't leading or driving anything on my own. It was my very first job in the Twin Cities and my first taste of agency life. It was the breeding ground for many of my foundations: how to talk to clients, how to serve on an account team, what work life in communications looked like. It was fun, fascinating, and very educational. I was part of a firm, and I was supporting the agency's consulting work for major companies and big well-known brands.

So I had a history with the company, but that was six years earlier and now I was living in Egypt, not Minnesota. I had the idea to see if Weber Shandwick would want to have offices in the Middle East. I decided to shoot my shot. Somehow I had the nerve to cold e-mail the actual chairman of the company, Jack Leslie, and introduce myself and tell him that I had an investor and partner lined up to be his business partner in the region. Just like that. It didn't dawn on me that I didn't know him or have any credibility to build a business for his firm in the region, but I made my case, sent over our credentials, and invited him to Egypt. We had some correspondence, and it wasn't immediate, but I told him if he came to Cairo we would organize an event with clients and media to show him the market potential and our capabilities. The company's initial feedback was that the Middle East wasn't a region they were interested in investing in at that time. Of course, how naive of me to think they would want to make a global investment to open offices if it wasn't part of their strategy and, for all I knew, it would require years of planning or maybe even board approvals. But like most things in business, it boils down to timing.

On September 11, 2001, the world came to a halt with something we have never witnessed before. The impact of that day changed everything—and for doing business in the Middle East it changed a lot—especially if you were an American company or brand. And immediately crisis communications took center stage. There was a boycott of American brands in the Middle East and for any PR firm, crisis and communications go hand in hand. Not only do they present enormous challenges for companies being targeted, they also present substantial business opportunities for agencies with experience in crisis communications to step in to support them. Weber Shandwick has significant experience in crisis management.

To do business with Weber Shandwick, it wasn't a matter of emailing the chairman in New York and asking them to set up offices. I learned that agencies are part of holding companies and networks of offices and brands. Weber Shandwick wasn't a stand-alone company; it was part of a holding company called IPG and the McCann Erickson Group, a conglomerate of advertising agencies with global reach.

In fact, their sister agencies already had offices in the Middle East, under the name of Promoseven advertising, but not PR firms. This was actually good news for our idea. We could open up PR satellite offices within their ad agencies and grow from there. Start small and share office space and resources; it was a lower lift and something we could implement immediately.

We worked quickly to formalize a partnership to open Weber Shandwick offices inside the satellites of the ad agencies. This move gave us immediate access to 18 countries with offices and I brokered a deal between Naguib Sawiris, Weber Shandwick and Promoseven. In October of 2001, I became the managing director of Promoseven Weber Shandwick. Months later Jack Leslie came to Egypt to celebrate the launch of the company and promote their presence in the region. A full circle moment for me: from intern to regional director.

This showed me how important it is to stay flexible, open-minded, and be willing to pivot when circumstances change. You also need to practice patience because you never know when an idea will come to fruition. The market is ever changing; and you need to change with it. When you stay low, keep moving, nothing stands in your way. You are ready to do your research about a situation and adapt when it is not what you imagined.

In 2014, when I left my job at Google, I had several meetings with inbound executives from Netflix who came to town from their European headquarters in Amsterdam. At the time, Netflix was only available in the United States. They were coming to Dubai to immerse themselves and learn about the market. The company was gearing up to launch globally and their services were going to be available in the Middle East. I remember at dinner explaining to them the importance of Ramadan, the most sacred holy month for Muslims, when they fast from sunrise to sunset. Today, about 1.8 billion people around the world observe Ramadan, but in 2014, I would say not many of the details about what Ramadan is and how it works was that mainstream. Ramadan is a religious time, but it comes with traditions: family traditions, cultural rituals and habits.

One tradition of Ramadan is when families gather around the television after breaking their fast to watch

TV; it's like the Super Bowl of viewing. The problem is the relentless ads that debut during Ramadan. Companies save up their budgets and campaigns to launch them during Ramadan because they know it's such a massive opportunity for a very captive audience. I advised Netflix to lean in to the culture and leverage this peak period of viewing to deliver ad-free content and explained how that would be a huge advantage. Although people in the region were hungry for American shows, not adapting to or understanding Arab culture would have been a huge blind spot.

The best way to integrate into a new market is to lean in to the culture and be relevant. Nothing could be more important to a content and entertainment company than understanding how people in the Arab world consumed content, what they care about, and their viewing habits. And if they leaned in to supporting big moments like Ramadan and took time to learn about the viewing habits of consumers during Ramadan, it would be a chance to win over hearts and minds in a new market they were entering.

Fast forward and Netflix went global and with it the Middle East was launched. I was hired to handle their launch into the region and I worked closely with them and built a team to support their business through my consulting firm. By the time Ramadan rolled around, they had shows about food, cooking, and family, as well as television serials that addressed the nuances of our culture. We were able to make that bridge between East and West, and today they have a whole Arabic content platform on Netflix dedicated to the Ramadan season and more than 88 million subscribers in the EMEA region and growing (as of January 2024).

RULE #1
STAY LOW, KEEP MOVING

It's how you succeed and achieve despite any obstacles that come your way. This rule is so important that it's the foundation for all the others.

Cheat Sheet

- **Be adaptable.** Be prepared to adjust your plans and strategies. Stay flexible, open-minded, and willing to pivot when circumstances change. The market is ever changing. Are you?
- **Prioritize action.** Don't waste time on things that don't matter. Make it a priority to take action toward your goals and move forward, even if progress is slow. Most actions are reversible, so don't waste time in "analysis paralysis."
- **Stay disciplined.** Stick to your plan and maintain relentless focus, even when things get tough. Don't give in to distractions or temptations that may derail your progress.
- **Keep a low profile.** Avoid drawing attention to yourself unnecessarily. Stay humble and focus on your goals rather than seeking recognition or accolades.
- **Stay connected.** Maintain strong relationships with people who can support and encourage you along the way. Build a network of people who can provide guidance, advice, and resources when needed.
- **Stay alert.** Always be aware of your environment and the opportunities or obstacles ahead. Keep your senses sharp.

Those Who Stay Low, Keep Moving

- Have relentless focus
- Understand that small things lead to the big things
- Do not seek attention for themselves; they seek attention for their work, efforts and contributions
- Know that rewards come to those who do not actively seek them as motivation
- Know that personal contributions are equal to or more important than professional contributions
- Face setbacks and understand that lessons come from the struggle
- Are capable of shifting gears and adapting; they are willing to adjust plans and strategies as needed and can pivot
- Are builders and problem solvers

Reflection Exercises

1. How do you embrace change and how do you adapt to new situations?

2. Reflect on a time that you faced a serious setback or challenge. How did it change your behavior afterwards?

3. Write down your proudest accomplishment and who you shared it with.

4. What are some ways you seek recognition and rewards from your work? And from important people in your personal life?

5. How do you manage a big problem you're faced with and who do you turn to for help, guidance or feedback?

> Hustle culture is out, value culture is in.

3

RULE # 2
BE A VALUE CREATOR

The meaning of life is to find your gift.
The purpose of life is to give it away.

— PABLO PICASSO

Everyone is motivated by different things. While some entrepreneurs are motivated by financial success or competition, I am motivated by creating value for others. This intrinsic drive to create value serves as my measuring stick for life both personally and professionally. It is the foundation of the second rule, Be a Value Creator, which is cemented around how you should approach relationships, opportunities, and life.

When I decided to write this book, I asked myself, *What's one consistent thing that people would say I've done well?* The common denominator in every single job success, positive business relationship, and how I treat my family and friends is that I always try to create value for the other person. It's delivering first to your customer, client, business partners or vendor to build credibility. It's based on the premise of creating something that the other person either didn't know they needed or didn't know that they would appreciate.

When you bring value to someone, you find out what's most important to them and how you can deliver it. The key is that it's something that they value, not something you value. This is not about what's in it for you. It's about what's in it for them. Then you have to lean in and deliver. And today, being a value creator is more critical than ever because your business is not just competing with others locally, but with companies and a talent pool all over the world. Here are examples of how I practice creating value daily:

- I ask a simple open-ended question: How can I help?
- I seek to understand the areas that the other person or business is struggling with the most.
- I put on my thinking cap and make the effort to look at a layer beneath the surface to anticipate needs.
- I do research in order to gather more knowledge and information about how they operate and what impacts them and their business.
- I invest in relationships by giving more time to people who matter to me, my team, and my business.
- I stay on top of culture, trends, and shifts. I invest in learning what's relevant to keep myself informed of my surroundings and

external environment. You cannot ideate without understanding how an idea, relationship, or proposal will play out in the real world.

- I pay attention to the news and what is happening in the market.
- I focus on dreaming up big, bold ideas and I'm not afraid of being too ambitious. I constantly ask, what if?

This way of operating has served me well my whole life and I truly believe that in order to stand out, you must add value. Now let's put this concept into action for you.

Discover Your Secret Sauce

When it comes to best positioning yourself to create value, it's important to know your superpower. We all have one; we just need to figure it out. Often, it comes from something unexpected or unlikely. Or it's something that is completely right in front of you but you didn't realize is worthy, valuable or desired by others.

Do you have a knack for solving problems or does tackling complex things excite you? Then that is your superpower. Are you good with people and love people? Then that is your superpower. Having that skill set lends itself to so many careers and fields where you can lean in to your superpowers. If you're a leader with empathy and strong interpersonal skills you would do well working in HR, customer service, sales, public relations, real estate, and education.

My parents came to the United States from Egypt when they were in their 20s. They wanted to give my older sister and me the best of the American dream, and they wanted us to have a strong sense of Egyptian values, to know where we came from and be proud of it. Inside the four walls of our house, it was all Egypt: the rules, food, language, even the music of Abdel Halim Hafez and Om Kalthoum that my parents played on repeat. But once I stepped outside our home, I was in Mankato, Minnesota, which is where I was born and raised, and everything I lived, breathed, and spoke was American. (After all, it was the hometown of Laura Ingalls Wilder of *Little House on the Prairie*.) It was a typical American childhood upbringing—4th of July parades, playing outside with the neighbor kids, cake walks, and high school traditions.

Growing up in the 80s in the U.S., the internet didn't exist. Nobody knew what Ramadan was or anything about Egypt beyond the camels and pyramids. I was the only diverse student in my class, and standing out wasn't cool—it was all about fitting in. But as I got older, I became more comfortable in my own skin. The internet brought people and cultures closer together, and I started to use my identity as a strength to build bridges and understanding between the East and Western worlds. I decided to use my culture and identity to help create powerful stories that connected my American roots with my Egyptian heritage. Growing up on a college campus around my dad's job meant that education was part of my DNA. Now, I was going to use my knowledge of both cultures and people to educate others through storytelling.

At the time, I didn't like this dual life, being Egyptian living in the Midwest. Balancing two cultures can be hard for anyone, but growing up Muslim in America during the 1970s and '80s was really challenging. I was often called "towel head" and "camel jockey." Everyone around me

RULE # 2 BE A VALUE CREATOR

was of Scandinavian descent with blonde hair and blue eyes, and Minnesota was famous for hotdish and lefse. A far cry from our traditional dishes served at home of *bamia* and rice (okra with red sauce served over white rice). As you can imagine, all I wanted was to be a normal American kid, something my parents didn't understand.

"Girls don't sleep outside of the house," my dad said firmly. "You can't go. I won't allow it."

"American girls do this all the time, Dad. It's fun . . . ," I said through tears, my 10-year-old mind searching for a convincing argument.

"No," he said, cutting me off mid-sentence and shaking his head.

"It's called a slumber party. . . . You're just in your pajamas with sleeping bags, watching movies, braiding hair and eating pizza. It's supervised."

"*Akher kalam*," my dad replied. This was one of his signature Arabic phrases which pretty much means "end of conversation." My dad liked to use Arabic phrases when he was fed up with me. (He didn't use them on my older sister because she never got in trouble. In contrast, all his gray hair came from me.) I'd already missed so many sleepover birthday parties and I thought this time would be different. Crushed, I ran into my room and flung myself onto my Holly Hobbie bedspread, my body shaking from deep, heavy sobs. *Being Egyptian is a curse,* I thought. I was the only brown girl in my community, a far cry from what Holly and her all-American features represented.

I should have been used to these moments of feeling left out, but I wasn't. Instead, each one made the wound deeper. For example, remember attendance roll call on the first day of school? It was a humiliating experience for me at Kennedy Elementary. Every year before the teacher read this list, she'd make some version of this statement, "If I pronounce your name wrong, please correct it for me. Or if you have a nickname—for example, your name is Elizabeth, and you prefer Liz—let me know." Then she'd look down at the alphabetized list, flabbergasted by the first name that she saw: "Abouelenein." As the teacher stuttered and fumbled trying to pronounce it, all eyes were on me. I sank in my chair, mortified that she was drawing the attention of the entire class to what made me different from them.

I dreaded the first day of school and dreaded having to explain to everyone where I was "from" and this is the '70s, folks. There wasn't any Internet, where people know what Egypt is beyond what they teach in history class of pharaohs, sand, the Nile River, camels and pyramids.

But my life felt like it was really over when the song "Walk Like an Egyptian" by the Bangles hit the Billboard charts when I was in high school and MTV played the music video on repeat. Kids would come up to me in the hallway, doing the dance—arms bent horizontally at their sides and moving in opposite directions—mocking me for being Egyptian. All of this made me loathe my dark hair and skin. I just wanted to fit in, not stand out. I wanted to belong, but I was never quite sure where. Although my name was Egyptian and I look Egyptian, I didn't feel connected to that culture and couldn't speak the language. When I was in Cairo in the summer and on holidays visiting relatives, no one thought I was Egyptian. I could barely say hello in Arabic and when I talked with a thick accent everyone giggled. When I was in America, no one thought I was American. Because I had a strange name, brown hair, dark skin, and even though I sounded American when I spoke, I certainly didn't look "American." I often wondered if I was *American* Egyptian, or if I was *Egyptian* American.

RULE # 2 BE A VALUE CREATOR

The fact that I had to ponder that still baffles me.

In the end, the balancing of two cultures that was so hard for me throughout my childhood turned out to be the best thing that ever happened to me; it became my superpower. The struggle became my strength and helped foster self-reliance. But that wasn't the only benefit.

It became the fuel, the fire and the purpose of my career, my personal brand and what set me apart from everyone else. Remember when we talked in the earlier chapter about life not being linear and the ebbs and flows of your journey? I started to appreciate how things worked in the Middle East and embrace it as I built my business.

When I moved to Egypt from Minnesota, I didn't understand how differently business was done in the Middle East. In America, it's all about results, deliverables, productivity, and the bottom line. It's about being efficient because time is money. It's about hustling, go-getting, and closing the deal. In contrast, at the core of the Middle Eastern approach is the idea that all business is personal. Relationships first, not transactions. Yes, you are going to get results, but you're going to do so in a very different way. The style of business is a culture. You must invest in your relationships and get to know someone in order to work with them. It's not just about trust but also establishing a connection that goes beyond the office: asking about his or her children, putting in the energy and making the effort and not small talk. Giving someone your time is highly valued; it shows respect, that you care about them, and that you understand the rules of engagement. In the U.S., people you do business with don't necessarily know anything about your background or family. In the Middle East, context is important. What family do you come from? Who do you know? Do we have any mutual friends? Often, people will do business with you without knowing your credentials if they know you come from a good family or if they know your circles and who you have relationships with.

The American way of working was ingrained in me, so I struggled at first. I got down to business too quickly in meetings and sent e-mails that went straight to the point. I was impatient and pushed to close the deal too soon. This wasn't well-received and luckily, a few people nudged me to take time to understand and adopt the Middle Eastern mentality. I had to change my tone and authentically settle into the culture, the people, and building relationships. I had to rewire how I worked and operated with a whole new playbook. For example, rather than getting right down to business in an e-mail, I am now more thoughtful about my approach and lead with a personal tone. I really enjoyed learning how to do this and once I did, my business took off and the connections I built were strong, authentic, and long-lasting.

Those who stay low, keep moving understand the importance of knowing their audience and adapting in order to avoid unnecessary mistakes. Some of the value I created for Gary Vaynerchuk (who you will read about later) was my ability to bring him to the Middle East. On that trip, I was nervous because Gary is in-your-face, very loud, and high-energy whereas people in the Middle East are quieter and more reserved. And I hadn't worked with Gary before, so I wasn't sure of his style in business meetings. But Gary was completely intuitive at reading the room, respecting the culture, letting them lead, and listening first. He was a natural and even focused on building personal connections and relationships, which went a long way.

And today, I spend time helping others build businesses in the Middle East the right way based on all the mistakes

RULE # 2 BE A VALUE CREATOR

and lessons I learned the hard way. What you say, how you say it, when to text vs. e-mail, when to be direct vs. back channel through a trusted source. It's a whole different way of working and every business culture, like a country's culture, has its ethos and ways of operating that must be followed. It cascades from how you build your partnership to how you communicate your values and even how you intend to bring value to the market.

Standing out versus fitting in made me who I am and today I take tremendous pride in my culture. I proudly say that I am American *and* Egyptian. I flow between the two seamlessly, understanding how each one thinks, the values of the people within them, and how to leverage this. In fact, I have mastered it to my advantage professionally and personally. Professionally, using this knowledge as a bridge between East and West has put me in a unique position. Creating value is all about finding what you have to offer that is important to the other person. The understanding of both markets gave me an edge and I realized that this was my point of differentiation. I started to help companies in the United States understand the Middle East and companies in the Middle East understand the United States It's one way I create value, not just for other people but for myself. This is my secret sauce, one that makes me different.

Deliver First

One big question when it comes to creating value is how to measure it, especially if it isn't tangible. How do we know whether what we're doing is valuable for others? What if we spend time and effort but we are completely off the mark? What about providing something that cannot be measured, like an introduction to someone? The answer is easy. It's not what you define as valuable, it's what the other person thinks is valuable. So the first act of how to give value to somebody is to start listening.

Value creators are always externally focused and culturally aware because you can't provide any value if you don't understand the other person, what they're up to, their business, where their gaps might be, or where you can best position yourself. What is going on with that potential client/co-worker/job/family member? Get to know what they're about so you can determine the best way to put yourself in the conversation. Find out what they value most and seek opportunities to create the work or build an idea they want to see happen. It's making an investment in the relationship, not just any investment but an insightful, strategic, and authentic one. This is how I came to work with Gary Vaynerchuk, the serial entrepreneur also known as GaryVee.

In the summer of 2017, I was at the bookstore in Dubai when my friend called.

"What are you up to?" she asked.

"I'm looking for something to read," I told her. "Any suggestions?"

"Yes. *Crush It!* by Gary Vaynerchuk."

"Who?"

"Just get it," she said. I love an emphatic book recommendation, so I took her advice and bought *Crush It!* The book is about using your passions and the power of the Internet to build a business based on you—your personal brand. I'd never thought of myself that way before. I just saw myself as someone who put her head down, stayed low and kept moving, tackling each project as it came to me. But when I paused to reflect on the totality of my career

RULE # 2 BE A VALUE CREATOR

to date, I realized I had done some unique and interesting things.

I took a step back and started to compound and group my experiences into skill sets: working in public policy, working in tech, launching companies, building a regional PR agency, managing teams, finding talent, managing crises and so forth. From running global communications and policy for Google, to launching Netflix in the Middle East, and serving the prime minister of Egypt, I realized these experiences gave me skills that could be put to work and translate to new opportunities.

I was also ambitious, driven, and hungry to continue this journey to see what I could do next with these skills. I read Gary's book and it was all about building your personal brand and using your experience and skills to "cash in on your passion." The insight Gary shared in his book intrigued me, so I started to follow him on social media. The more I learned about him, the more I was determined to find a way to meet him and find a way to work with him. I was curious and for the first time, I started to think about all my experiences and skills not as a job or career path but something that I could scale and market differently into a personal brand.

One day I saw a video where Gary interviewed Cy Wakeman, a researcher who studies drama in the workplace. She was launching a new book, *No Ego: How Leaders Can Cut the Cost of Workplace Drama, End Entitlement, and Drive Big Results,* and she was on Gary's podcast to promote it. I was fascinated by her, her story, and everything she talked about. In his book, Gary advises you to DM somebody you want to work with or make a comment on one of their posts. Although I'd never done this before, I took his advice and DM'd Cy, telling her how much I enjoyed her book. I also said, "I'd love to have you come speak in the Middle East." I don't even know why I wrote that because I was not in the business of booking speakers and didn't have any events for her to speak at.

That was until two months later when I was in Egypt with friends who were organizing a big tech event called Rise Up. We were sitting outside on the grounds of the old GrEEK Campus of the American University of Cairo.

"We want to bring someone in who can talk about culture in the workplace," they said. I immediately thought of Cy.

"I know somebody I could reach out to," I said. "Well, I don't actually know her, but I can write an e-mail and pitch her to come to your event."

"That would be great," they said. So I went back and DM'd Cy again, this time saying something along the lines of, "I'm working with the company that's organizing Rise Up and they'd love to have you come speak in Egypt. If you could give me your assistant's e-mail, I'll send over some more information." This way I could send a more formal e-mail and establish my credibility so I didn't seem like a fangirl or stalker. Soon after, Cy shared her assistant's contact info and I sent an e-mail with my bio and what I do for work as background. I also shared a link to the event. The assistant replied saying that Cy would like to talk. I was totally excited; I couldn't believe the advice worked. Next, my friends from Rise Up and I got on a call with Cy to discuss the event, what topic she'd speak about and logistics. Cy said yes to speaking and my friends were thrilled. Although I wasn't working for Rise Up or Cy, I felt good because I love creating value for others.

Two days before Cy arrived for the event, I flew from Dubai (where I was living at the time) to Egypt to help organize her all-expenses-paid visit. This included getting

RULE # 2 BE A VALUE CREATOR

picked up at the airport, rooms at the Four Seasons and a tourism package so she could do things like see the pyramids. I wasn't being paid to do any of this, and I had to pay for my plane ticket to go from Dubai to Cairo to receive her. I held her hand through the whole trip acting as her host. I had a get-together for her at my home, which is a typical gesture of Arab hospitality, and took her sight-seeing to the pyramids. Cy spoke at the event and did a big book signing. It was a huge success. People loved her and she had the time of her life. She'd brought a videographer, Matthew, to capture the trip and after talking with him over the course of those few days, I learned that he actually didn't work for Cy Wakeman, he worked for Gary's company VaynerMedia. I couldn't believe it. This is an example of how doing something with intention and giving value to others can lead to unexpected benefits.

"Can you introduce me to Gary when you get back to the U.S.?" I asked.

"I work on a different team so I can't do that," he said, "but I'll connect you via e-mail to his head of business development, Alex De Simone."

After Matthew connected us, I sent an e-mail telling Alex who I was and that I'd love to meet Gary. Alex wrote back, "Let me know the next time you're coming to New York and I will meet with you." It turned out, I was actually going to NY in two weeks because my sister was getting remarried and I was flying from Dubai to Minnesota through New York. I was only there for one day, so I went from the airport into Manhattan and met with Alex. I explained what I do and how I thought I could help Gary business-wise.

"I launched Weber Shandwick in the Middle East," I told him. "and I really think we can launch VaynerMedia there, too. I know all the clients, media, and dignitaries and I'll set it up. Is doing business in the Middle East something you're interested in?"

"That's a question for Gary," Alex replied. "Can you stay until tomorrow, and I will try to make a meeting happen?" I was really nervous about changing all my plans. I was supposed to leave New York that night so I could arrive in Minnesota with plenty of time for my sister's pre-wedding spa day at 1:00 P.M. the next day. The other issue was the additional expenses I'd incur to change my plane ticket and book a hotel room. New York is not cheap. I also knew Gary was super busy and that trying to get a meeting on short notice would be challenging. And even if I did get that meeting, there were no guarantees about how it would go or whether I'd get to share all my ideas. Regardless, I decided if I can make both work—meet my personal commitments to my family and get a chance to see Gary—that I would do it and if it was meant to be—then it was meant to be! I had to jump through a few logistical hoops with my flight and hotel, and Alex did some calendar magic with Gary; he was able to secure me a meeting first thing so I could get on the flight home in time to make the wedding festivities including a pre-wedding girls day at the spa!

My big idea was to help Gary learn about the Middle East market, an important economic and consumer block for any company looking to expand into global regions. It offered an oasis of opportunities for entrepreneurs and the marketplace was thriving like never before.

I shared this with Gary during our meeting, which went really well. In fact, our rapport was so great that what was supposed to be a fifteen-minute meeting, turned into an hour. (You can't imagine the turmoil I was experiencing

RULE # 2 BE A VALUE CREATOR

at the time: I loved every extra minute with Gary but also had a flight to catch. My sister was going to kill me if I didn't make it.) As the meeting ended, we agreed that we were going to continue talking to explore working together. I was really excited. And yes, I made it to the spa four minutes before my sister arrived.

That meeting led to 14 months of watching and listening. I spent time with key executives in his company to learn about how they operate and what they prioritize. I had to learn about his business if I wanted to be able to recommend a market entry strategy for him. I met with everyone from the e-commerce lead to events and even connected with key leadership from the UK office. This time was crucial because Gary already had an empire with 1,000 employees, including a robust content machine team. I had to find a lane to bring value. I also didn't want to step on someone else's toes. I had to discover what I could offer that no one else could. So this meant thinking through everything from new opportunities and revenue streams to new audiences or strategic relationships I could create for Gary or the company.

It took months of calls, touching base with Gary, developing decks, and doing presentations about my company and the Middle East to various members of his team—all without getting paid a penny. I was so heavily invested even though I didn't know where this was going and what the end result would be. Now, this is a calculated risk I took. I had other paying clients and income that I focused on and did all this business development as extra credit that didn't take away from income-generating opportunities. I was playing long term (another self-reliance rule). I was building and planting seeds for the future. It could or could not play out to reap results. And that's why this story is a perfect example of putting in the time to create value and being patient.

It sounds counterintuitive, but the most financially lucrative business deals I've ever made have been the direct result of doing work for free. If you're like most people, you struggle with the idea of giving away your work. I get it. No one ever wants to feel like they're opening themselves up to the possibility of being taken advantage of or worry that they're wasting the most valuable resource they have—their time.

But what many people don't understand is that if you have confidence in the value you're able to provide—and you should!—the best way to maximize your opportunity, in the long run, is to demonstrate what you can do, even if it costs you upfront. With more than 30 years of experience in the communications industry, I've learned that a good client, boss, or hiring manager will be smart enough to realize how much you're worth and reward you—and if they don't, that tells you everything you need to know about whether they'd ever appreciate your value, and whether they're the right client or organization to work for.

Five months in, I asked Gary if he was ready to work together.

"Meet me in France," Gary said.

"What?"

"My team's going to Cannes Lions," he said, referring to the international festival of creativity. It's a big advertising event in France where agencies, the creative industry and brands come together in the South of France. "Come spend time with us."

"Okay," I said, even though I didn't have an airline ticket, hotel or credentials and it was just weeks away. More than one person couldn't believe that I was giving so much and now spending more money and time to fly to the South

RULE # 2 BE A VALUE CREATOR

of France with no guarantees. But I knew what I was doing. Gary valued spending time with people before doing business together. He also valued seeing how they operated and the chemistry between that person and members of his team. This was one of the important things I learned in my five months of spending time with him and his team. It was a valuable insight.

In Cannes, I spent every day going to events with Gary, having coffee with him, walking to meetings, and just hanging out. I was investing in our relationship and making deposits in his trust bank—investments that I was willing to make in order to establish myself with him.

For a while, I had been pushing Gary to come to the Middle East, and he agreed that he couldn't entertain the idea of doing business in the region if he'd never been there before. I kept selling the idea and trying to get him to come. He agreed it was important, but there was a catch.

"But if I'm going to come, I need a speaking gig," he said.

"Okay," I replied.

"And I have to get paid," he added. He went on to tell me how much he typically gets paid for 45 minutes and that he also needed his expenses covered and those of a videographer who would document the whole trip. So now I needed to find a speaking gig that would pay for all of this. I needed to find an event who wanted a speaker that covered Gary's topics, and I needed to find an event that could pay his fees and expenses. Gary is a well-known serial entrepreneur and a guru when it comes to digital marketing, social media and how to be relevant with pop culture. He was also going to be coming for the "first time," so I had that in my favor that I would be able to bring a headliner that was new to the market and that was appealing for any event organizer needing to sell tickets and fill seats! I called the one person I knew who was having an upcoming event in the UAE and asked if they needed a speaker. I hit a jackpot—luck couldn't have been on my side any better—the Sharjah Entrepreneurship Festival was taking place later that fall and they needed a headliner who was a famous entrepreneur!

"He's a big headliner, so this could be a big deal, but there's a catch," I told them. "We need to cover his fees and pay according to their terms to confirm he can come." I learned that unless a contract is signed and a payment is made a speaking gig is not confirmed.

"No problem," they said.

A week later the money was in Gary's account. This created value for him as well as the event organizers and attendees. (I love a double-whammy, but we'll talk about secondary value later on in this chapter.) And once we had a booked speaking engagement that meant he would be coming to visit the region. He said, "I will let you book my entire schedule and program for my trip; I am coming!" And he left everything open ended. I learned this was also on purpose. He was going to see what I came up with and how I operated, and he was leaning on my expertise to drive what was important and what would make the most cultural and business sense. I was pumped! Nearly 11 months since our first meeting, he was finally coming to the region.

At that point, Gary had a sense of what I could do for him and suggested I give him a PR proposal to work together. But since the Dubai trip was just weeks away, I decided to wait and show rather than tell him.

In November of 2018, almost a year after we'd first met, I was standing at the airport in Dubai to receive Gary for his first trip to the Middle East. I had organized the entire visit from beginning to end. This is typically a service that the client pays for as it requires an incredible amount of time and effort to curate an inbound executive visit.

RULE # 2 BE A VALUE CREATOR

But I came this far and decided that this trip would reveal a lot—for both of us—if this was a good fit for me and for him and if there was future work we could do together. I wanted to see this through and deliver and then decide if this was worth working on further—and formally or not.

Putting together an executive visit is a function of strategy, education, and value creation. Strategy is using the time I have to build a high-impact, high-value agenda that maximizes his time and those who I am connecting him to. Education is using the trip as an opportunity to educate him on the market through the experiences and people I introduce him to. And lastly, at the heart of it all is value creation—value for the partners and value for Gary.

I had to think about whom to approach, package the information that would be the most compelling and informative, and then reach out to a wide range of people to set up meetings for Gary. Then it's a jigsaw puzzle to masterfully ensure his schedule was booked with no idle time because he was only on the ground for 24 hours and then juggle the schedules of the people I want him to meet. As Gary was new to the market (a first-timer), it was a heavier lift. I was organizing not only business meetings, but also press, a big speaking engagement, a book signing, and a meet and greet with fans.

In addition to the speaking gig where he spoke to more than 4000 entrepreneurs, he went live on the UAE's number one show, Virgin Radio's *The Kris Fade's Show*, spoke at Facebook headquarters to a room of CMOs, was featured on a billboard on Sheikh Zayed—the main highway in the UAE—and met about 100 CEOs and CMOs. One night, I hosted a dinner party in his honor for almost 50 guests. Remember, Gary wasn't a client or financing any of this, but I knew this investment would pay off more than financially in the long run.

His first trip to the Middle East was a success and Gary posted a seven-hour video about it that you can watch on YouTube. It was also the a-ha moment when he understood what I could bring to his table because he was able to see me in action. At least that is what he told me.

At the end of the trip, we were both flying back to the United States the day before Thanksgiving, and as we sat in the Emirates lounge at 1:00 A.M., Gary said, "We should work together." *Finally*! I said to myself. And it was the right time. We both got to see how we work together. Anything decided earlier would have not been the right timing because I also had to learn how he operates in the region and what he is curious about and where I can really bring value. It was just as important learning for me as it was for him. I was excited and I felt that the work, the patience, and the process paid off the right way at the right time.

Why did all those months finally turn into us signing a contract? I believe it's because I listened, observed, and got to know Gary on his terms. I also used the time to understand and learn his business. I needed time to truly understand what role I could play and then I showed him my value by delivering first. To me it felt he kept giving me hurdles—come to Cannes, find a paid speaking gig, etc.— but these weren't hurdles, it was training. I didn't see this as onboarding but it was and I did my part and delivered first. That's why listening is so important. That's the entry point. And it worked.

Seven years later, Gary is still a client, and we have built an entire team at my company to support his work.

It took more than a year for us to formalize our working relationship. And it did require me to invest significant time, effort and money. But to me, it was worth the investment because the rewards we both reap today are incredible.

RULE # 2 BE A VALUE CREATOR

> By creating value for others, you ultimately create value for yourself.

I hope this story makes it clear why creating value for others needs to be your default and why you sometimes have to be patient. Creating value can mean many things: sharing something you think they would appreciate, making an important introduction, giving someone access to an important event, suggesting speakers for their upcoming event, doing research for a company they thought about investing in? It's simply stepping up and giving them something without them directly or overtly asking for it.

Give the other person or company a reason why they should care or why they should listen. Giving and delivering first shows them your intentions are to do good for them. This builds credibility and equity with the other person. (It's also a good example of being a long-term player, which we'll talk more about in Chapter 6.)

People struggle with the concept of being patient and the concept of giving without having any idea whether they will get anything in return. But if you rely on your skills and confidence to drive the value you're creating, it will pay off.

It's normal to have a fear of giving something away and receiving nothing in return. I am not saying do things for free, be naïve, and open the floodgates. Be selective in how you create value for others. Do just enough to demonstrate your skills, power, what you are capable of, and the value you can bring, but don't do everything all at once so you don't deplete your resources.

For example, I used my time to serve Gary, but I didn't use any of my team resources or team billable hours to do non-billable work. I kept them focused on the business. I didn't incur any incremental travel expenses after the Cannes trip or pay anything out of pocket in preparation

RULE # 2 BE A VALUE CREATOR

for the trip. I was willing to invest time but not any additional expenses.

Also, be selective in who you give value to. Make sure you have a relationship with the other person, know who they are and what they are about. If you don't know them, gather some information first to see whether they are trustworthy, ethical, and good business people. You will have to take a risk but at least it will be calculated.

The very nature and premise of business is a transaction, which is where you give to receive. What I am suggesting is that you look beyond the transaction and think long term. I have done this for 30 years. In that time, I have had to sacrifice a lot of transactions that would have been good business decisions (good money, short-term gains), but I chose to go for a longer-term view to be a value creator and, I was learning and having fun at the same time. If this model sounds different than those you've heard before, that's because it is. I practice this in situations I care deeply about and where I strategically know the returns and risks. I also do it for those who will appreciate it and benefit.

Being a value creator is based on a long-term mindset and on potential opportunities for additional benefits. These include gaining access, learning something new, developing a connection for a relationship, and building your profile or brand in a meaningful way. But paving the road for future outcomes like these starts with lifting first; putting in time, effort, and equity first; and delivering first. And doing all these things well.

Execution Is Everything

A lot of people ask, "What's in it for me? Why would I just do that?" Well, if you're good at what you do and you do it well, no one's going to be able to replicate it. Ideas are a dime a dozen, it's the execution that is the difference. It's your experience, relationships and strategy that you bring to an idea that is your value.

There are a million ideas out there, but the hardest thing is execution. So why did I work for Gary for all that time for free? Because I really wanted to do business with him. So I discovered what he valued and gave it to him authentically with good intentions and fully committing to the entire process. I was constantly listening, culturally aware, and externally focused. Could Gary organize a trip to the Middle East? Absolutely! Did he have the time to build a full itinerary with the who's who of Dubai, book a prestigious speaking gig, and manage all his press? Probably but not as quickly and efficiently as I could because these relationships take years to foster and build. That was the value I created and shared with him. That's another important aspect of creating value for others: you must be able to deliver and repeat it. This is where the magic happens and when you can really reap benefits. You can't be a one-hit wonder.

> To be a value creator, you must listen first.

Create Opportunities That Offer Value for Others

It's one thing to create value for a client or business partner that you know they want or expect, but what is even better is identifying new opportunities or linkages that they haven't made yet. In other words, see around corners. This strategic insight is another way to create value. You've got to seek and create opportunities to offer value because they're not always going to present themselves or

RULE #2 BE A VALUE CREATOR

be obvious. Think and listen. Pay close attention to what the other person is saying, doing, not saying, and not doing. In other words, flip how you operate on its head. Instead of thinking that you will deliver what is asked of you or build something based on what is expected, do the reverse. Find ways to proactively bring value without being asked or before being asked. This is not just about anticipating needs; it's also about thinking strategically and building on that idea to create something of value, or even a whole new opportunity. Let me give you an example.

One way I do this is by looking at a layer beneath the surface. This is what happened when I went to the NBA All-Star weekend in Salt Lake City, Utah. A week before the event at the Super Bowl in Arizona, Gayle King told me she was speaking at the NBA All-Star weekend media breakfast. I knew nothing else about the breakfast except that Adam Silver, the NBA commissioner, would be speaking there too. So I did something else that helps create value: researched more information. A media breakfast could be really valuable for my work in PR and I had just signed a contract to support the NBPA (National Basketball Players Association) Foundation, so I was in learning mode.

Being in learning mode meant I needed to understand how they work, what is important to them, and how these seasonal league events operate so I can find out where I can add value for future events. Learning comes from talking to people, trying to uncover formal and informal activities around an event, and making sure you know the rules and parameters that you have to work with.

I asked around to find out what the media breakfast is. What happens there? Are there awards? How big is it? Is it a panel or just one speaker? After all the info gathering, I realized it was a worthwhile event for my client to attend so we could network and create new relationships. There was one problem: I didn't have an invitation, there were limited tickets, and it was sold out. Thankfully, a good friend and NBA reporter (thank you Ros Gold-Onwude) came through and sent me two tickets the night before the event. I was so grateful.

But then I noticed the mobile tickets were "general entry." I had no idea what those tickets meant or how seating worked. I normally don't bring a client to an event "cold"—meaning walking into an event without doing the advance work. Advance work is understanding all the details about an event; it can be simple things like knowing where people arrive and exit, to how the agenda and seating work to learning about media and networking opportunities. I arrived at the venue before it started to figure out the lay of the land and crash course my advance work checklist.

I asked around and found a table in the front and asked the table managers if that table was available and they said yes! Great . . . now I need to get to work and curate a table for us! I wanted to create an opportunity to network within our table and bring value to the guests by helping them meet and network with each other. I knew right away to save seats for Will and his friend, me and my client, Gary. As people started to arrive, I saw the filmmaker and actor Spike Lee, who I knew from several previous events. He was about to take a seat at a table farther back, so I walked up to him.

"Spike," I said. "Come sit with us." I knew that he and Gary knew each other really well because they sit courtside together at New York Knicks NBA games. Spike and his son took seats next to mine. Then I noticed the newly announced CEO of YouTube, Neal Mohan, walking toward a table in the back row. We'd met the day before, so I waved him over and he joined us. I was excited to introduce him

RULE #2 BE A VALUE CREATOR

to Will and help connect everyone at the table together. I knew Gary hadn't met him either, so I was excited to help make a new intro there as well. I wanted to make sure that all the guests at the table were able to meet each other and connect even if it was for a hello and to break bread over breakfast. This is how I approach creating value for others—something as simple as curating a table for others to have the opportunity to meet. Networking can bring tremendous value and deposits for future cooperation. I believe the most important reason to attend an event is to leverage the relationships you can create from attending them. When you go to an event, have the mindset of extracting the most value from them—especially since you are away from your families, jobs, and other responsibilities. That includes introducing people to each other—be a super connector.

Be quick on your feet and nimble at events where you can create the most value for yourself and others. Proactively think about how to create value for other people and seize those opportunities. It's a mindset. Creating value behind the scenes is knowing how to choose the right strategy, how to put in the work, and how to build the right network.

For example, if you're at an event and there is a professional photographer there, such as a Getty photographer, pay attention and suggest a group photo. You never know if that photo will go viral or create news. Small things like that can make a difference; it could end up on the news or the event could feature it on their website for more reach to their audience.

Value Creators Know Their Strengths

Value creators are willing to do the research and are self-aware enough to know what they don't know. For me,

I'm willing to put in the effort to gather as much information as possible when I feel I am not on the front foot. This has been a key to my success as an entrepreneur, but I learned it way back before I had my own company.

I am willing to outwork others to fill gaps, especially for my weaknesses. To outwork others means to put in more effort, dedication, and hours into your tasks or goals compared to those around you. Especially if you are not familiar with a topic or area, it will take more effort from you to get up to speed. Do you have a strong work ethic and the willingness to do what it takes to achieve success, surpass expectations, and stand out in a competitive environment? Outworking others can involve starting earlier, staying later, focusing on continuous improvement, seeking additional responsibilities, and being proactive in facing challenges, especially when there's a steep learning curve.

When I was working at General Mills in Minnesota, I was in the promotions department, and one of my first projects was to determine how General Mills brands like Cheerios, Betty Crocker, and Pop Secret could get involved with NASCAR. NASCAR was a big part of the culture in the southeastern part of the United States and the company wanted to learn how to benefit from a potential sponsorship or licensing agreement with NASCAR. The benefits would be tremendous: connecting with a massive and dedicated fan base, brand exposure and visibility, the chance to reach a diverse audience, and networking opportunities. A well-positioned partnership could also present strong marketing opportunities with key grocery stores and their sales teams. My boss basically said go figure it out. But I knew nothing about motorsports. So I started asking around to get help. Those who are self-reliant know when to ask others for help.

RULE # 2 BE A VALUE CREATOR

My friend Kevin McNulty was working in sports marketing, and when I told him what I needed, he invited me to Florida.

"I'll take you to your first NASCAR race," he said.

It turned out it was the Daytona 500. And it was there that I continued my research. It's also where I became a NASCAR junkie. I was in the pit with the racing teams and it was thrilling. We were in the actual pit where we could feel the pulse of the engines, the sounds of pit crews installing lug nuts on the tires, and the hustle and bustle of teams working fast and talking to engineers through headsets! So much was moving so fast, and I was seeing how fast they work in sync to compete. I also learned who the drivers were and asked the teams all about the role of sponsors and partners, which brands were doing it well and why. It was fascinating. I went from knowing nothing to being in the center of all the action.

The access that Kevin gave me provided all the intel I needed to know about the sport, including how the fans engage with the sport, which for any sponsoring brands is very important. Knowing how to integrate with fans is really important.

In the end, General Mills built a whole strategic platform around motorsports, negotiated a licensing deal, and sponsored their very first car with Mark Martin of Roush Racing signed as the driver. The number six car proudly displayed the logo for General Mills's Bugles brand of snacks. I earned a Chairman's Award for my work from the chairman of General Mills during the company's annual meeting. Since then, this successful relationship between NASCAR and General Mills has grown and now includes cars sponsored by other brands such as Cheerios, Betty Crocker, Pillsbury, Totino's, Chex, and Wheaties. I am so proud to have been there from day one and I have a framed signed photo of the 1998 Roush Racing Mark Martin car in the pit from race day when it debuted. He finished second that day behind Jeff Gordon.

General Mills was one of my first jobs, and this ability to know what I didn't know, then go above and beyond to create value, has served me well at every job I've had since. It also helped me get and retain clients when I started my own company and is something my team practices daily. For example, when we get hired by a new client, we take the time to do an audit of where they've been in the press in the previous two to five years. This includes doing research to check whether they've had any media exposure and what kind of press it's been. We look for positive and negative stories and what types of outlets are covering them. We don't have to do this; we could easily just go forward with whatever information they choose to share. But it's so valuable to study their public track record and see their positioning in order to understand where they are today and what their strategy should be in the future. And we don't just do this for paying clients. Often, we do an audit when we're pitching new business or before we enter a meeting where a client is briefing us. Yes, this research is extra work but we see it as a core part of our job. Armed with this added information we can build the best strategy, which provides even more value.

Step up and stand out—show your value.

Be the First

One way you can create value for others is to seek first-time experiences or business opportunities—creating something new or facilitating the discovery of something new. For example, I like to be the first to show a potential client

RULE # 2 BE A VALUE CREATOR

a new city, or introduce them to a new event or experience. They have nothing to compare it to and chances are they are never going to forget their first visit. This puts the operative word of *creation* in *value creation*. By relying on yourself to look for new "firsts" you can set your own rules and that is very exciting and empowering. Let me put it into action for you to demonstrate this idea.

I met Dr. Deepak Chopra through his business manager for the first time over Zoom and introduced myself and my work. We stayed in touch and I met him several more times. Over the course of a conversation, I realized that we were both going to be in Dubai in the upcoming month and overlap by one day. Deepak is a busy, world-renowned person, and I knew he had been to Dubai before, but I reached out to him and said, "If you can just give me half a day, I'll arrange something meaningful for you there." I had no idea what I was going to do, but I was determined to use my thinking cap and connections in Dubai to create value in my way.

First, I reached out to a minister—and not just any minister but one of the most important in the UAE—and asked him whether he would appreciate time with Dr. Deepak Chopra. Luckily, he was available during the only window I had to work with. I had also done work for the Dubai Future Foundation, which just recently opened the Museum of the Future. The Museum of the Future, dubbed "the most beautiful building in the world," is a six floor building that exhibits life in the year 2071, from health and wellness, to science and technology. Since Deepak had launched an AI app and is all about the future in terms of mindfulness and wellness, I thought that might be a valuable visit for us. I arranged to get him a private guided tour with the executive director.

When the day arrived, Deepak was taken on a private tour of the museum and then met with the minister. The meeting with the minister was supposed to be 20 minutes and went well over an hour. In the end, the half day was of tremendous value. The meeting went so well that the Dubai Future Foundation agreed to host him for a private event and bought his books to share with guests. The UAE minister was happy because he got to spend time with Deepak and Deepak was thrilled because he was able to talk about important things on his agenda. Deepak also seemed to enjoy it and shared the experience on his social media, which was a nice surprise.

This experience also created value for me because I got to learn more about both of them. Building a relationship is about investing time, and once you spend time with someone you are able to understand how they tick, and more importantly what they care about.

This is all about how you take an opportunity and try to create value for somebody. Or in this case for two parties. Both Deepak and the minister saw the value; and for me, it was an important mission to land. Deepak put his trust in me, and I didn't want to do anything to jeopardize it.

Think of doing this for any potential client so they get to see how you operate and what value you can create when you are not paid. They see your authentic way of contributing. They might think, *If this is what you do when I'm not a client, imagine what you will do if I become one.* In my case, it was a springboard for my business relationship with Deepak for a special short-term assignment.

I've done this countless times in my career and continue to do so in the hopes that planting seeds and creating value will lead to long-term benefits. Maybe the other person will become a client. Or maybe it's someone I just want to be in good standing with. Perhaps they might connect me to somebody I'm trying to work with. That brings me to

RULE # 2 BE A VALUE CREATOR

a critical point about value creation: when I'm creating that value, I don't know what the outcome will be and I don't focus on that. I focus on the deliverable right in front of me because there might not be an outcome.

What are you adding to the value equation?

Four Principles for Creating Value

I have value creation boiled down to four key principles:

1. Be consistent with your behavior. Creating value is not just what you do, but it's also how you do it. The way you conduct yourself is what defines a value creator. For me, it's the culture of my company. The number one reason we exist is to create value for clients, and the only way we keep them is if we continue to add value and do it very well.

On the first day of work for every member of my team, we emphasize and train on this principle. We share examples of what we mean by creating value: being on time and on budget, being proactive, delivering outstanding results, coming up with breakthrough ideas, making outstanding connections, seeing them through tough situations, and closing space.

"Closing space" means we are making efforts to become closer to clients or customers through relationship building. Are we treating clients like true partners and closing space by speaking to them frequently? Are we closing space by having difficult conversations with them when necessary? Our job is to protect their reputation and sometimes we have to share bad news—i.e., a story broke that is not favorable and it's going viral. We need to be honest with them about what it's going to take to manage it.

Creating value is so important to me that we ask two questions at every weekly staff meeting: What's happening in culture? And what are we doing to create value for our clients this week? The reason we put these two topics on a pedestal is simple. We must understand what's happening in culture, the marketplace, and the news to deliver a story that is relevant, not tone deaf. Consistent behavior and adjusting your behavior to suit who you are working with or creating value for is what matters.

2. Share knowledge. One way that my company creates value is that we offer media training to all our clients. We do this to help them communicate confidently in a variety of interactions with the media and other situations. And we don't charge them for this added service. The mock interviews we conduct are similar to those they'll actually take part in, complete with curveballs and questions that get progressively harder. Then we provide feedback. This includes insight into how to handle challenging questions, maintain control of their answers, and leave a positive impression. We talk about the importance of delivering your key messages and doing it consistently. For example, we practice the main ideas the client needs to get across before the interview and then train them on how to communicate them in a concise manner that can be used as sound bites. We also work on body language. Are they making eye contact? What are their hand gestures? Clients love this added value because it gives them confidence, makes them feel prepared, and puts them in control. For your company, think about how team members can share knowledge and information with each other. We have a WhatsApp group where we share interesting new apps, articles, or things we see in the market. We also send these notes to clients, because knowledge brings value—and it's even better if the timing is right.

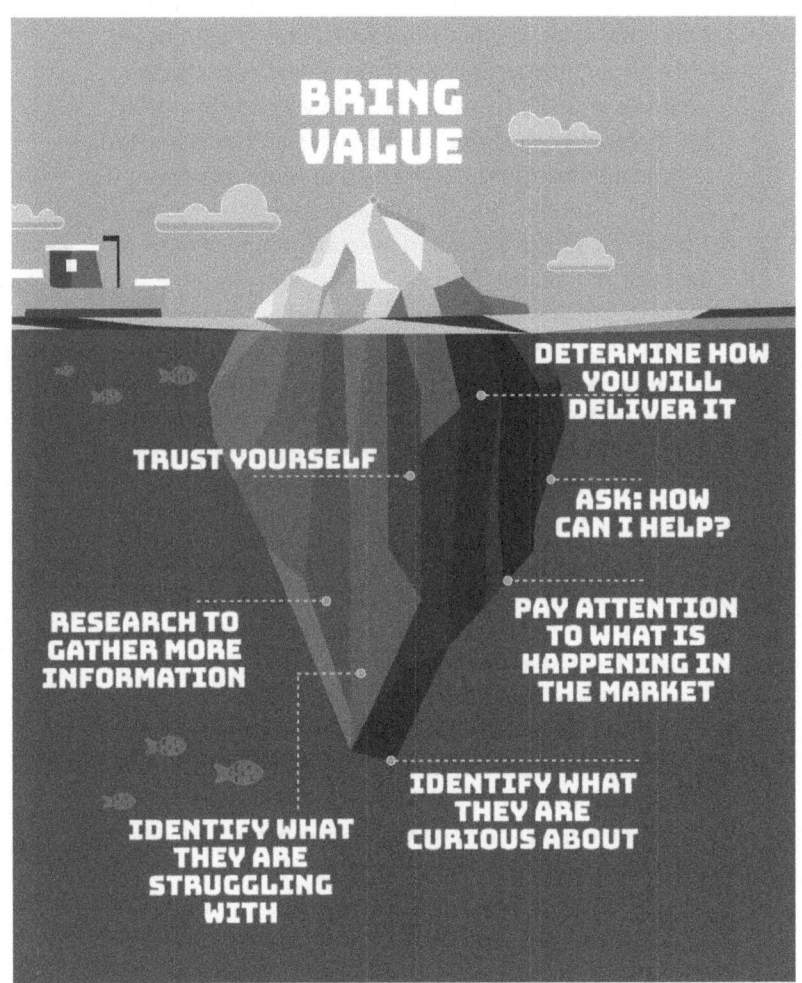

Sprinting for Obama: It's Classified

If you have knowledge, share it. Never underestimate the value of what you know and how your point of view and expertise can make a difference. In September of 2015, I was contacted by the former chief technical officer of the United States and assistant to President Obama who was given my contact information by a former Google colleague. President Obama began an initiative to bring in small groups of outside experts to conduct "sprints," aimed at exploring ways to improve how the government works. These professional experts volunteer three weeks to work full time on a mission and are handpicked based on their experience. At the time I was living in Dubai, and I was asked to be on the first-ever sprint team dedicated to strategic communications. This six-member sprint team would be the first one housed at the U.S. State Department under the direction of public diplomacy. The assignment was to assess counterterrorism communications strategies to leverage emerging communications platforms, techniques, and technologies.

Trust me, I was wondering how I ended up there too. *What do I know about counterterrorism strategies? Nothing.* But I do know how the media works and how communications works, so, like me, when you're faced with something you have never done before, ask what you CAN bring to the table and focus on that.

I was the only one on the team who was from the Arab world, who actually lived in the region, was fluent in Arabic *and* had direct experience doing strategic communications in the Middle East. The other members of the team worked in public policy, branding,

RULE # 2 BE A VALUE CREATOR

data analysis, political organizing, and tech. All were based in the United States and all had incredible pedigrees and credentials. I was super intimidated until I learned that none of them had any direct experience in the region whatsoever. I was honored to be selected, but three weeks was a long time to "volunteer." However, I knew it would be a valuable learning experience and I felt my participation would be beneficial, especially after I learned I was the only one from the region. I would be in an advantageous position and bring a lot to the table.

Before I could join the team, I had to acquire security clearance from National Security and the FBI. This is a very complicated and lengthy process, where I had to answer several questions and then submit fingerprint cards they shipped to me that had to be inked at the Dubai police station. I had to go to three police stations before they agreed to help me. I passed all U.S. government security measures and took off for Washington, D.C. I was basically going on a field trip in the United States to work on a group homework assignment where we had to turn in the paper to President Obama. Imagine that.

The three weeks were highly organized. During week one, we were briefed by officials in different agencies and departments across government. During this process they fed us boatloads of information and outlined the problem they wanted us to work on. It was an avalanche of information to digest in one week. During week two, we worked long intense hours as a group to address the mission we were assigned. These were long days and laborious work of debating, thinking, strategizing, organizing, researching, and collaborating. We went through all the stages of teamwork: forming, storming, norming, performing. It was not free of drama, that's for sure. After all, we didn't know each other and were thrown together in a conference room, like a professional escape room that we couldn't get out of until we solved how to improve counterterrorism communications strategies for the U.S. government. Simple, right?

Finally, during week three, we presented our recommendations and innovative ideas to a variety of officials in a mini-roadshow across government branches. This was the fun part and the only highlight I can actually share is that we got to do a presentation in the Situation Room. Yes, *the* Situation Room that you see on TV. The Situation Room is a secure conference room where the U.S. president and senior government officials convene during crisis situations and is also a well-known TV show on CNN—ha!

During the course of week three, we presented our work to some heavy hitters including John Kerry, secretary of state; Tony Blinken, deputy secretary of state (currently secretary of state under President Biden); Lisa Monaco, chief counterterrorism advisor to President Obama; Jen Easterly, special assistant to President Obama and senior director for counterterrorism on the National Security Council; and countless others. After the three weeks ended, we all flew home and back to our normal workdays. Four months later the White House issued an executive order based on the recommendations we shared for the establishment of a global engagement center. Executive Orders are directives issued by the president of the United States and they carry the force of law, are legally binding, and are used

> to establish new policies or procedures. It was a pretty cool moment for all of us when it was issued. It was later abolished when President Trump came into office.
>
> This experience taught me so much, but what I want to underscore for you is the importance of sharing the knowledge you have acquired over time. You can share knowledge through so many ways and platforms: one-to-one relationships, in business or through social media. The biggest insecurity we have about sharing what we know is wondering if anyone will care or find it helpful. The only way you will find out is if you make an effort to share your knowledge with as many people as you can. This not only enhances your ability to learn new things, it can also foster innovation by sparking new ideas as people come together to share insights and expertise. It can also help build relationships. When people educate me and share knowledge with me, it helps build trust and strengthen those relationships, which creates a culture of openness and mutual respect. Lastly, people feel more engaged and motivated when they are learning and growing. So, if you share knowledge with others you're actually increasing their engagement and interest levels too.

3. Sell your vision. If you want to create value for someone, they must see the value you are bringing to them. If you come up with a good idea, but the other party doesn't find it valuable, then you have a losing proposition. What you propose and how you propose it is a form of selling. How good are you at selling your vision to your customer? Are you clearly articulating your value proposition? Good ideas travel faster when you share your vision with conviction but also with facts, context and meaning. Give your ideas meaning by bringing your expertise into the story.

For example, I am a self-appointed ambassador for doing business in the Middle East with leaders based in the United States. There are tremendous opportunities for U.S. companies and brands to work in the region across multiple sectors and industries. In order for me to convince them to even look at the region, I need to sell them my vision.

My vision is that when people look at me or look at the Middle East, they see ambition and opportunities, and are inspired by the region, not just from a monetary standpoint but from a true place of cultural and economic optimism and promise. So many people want to come to the region to collect a "bag" (of money). My role is to ensure that we have a real purpose: to create jobs, transfer knowledge, build new opportunities in the market, bring value, teach new skills, and grow the ecosystem. Period.

This means I need to make the case for why they should invest time and money exploring the region when they have other priorities, other business markets to look at or other strategic needs that have nothing to do with expansion to the Middle East. For many leaders it's a very heavy lift. Dubai, for example, is a 10-hour time difference and a 14-hour flight away from New York. It's not exactly conducive for workflows and business streams. I navigate this in three ways: first, I explain the value proposition; second, I spend time educating and sharing information such as helpful links, data, and articles; and lastly, I ask them to come with me on a trip. This way, I can curate a visit and let them see everything for themselves; after all, seeing is believing. It's the easiest way to see the vision I proposed live in action.

RULE # 2 BE A VALUE CREATOR

A Tale of Two Sisters

When my dad was the dean of the business school at Minnesota State University, Mankato, he started a program called "Executive Lectures," where he would invite former alumni who were entrepreneurs, executives, and leaders in their fields to come speak to students about their career paths. Eleven years after my dad passed away, the university asked if my sister and I would be guest speakers. It was a full-circle moment for us and we immediately said yes; our dad would have been so proud. The goal of these fireside chats is to inspire students by sharing personal stories and experiences.

My sister and I couldn't have shared more polar opposite stories. We have completely different career paths and journeys, which was cool to share with the audience. Once Amany graduated from university, she joined General Mills and has been there for more than 30 years. She's had various roles within the organization and worked her way up the ranks to company officer and has spent her entire career there. I, on the other hand, have the complete opposite story. I changed jobs and switched from corporate life to entrepreneur life. I've worked for governments and companies and done everything in between. Where she was a straight line, I was a zig zag in comparison. Same level of texture and difficulty, just different paths.

We actually had to sell our visions to students based on our careers. Should you work for a company and be a dedicated employee climbing your way through the roles and ranks or become an entrepreneur? My vision was simple: follow your passions and don't be afraid

> to test and taste new things on your journey as we all change and so should our careers. My sister's vision was also simple: if you invest in your career and your relationships in the company you work for, you can grow within the organization and rich experiences are yours for the taking—if you're willing to put in the hard work, take initiative, and deliver results. We shared our paths and we actually learned a lot about each other in the process. I walked away with newfound respect for my sister and what she has accomplished.

4. Anticipate needs. Value creators know how to anticipate needs. If you can anticipate the needs of your manager, customer, or client, then you bring tremendous value, which will build stronger relationships and improve your effectiveness. It's an important skill to have and requires you to be an active observer so you can jump on opportunities to add value to someone at the right time. To anticipate needs you must also be patient, be a problem solver, and be proactive. You also need to deploy empathy and find ways to put yourself in someone else's shoes, understand cultural nuances and be resourceful. Anticipating needs is about thinking ahead and completing a task someone needs or might appreciate. I love how my executive assistant does this for me by thinking things through, especially when I have a hectic travel schedule. For example, it can be something small like thinking through what I am going to do with my bags if I go straight from the airport to a meeting, to seeing on my calendar a client's birthday and sending me ideas for a gift and how to arrange its delivery. This creates so much value for me and saves so much time. How can you anticipate the needs of your customers, team members or employees?

RULE # 2 BE A VALUE CREATOR

Stand Up and Smile

When I graduated from college my first job was as a customer service representative of a software company called Clear with Computers (CWC). The company sold software on floppy disks to the manufacturers of medium- and heavy-duty trucks. Their customers included Peterbilt, Mack, Kenworth, Scania, Renault, and Freightliner, among others. The software was designed to help truck manufacturers customize their orders, from selecting the wheelbase and chassis sizes to outfitting the cabins where drivers sit to their decked-out sleeping amenities.

My job was to answer the helpline and help customers who had problems installing the software and get them through it. You have to be a very good listener to understand the prompts on their computer that you couldn't even see and you had to be able to disarm frustrated customers who were having problems with the installation process. I can't believe I did this job for two full years. Customers who call a helpline are usually at their wits' end. This entry-level job taught me everything I know about anticipating needs and creating value for customers. I learned how to express empathy for frustrated customers. I had to be patient and absorb their energy, and I had to be a problem solver. They weren't hanging up until their problem was fixed! I had to be an active listener and a good communicator. The company gave us very good training on how to handle various situations, but the most valuable tool they gave us was a mirror.

Yes, a mirror.

I couldn't understand why we needed a mirror to do our jobs over the phone, but then they explained.

Every customer service agent was given a mirror that said "Stand Up and Smile." They trained us that when we are dealing with an upset customer, stand up. It will give you power and is empowering. Secondly, they wanted us to smile. A smile is disarming and immediately changes your demeanor and attitude in a matter of seconds. This move can change the trajectory of a customer experience and help you close a call. After all, our aim is to get off the phone as fast as possible with happy customers *and* a successful installation. It was such a simple tool, but it was so effective I couldn't believe it worked like a charm—every single time!

The job wasn't easy, but being on the front lines handling customers gave me tremendous insight into how a business works. When the new CEO of Uber, Dara Khosrowshahi, took over the company, you know the first thing he did? He became an Uber driver to get firsthand insights on the end-to-end customer experience. The CEO of Airbnb, Brian Chesky, decided to live in Airbnb properties to learn how to anticipate the needs of hosts and customers. And he documented the whole thing on social media. By sharing his insights, he not only sent a strong message to his employees, but he also built trust and connected with future customers.

Being on the front lines gives you incredible insights and perspectives, and firsthand information helps you to learn things by actually seeing them and experiencing them yourself.

RULE # 2 BE A VALUE CREATOR

Once you understand this second rule, "become a value creator," to master self-reliance and you go all in, you become unstoppable and invaluable to others. The playbook to winning doesn't involve luck. And it doesn't need to. If you live your life creating value for others and do so authentically, you ultimately create value for yourself. You get a sense of purpose and satisfaction that you are doing good in this world. It's a way to live. It's a way of bestowing generosity on others: generous with your time, generous with your words, generous with your intentions. Creating value for other people is my random act of kindness; it's giving back to the world. By thinking of others, you can build the life you want. It's worked in my personal life and in my professional life. And I know that if the value doesn't show up today, it'll show up later.

Creating value is the underlying thread of everything I do. However, I'd never named it until I was brainstorming with Gary on a job title to reflect the PR and business development work I do for him. Typically, you do one or the other, not both. We came up with *chief value officer*. My secret sauce is finding out what others value the most and then delivering that.

It should be your secret sauce too.

How can you be the chief value officer of your life?

RULE #2
BECOME A VALUE CREATOR

It's how you create authentic relationships, build credibility, achieve a sense of purpose and make yourself indispensable to clients or customers.

RULE # 2 BE A VALUE CREATOR

> **Cheat Sheet**

- **Solve a problem:** Identify a problem that people are facing and find a way to solve it or take something off their plates. This could be as simple as making an introduction or providing a service that addresses the issue or as complex as developing a new technology or innovation. Value is directly tied to performance. Value creators are problem solvers and solution providers.
- **Share knowledge:** If you have expertise in a particular area, share your knowledge with others. You can write blog posts, create videos, or teach courses to help others learn and improve their skills.
- **Provide support:** Showing up and providing support is a great way to bring value to others. This is especially the case when you don't have all the answers or skills, but you are there when they need you the most.
- **Volunteer:** Giving your time and energy to a cause or organization that you care about can create immense value for others. Whether you're working with people in your local community or contributing to a global effort, your can make a meaningful difference.
- **Create something new:** Whether it's a piece of art, a new product, or a unique service, creating something that didn't exist before can provide value to others. Your creation can inspire others, solve a problem, or simply bring joy to people's lives.

7 RULES OF SELF-RELIANCE

Those Who Create Value

- Value themselves; they know that they have something special to offer and are worthy and willing to share it with others
- Identify who needs or will benefit from their value
- Identify opportunities or linkages that others can't make or execute and use them to create value. They see around corners, taking information from multiple sources. Their strategic insight is the value
- Are always listening, culturally aware, and externally focused
- Have a strong sense of self-awareness
- Are able to see challenges as opportunities
- Are willing to work a blank page
- Learn how to collaborate with others; value creators never work alone
- Create the work or idea they want to see happen
- Consistently execute
- Have somebody who is willing to pay for their value; the customer must see the value they are presenting/ proposing

RULE # 2 BE A VALUE CREATOR

How to Hire Value Creators

When building your team, there are five dynamic qualities you should look for if you want to hire value creators and bring them into your organization.

1. **Consumer centric**: They are relentlessly focused on bringing value to their customers and obsess over meeting them where they are so they can build from that standpoint.
2. **Strong communicators**: They are skilled at articulating their ideas and building a rapport with their partners, customers, and audience. They can successfully sell their ideas and explain their thought processes.
3. **Resourceful**: They are externally focused and know where to go to find answers and solve problems. Resourceful team members know the value of collaboration and asking for help. They also know when to dig deeper on their own before escalating a key issue.
4. **Curious**: They have a keen interest in knowing more and going beyond the surface. Their curiosity motivates others in the workplace, contributes to the company culture and stimulates innovation. Curiosity players also have a growth mindset which is essential to creating value for others.
5. **Confidence**: They have a sense of confidence and urgency in their approach.

Reflection Exercises

1. What value can you bring to others?

2. What gaps exist that you can fill?

3. What connections can you make for others?

4. Do you have the ability to bring value to the other party?

5. List skills or qualities that you bring to the table.

6. Identify the most rewarding experiences you've had and what you did that made the difference. (P.S. That's the value!)

7. How can you stretch outside your comfort zone?

8. Recall a moment when someone created value for you. What did they do? How did that make you feel?

> Nobody is going to put you at the top of their priority list.

4

RULE #3
DON'T BE A
WAITER

*I never dreamed about success.
I worked for it.*

— ESTÉE LAUDER

You can be one of two things in this world: a waiter or a creator.

Waiters rely on other people to bring them opportunities, are reluctant to make decisions, and prefer to stay in their comfort zones. They go along with the status quo and are averse to taking chances and putting themselves in vulnerable positions. In contrast, creators search for and produce their own opportunities. They are bold enough to take a stand, make difficult decisions, and navigate unchartered territory—even if they are nervous or there is a risk of failure. Creators don't need anyone to give them permission to change and grow. When you stop being a waiter, you learn how to rely on yourself.

Chances are, no one is going to just hand you the opportunity that you actually want. You must create it for yourself. Nobody is going to put you at the top of their priority list. Not your parents, not your spouse, not your co-workers. Only you can do that. No one is going to prepare you or teach you new skills, which are crucial as the ways of working and living have evolved. No one is going to say, "I anoint you with this project or client that's going to make you a star." That just doesn't happen. There's no fairy godmother of business. There's no magic wand of entrepreneurship wizardry that will bestow gold dust upon your shoulders. This is especially the case if you want to survive in today's business environment, where you've got more control but also more responsibility and must be accountable. As an entrepreneur running your own company, you certainly can't rely on others to tell you what's important, to take charge or make decisions. The good news is that going from a waiter to a creator is easier than you think.

Are You a Waiter or Creator?

Of course, the first step is identifying whether you are a waiter or a creator. I actually had no clue that I was a waiter until my friend Alaa was brutally honest with me.

"What's your sign?" he asked one day over tea.

"Scorpio," I said.

"I knew it!" he exclaimed. "Scorpios are passionate and loyal, but they're also waiters."

"What??" I said, feeling defensive.

"Scorpios tend to lay in wait," he repeated, that word stinging as he said it. "You wait for things to happen to you. You wait for the next job or event. You wait for Mr. Right to arrive. There's no end in sight and you don't have a sense

RULE #3 DON'T BE A WAITER

of timing. Maha, please don't be one of those people who waits for things to come to you or for your circumstances to change."

The conversation hit me hard because it was the truth. Dammit, I was a waiter. You know when someone tells you something and you know it to be true but you never zeroed in on it or said it out loud—that is what I felt in this moment. I never had a label for my behavior—until he said it out loud and then I couldn't unhear it being attached to me. At the time, I was in Egypt, working at Orascom Telecom and going through the motions of my day-to-day life. My parents were both sick and I was waiting for their conditions to improve or get worse. At work, I was doing the projects I was given, but not going outside my comfort zone. I wasn't particularly unhappy about anything; I was just waiting for something good to come along, waiting for life to happen to me. I thought that you just had to win the day. You go to work, you go to the gym, you see your friends, you're a good daughter. That was it. I didn't know that I should have broader ambitions or focus on achieving more. I didn't plan things. I was just doing what I thought I was supposed to. I was reliable and responsible. But I wasn't going beyond that. I realized that I was just an executor. Yes, I was skilled at it, but I was not stretching or reaching. I was basically catching all the balls life was throwing at me.

After tea with Alaa, I couldn't stop thinking about being a waiter. I am not exactly sure how I saw myself before — a go-getter or something else — but I never would have called myself a waiter. Now that he named it, I became it. So what did this mean for me?

I wanted to move from being a waiter to being a creator, but how? It's not like I could flick a light switch and immediately change. Instead, I focused on the little things that I had to do to become a creator, starting with taking a mental inventory. My list included things like: What insecurities do I need to address? What dreams am I not focusing on? What do I need to stop doing that is no longer serving me? How do I spend my time and am I focusing on the things that are best for me?

I started to reflect on my job and wondered if it was dictating my future, my happiness, and my success. Or was I just going along with the status quo? Was I in Egypt only to take care of my parents and work to pay our bills? Or was I going to go after my dreams? And by the way, what were they because I never stopped to think about them? Back then, we didn't journal or manifest our dreams into the universe. I do recall the book *The Secret* was out, but nobody actually believed it worked. Raise your hand if you bought the book!

The truth is most of us are waiting; waiting for a co-worker or partner to tell us what to do, waiting for that new client or love interest, waiting for the right apartment/time to have kids/fill in the blank. You don't have to be a Scorpio to be a waiter. To change any behavior, it's important to understand why we do it.

So why are so many of us in waiting mode?

What is it about society or our upbringing that values waiting. Is it not wanting to be seen as aggressive? Is it because we were told to wait our turns and follow hierarchy? I'm not sure, but what I am sure of is that everyone can wait, but only those who want to own their lives choose to become creators.

Maybe so many of us fall in waiting mode because it's safe. It's our bubble of comfort.

RULE #3 DON'T BE A WAITER

Want to stay in your comfort zone? Well, then say hello to:

- Limiting your growth
- Missed opportunities
- Potential for regret
- Complacency, social isolation, anxiety, and more

Taking a risk is scary and makes our hearts skip a few beats while waiting helps us avoid putting ourselves in vulnerable positions and keeps our nervous systems in check. We don't want to open ourselves to stress and anxiety. And it's not just that people wait to seek opportunities or take chances, they also stay in bad situations because they're afraid of the unknown. We also wait because we fear what others will think of us. Although their relationship/job/fill-in-the-blank isn't satisfying and makes them unhappy, they don't do anything about it. However, it's when you get out of your comfort zone and the waiting mindset that the magic happens.

Taylor Swift is the ultimate example of "don't be a waiter" in action. In 2019, music mogul and producer Scooter Braun purchased *Big Machine Records,* which owned the master recordings of her first six albums. Swift took to Tumbler and said, "Now Scooter has stripped me of my life's work, that I wasn't given an opportunity to buy," because she wanted the chance to own her life's work. He owned the right to when and how her songs were played, including in Netflix documentaries and even in live performances for music award shows.

Then artist Kelly Clarkson suggested Swift do something that has never been done before in the music industry. She encouraged her to do the ultimate "don't be a waiter" move and immediately catapulted her to the front of the trail blazing creator line!

Clarkson suggested that Swift re-record all of her old albums to create new masters and re-release them. This way Swift would get full control and ownership over her complete music library. She could have waited for the music industry to change their rules, but instead she created a new industry standard. Swift re-recorded all of her old music and re-released them as "Taylor's Version" and she even included songs composed for each album that never made the cut and called them original songs "From the Vault." Not only did she re-release the albums successfully, but they also smashed records. Swift is the first woman—and first living soloist—to have 11 concurrently charting albums on the Billboard 200 since the list combined stereo and mono albums in 1963.

Some people stay in waiting mode without realizing it. For example, Oprah Winfrey has famously talked about being fired from her first job as a news anchor in Baltimore because she was told she wasn't fit for TV. I wonder how that producer feels now! And founder of IT Cosmetics, Jamie Kern Lima, was told that no one would buy makeup from someone who "looks like you" because she was not a size zero. Thankfully, she didn't listen because her company was the largest beauty brand on QVC and was then acquired by makeup giant L'Oréal for $1.2 billion. But many of us are not that thick-skinned or able to block out the naysayers, so we retreat back into the waiting room. However, standing still is not progress and you won't get anywhere without taking action.

RULE #3 DON'T BE A WAITER

No Office No Problem

When I wanted to start my own business, I couldn't wait. I wanted to start my new chapter immediately. I was cash-strapped and I could barely afford to pay my only full-time employee. Her name was also Maha, and we needed to get to work and get clients. But I wasn't going to work at an Internet cafe. I needed a home base where we could start the company. You have heard the stories of companies that started in basements or even garages. Apple, Google, Microsoft, Amazon, and HP all started in a garage. I didn't have a garage. But I did have a friend with an ad agency, and he let me set up shop in his conference room temporarily. Every day, we went to work in Hatem Hashad's office, Advision. We heard the office space downstairs was going to be available, but it needed to be renovated first before we could move in. Hatem let us work out of his office until we were ready to be on our own. Hatem was a gem; my team had swelled to six people and he continued to support us and gave us a home to work from. I am forever grateful that he gave me my first start by opening his office and his heart to support me and my dream to have my own business.

We did overstay our stay, for nearly a year, but soon we would become neighbors. As entrepreneurs, you never forget your startup story. I knew if I waited for the right things to align—like waiting to have money to afford an office space—I might not have gotten started.

Make a Choice to Not Wait

From the moment I had that conversation with Alaa, I pivoted. As soon as I realized that I could be a waiter forever, I've spent every waking minute trying to be the opposite—a value creator, opportunity seeker, and lifelong learner—not a victim of circumstance.

In 2007, even though I was living in Egypt, I was very excited about the first female presidential candidate, Hillary Clinton, and was glued to U.S. news. But I had a good friend who worked as the bureau chief for CNN, and he kept telling me to pay attention to this new guy Barack Obama. It became a little rivalry, the two of us badgering each other because I was Team Hillary and he was Team Obama. One day he told me he'd quit his job to move from Egypt to the United States to volunteer for the Obama campaign.

"You're taking this a little too far, don't you think?" I asked. "You can't just quit your job at CNN to volunteer and not make any money. Nobody does that."

But he did. Just like that he showed up at campaign headquarters in Chicago and offered to canvass, stuff envelopes, and do whatever else they needed. He's so smart and hardworking that after about a month, when they had just announced Joe Biden as Obama's running mate, my friend got assigned to be part of Biden's speech writing team. At that point, he was entrenched in the Obama world and U.S. race for president.

"You've got to come here and be part of this," he said. "It's the most incredible thing. I can't even put it into words."

But he didn't have to. His enthusiasm was contagious and actually made me jealous. So I decided to go to the Democratic National Convention (DNC) in Denver that

RULE #3 DON'T BE A WAITER

summer. Of course, this was easier said than done. It's not a public event, so you can't just buy tickets.

I went into learning mode to find everything and anything I could about this event. I had to search online and reach out through Facebook to as many people I knew that were remotely or loosely tied to Minnesota politics.

First, I tried to figure out how I could be a part of the Minnesota delegation. I called around, but no one had an answer for me. They basically saw me as some superfan girl in Egypt who wanted to come to the DNC. But I was determined, so I asked all my friends in Washington and in the media. Still no luck. Then a friend told me that a friend of a friend of a friend ran an operation that managed volunteers who worked the DNC event. These volunteers supported various jobs to put on the convention, like tracking and escorting speakers, making sure the convention ran on time, and helping load speeches into the teleprompter.

"How do I get to be one of those volunteers?" I asked.

"Talk to this woman named Margaret," she said.

Long story short, I called Margaret and told her I was in Egypt and wanted to come to the convention and be one of her volunteers. Margaret is a big-time lobbyist and lawyer who did work for the Screen Actors Guild and was an active member of the DNC.

"Great. Then I'll see you on Monday," she said.

This was a Friday. So basically, after a three-minute conversation, all I had was her phone number and a time to meet her outside the Ball Arena (formerly the Pepsi Center) where the convention was being held. She didn't tell me if I had tickets, if I'd get credentials, or if I'd even get into the DNC, but I didn't care. I was taking a chance and grabbing the opportunity. I booked a plane ticket and started looking for a hotel. This is when I learned that the DNC had taken over all the hotels in and around Denver and allocated them to the delegations from each state. (Blogs reported that even Oprah couldn't get a hotel room, so she rented a house at a whopping $50,000 for the week.) Next, I searched Craigslist and found a guy who had listed his apartment because he wanted to escape town during the convention. It turned out to be an amazing loft in the heart of all the action just a quick walk from the Ball Arena and the price was much less than a hotel would have been. Even though I still didn't have a ticket and no assurance I'd even get into the convention, I rationalized that worst-case scenario I'd just go hiking and do yoga in Denver and watch the convention on TV.

On Monday, I met Margaret as planned. She was captivating, snappy, and commanding. She was on the phone when we met, and I could immediately tell she was a powerhouse. She had that New York fashion style too; she wore a tight pencil skirt and her signature Roger Vivier heels every time I saw her from that day forward.

"Come with me," she said, as I followed her like a lap dog, marveling at the fact that she could walk so briskly in that pencil skirt and high heels. Then she gave me my first job of the week. "You're in charge of working the speaker tracker," she said.

I had no idea what that meant, so I asked. This meant meeting the various speakers at the door and tracking their movements. We needed to meet them, take them backstage, and pace them through the process to prepare for the big show. Every single speaker had to rehearse and work with the famous speech coach and writer Michael Sheehan. He trained them on the teleprompter and went over their delivery. Also, backstage there were two rooms with signs that said, "Speech Writing" and "Speech Tracker," where

RULE #3 DON'T BE A WAITER

a team of professional writers labored over every word of every speech. Then Barack Obama's team would proofread and approve them. Obama's team had a big sign outside of their door that said, "Edits you can believe in" with the word *Edits* crossed out and the word *Changes* written above it. "Changes you can believe in," a play on Obama's campaign slogan. I loved it and couldn't believe I was a part of all this action.

This was an opportunity of a lifetime. I was pinching myself. How many other Egyptian girls were going to be on the floor of the Democratic National Convention and backstage no less. I told myself that every night I would go home and journal this. I wanted to capture this in a bottle forever!

Just being "on the floor," as they call it, was so thrilling. It was like taking the field before a big game. I loved watching the sound and production guys tweaking the lights, cameras, and teleprompters to perfection. I also loved looking up at the boxes around the perimeter, each one representing NBC, MSNBC, CNN, FOX, ABC, BBC, etc. I've always been a news junkie obsessed with various anchors. Now I got to see them do their jobs live right in front of me. (By the way, Katie Couric did the evening news in flip flops one night.) One evening, I wanted to prove to my then six-year-old niece that Auntie Maha was actually at the convention. Michelle Obama was on stage and David Gregory from MSNBC was doing live cutaway shots from the floor. Perched in a director's chair with a clear view of the speaker's podium behind him, I stepped into the camera shot for 30 seconds until my niece confirmed that she saw me—in white sleeves!!

My next assignment was escorting some of the speakers during the convention. I was given a map and had to learn where the various suites were located and where to bring each speaker when it was time for them to take the stage. I was stationed outside at the VIP drop-off zone waiting for people to get out of their cars. Most were people I didn't know, although I did get to escort Steven Spielberg to his suite. I came back and next was assigned to escort Teresa Heinz Kerry to suite 256. When we got to the suite, the person working the door said that I needed to get Mrs. Kerry settled because, "Michelle and the girls are coming." *Michelle and the girls?* Yes, *that* Michelle and the girls.

"Shut the door and don't leave because they're locking the room for security sweeps," she told me. Talk about not being a waiter! Just a week earlier, I had no clue how I was going to get into the convention and now I found myself with the best seat in the house. While Barack Obama gave his acceptance speech, I was sitting in the box with Michelle Obama and their daughters. And it gets better.

Next thing I knew, I was talking to Michelle about Egypt. (I can't believe that Barack Obama's first state visit as president was to Egypt.) After that I went to several private parties, got introduced to members of the Obama transition team, and met a lot of new and important people. In the end, many of these people became good friends and future business connections. Why? All because I chose to create my own value and fly to Denver with no guarantees rather than wait for something to happen to me.

In 2014, I made another huge don't-be-a-waiter move and left my job at Google to go back to my company. I had accepted the position of head of global communications and public policy the morning of January 25, 2011—the day the uprising in Egypt began. Of course, at the time I had no idea how this would impact me. And that wasn't the only major moment. Through my role there, I was a part of a team that launched some of their largest brands in the Middle East for the first time: YouTube, Google Maps, and

RULE #3 DON'T BE A WAITER

Street View to name a few. But after three and a half years at the tech giant, it was time.

It isn't easy to say good-bye to a regular paycheck no matter where you work, but it's even harder when your employer is considered the ultimate. Voted the top company to work for five years in a row by *Forbes*, Google's name is enough to make anyone in the room turn around and listen. The perks, the technology, the spirit of innovation: it's the job so many people dream of landing, and I knew how lucky I was to work there.

Google was the cutting edge of all things tech—and still is. Being in such a global organization gave me firsthand experience on how major multinational companies work. This company is known for its innovative culture and its place in history as one of the leading global tech giants next to Apple, Microsoft, and Amazon. And it's not a secret, working for a globally recognized and respected company like Google can be a significant boost to one's career. The experience and network one builds at Google can open doors to numerous opportunities.

But I loved being an entrepreneur and having the freedom to choose what I worked on and how I spent my time. I loved having full control of my day, picking the projects and clients I felt uniquely qualified to do. And I also wanted to challenge myself as I moved forward in my career. For example, a lot of qualified professionals can write press releases for Coca-Cola, but not everyone is cut out to do crisis communications after a terrorist attack on a hotel. There were hundreds of PR agencies who were capable of handling press conferences and product launches. I wanted difficult projects that would help me grow and learn. You don't get stronger by going to the gym and lifting the same 5-pound weights for 10 years. Eventually, you need to up your game.

So you need to lift heavier to see results. I really had no idea what I was signing up for, but I was willing to put in the hard work to find out. I started making lists: lists of people in my network, lists of things I needed to study and learn, lists of industries I could or could not approach. You cannot edit a blank page so I started to put ideas to paper to help me think it through.

Also, I was tired of making money for other people. I was the expert and yet I was lining everybody else's pockets but my own. I was building value for them, but I wasn't building value for myself long term. I wanted to be self-reliant and not depend on others. I became aware that I should put that time and effort into myself. And I realized the ultimate self-reliant move was to become an entrepreneur again and it was time to see what was next. I was scared to take the leap again but kept hearing my dad's words in my head, "If you're passionate about something, put your head down and pursue it. Hard work always pays off."

My dad passed away Thanksgiving weekend of 2004, but he will always be my north star. He is why I am who I am. So I had to make the move—no matter how scary and uncertain that move was.

His voice was in my head, and I know what it's like to be faced with uncertainty and making pros and cons lists! You start to question yourself and self-doubt creeps in but what's meant for you will unfold for you. I firmly believe that.

Has my entrepreneurial journey been perfect? Not at all. I've dealt with cash flow issues and struggled to pay suppliers and meet payroll. (Being on the hook for other people's salaries has given me plenty of sleepless nights in the last 20 years.) I've made a lot of bad business decisions too. I've hired the wrong people and kept them too long.

RULE #3 DON'T BE A WAITER

Countless times, I should have resigned an account after being treated poorly by a client who didn't respect us and exercised grotesque abuse of power. But has it been worth it? Yes, yes, and yes! Taking risks is part of growth and can lead to success. While many of us know this is true, we wait because we're afraid to fail. But failing is part of the process. If you take a risk and it doesn't work out, you learn from it. Failing helps you figure out how to get better and deliver on the next job, career move or version of yourself.

When you embrace the principles of self-reliance, your relationship with failure and fear changes dramatically. I used to put enormous pressure on myself, but once I started to rely on myself more, I realized that not only was self-imposed pressure paralyzing me, but also that the pressure was rooted in fear of failure. I got more confidence in myself and trusted that my skills and know-how would be what moved me ahead, not pressure or fear of failure. It was extremely counterintuitive to where I wanted to spend my energy.

We fear failure for so many reasons, whether it's related to past experiences or pressure from society fueled by social media. The fear of failure is also related to identity. I was tying my self-worth and identity to my achievements, so failure felt like a direct hit to my self-esteem, leading to feelings of inadequacy and diminished self-worth. This is why I often say self-reliance is related to self-confidence and self-worth. If you start to believe you can achieve your personal and professional goals, you gain confidence. Once you gain confidence by knowing your self-worth, your relationship with fear and failure shifts dramatically.

Mistakes have helped me pivot and grow. I didn't walk into any part of my life knowing what I was doing, from taking care of my parents to being an entrepreneur. Most of the time, I had no idea. I've failed plenty, but I've always had the resilience and determination to want to challenge myself. No experience is wasted if you embrace it as an opportunity to learn and reframe it as valuable insight. Then you can let go of the fear of making mistakes and take more risks. Don't be afraid to try new things, especially if it means leaving your comfort zone and pushing yourself. You will be surprised at what you are capable of if you just challenge yourself. Of course, your risks should be calculated, so think them through. Always take risks where you are betting on yourself, thus automatically stacking the odds in your favor.

Five Ways to Go from Waiter to Creator

1. Be curious. People who are curious don't wait. They learn and discover new skills or interests that they had no idea they possessed. This puts you on the front foot to step up to new experiences and helps you search for and create your own opportunities. After all, the more you learn about the world, the better equipped you will be to leverage new ideas.

For example, one of my friends recently bought a keyboard and was telling me how playing music helps her relax—it's sort of like meditation—and how much she loves learning something new. Hearing about this made me curious. Would I be good at music? Would I be interested in playing the keyboard and taking lessons and working to get better at it? It's something I never ever thought about because music wasn't part of my life in high school or college. My mom tried to teach me piano when I was little but I wasn't good at it. I often cheated on our piano lessons when our teacher would call asking us to play over the phone for her and I would beg my sister to play twice to save me.

2. **Get an accountability partner.** If you have a goal, sharing it with another person can keep you honest and increase the chances that you'll achieve it.

I recommend having a personal board of directors: a group of people who care about you, have your best interests at heart, but will also give you some tough love when you need it (more on this in Chapter 6). Pick people you can confide in honestly about where you are with your goals and aspirations. My accountability partners are my sister, a former client, and a former co-worker. Plan regular check-ins with each person on your board. Whether you do it monthly, quarterly, or annually, schedule this time to go over your vision for the future and the steps you're taking to achieve it. I create a quarterly report for my board so that I can honestly assess how I'm doing. Also, make time to get feedback. Having an accountability partner is an effective way to stay focused and on track because you know somebody is checking up on you.

3. **10X your strengths**. Take some time to think about things that you're good at and write them down. Often, we don't celebrate our strengths. In fact, many of us spend a lot more time dwelling on our weaknesses and thinking about all the things we haven't done or aren't good at. I think this has gotten worse with the advent of social media because we are constantly comparing our lives to other people's highlight reels. But you are capable of doing so many things and have so much going for you, so redirect your focus. Invest to become 10X of your strengths rather than focus on your weaknesses.

List everything you can think of; putting it on paper helps you see it more clearly. Then ask yourself: What skills and abilities do other people tend to compliment me on?

(Often, you don't see yourself the way your friends, family and colleagues do.) Maybe you're good at meeting deadlines, coming up with ideas and dealing with confrontation. This is a good way to find things you can lean in to and opportunities to not be a waiter. If you give really good advice maybe you should start coaching. If you're skilled at teaching yourself new things, pick something you're curious about—a new technology or the stock market, for example—and commit to learning about it several days per week. This exercise is empowering because you're focusing on the positive and may discover a new area that is your secret sauce. Then you can figure out how to take this superpower to the next level professionally and personally.

4. Be a dreamer. Think about things that you really want to do, then figure out HOW. Dreams don't magically appear. You need to manifest, journal, and ideate around them. For me, this starts with a goal and being curious.

For example, three years ago, I was thinking about how to take one of my clients to the Super Bowl and create new relationships and opportunities. I had never been there before and had no idea how it works or how to plan things there. I just knew that it was a perfect storm of media, brands, celebrities, and business. But no one was going to just invite me to the biggest sporting event in the country, so I had to do my homework.

I reached out to a ton of people and asked questions about how the Super Bowl works. I found out about something called Radio Row, an enormous ballroom where every TV and radio station from CBS and FOX Sports to ESPN had a beautiful set ready to do interviews. Although my client had been to the Super Bowl, I never supported him to conquer Radio Row so I figured out how to get him in to do interviews at every booth, in the mix with Hall of Famers, current athletes, news anchors and celebrities. At

RULE #3 DON'T BE A WAITER

one point, I noticed that Twitter was doing rapid-fire interviews with celebs and culture makers. I told them that my client could swing by and they jumped at the chance.

The client was Gary Vaynerchuk and the Twitter interviewer asked him questions about all sorts of topics and whether they were overrated or underrated. Gary had a blast and it worked out so well that he turned "Overrated vs. Underrated" into his own wildly popular content series that does hot takes on all things in culture. You can watch it on YouTube.

That year after my work was done, I flew home and watched the game with my family in Minnesota. But the next year, I was offered a ticket to attend the game at SoFi Stadium in LA. It was awesome. My point is that I didn't wait for a client to give me a brief to go execute at Radio Row at the Super Bowl, I created the opportunity to offer value in my way. In addition to helping my client, I was able to create content for my audience and share the experiences, meet new people, expand my network, and plant seeds for next year.

By authentic value I mean having good intentions. So much about business is hit and run, short-term gain and instant gratification. I operate totally differently. I almost run away from things that have short term written all over them; they suck up too much time and pose greater risks.

The NBA All-Star weekend was right after the Super Bowl and Gary was going. I told him, "I have never been to the NBA All-Star weekend and I have no clue how it works, so I won't be going."

He looked at me and said, "Maha, if you don't go, how will you know how to work it next year?"

Gary is the kind of leader who is open to learning the first year to pay dividends for the next. He is a long-term thinker and player (a self-reliance rule!). He loves to operate through osmosis. He strongly believes you can learn by simply being around the learning opportunity. So, I decided to go and figure it out. And, he was right. I went, got to work, and hustled my heart out. Not only did I figure it out, but I ended up at Michael Jordan's birthday party hosted by Nike. I learned about all the press and brand events, ended up building a relationship with the National Basketball Players Association (NBPA) and watching the Slam Dunk contest from their suite! (Thank you, TTT).

5. Explore your options. Be open to exploring different options and taking on new challenges, even if they're outside of your comfort zone.

Last year I started to wonder how my public relations skills could serve the private equity industry and clients. And what I discovered was that their needs and my skills complemented each other:

- **Relationship management:** Both private equity and public relations professionals need to excel in building and maintaining relationships.

- **Strategic thinking:** Success in both roles requires a strategic mindset.

- **Reputation management:** While the contexts differ, managing reputation is a common goal. Private equity firms often work to enhance the reputation and brand value of their portfolio companies to achieve a successful exit strategy. Public relations focuses on managing the public image and reputation of their clients through media and communication strategies.

- **Research and analysis:** Both fields require a strong foundation in research and analysis. Private equity involves analyzing market trends, financial statements, and potential investments. Public relations requires understanding media landscapes, audience sentiment, and crafting messages that resonate with target demographics.
- **Communication skills:** Effective communication is key to both private equity and public relations. Whether it's communicating with investors and stakeholders or crafting press releases and media pitches, the ability to convey information clearly and persuasively is critical.

So, then I reached out to some private equity firms to see if I could support communications for their companies and portfolio investments. This way of operating has served me my entire life. Don't just wait for someone to give you that opportunity. Go out and create it. Rely on yourself to think about how you can seek things that are bigger and better. Those answers are within you—so don't wait, create.

Waiters are on the receiving end of opportunities that others bring them, but it's much more fun and satisfying to create your own prospects. As Mel Robbins said, "You're missing out on everything because you are waiting for someday. Make today that someday." Think about things that you really want to do, then figure out HOW and get started. It just takes one tiny step at a time. You will create opportunities for yourself that you never imagined were possible.

How I Created a New Life for Myself Because of the Pandemic and Decided Not to Be a Waiter in the Middle of a Global Crisis

From January 2020 to March 2020, I was on business in the U.S. from Dubai. I usually fly back and forth to Dubai, but after tracking 16 flights between Dubai and the U.S. in 2019, I wasn't willing to put my body through that for Q1 of 2020. I had a series of events to attend for work, and instead of flying back and forth, I used my sister's home in Minnesota as a basecamp between work functions.

I kicked off on January 7th with Oprah's Vision Tour, then the NFL's Super Bowl in Miami, the NBA All-Star Game in Chicago, and the Grammys in LA. Between events, I would go back to my sister's. After all my work was done, I finally flew home to Dubai on March 7th, 2020. When I got there, everyone was talking about "coronavirus," and the news from Asia was dominating headlines in Dubai much more than in the U.S.

I remember talking to my sister about what I was reading and said, "This looks serious, and I am worried." I always spend my summers in Minnesota, but this particular year I had booked my trip for May instead of June because my niece was graduating from high school, and I was going to attend the ceremony. So, I was planning to be in the U.S. earlier and longer than usual. I would usually go to the U.S. for the summer, and my housekeeper in Dubai would watch my dogs. Summers in Dubai are very hot and humid, and it's common for many executives to escape the heat and work remotely from Europe or elsewhere in the Middle East, like Lebanon or Cairo. Working from the U.S. is

RULE #3 DON'T BE A WAITER

not that common due to the time zone differences, but for me, spending summers in Minnesota with my family was what I did every single summer after moving to the region.

The news was overwhelming, and I wondered what if this spreads and they lock down Dubai or, worse, cancel flights or limit my ability to get home this summer. I didn't want to miss Kenzie's graduation. I started to panic that Armageddon was coming, and the thought of not being able to see my family again or having access to go see them scared me. My sister assured me everything was going to be okay, saying this was like bird flu and everything would be fine. She said, "When have you ever heard of any global airports closing or travel being restricted where you won't be able to come home? Don't worry."

On March 11th, the World Health Organization categorized the coronavirus as a pandemic due to its alarming spread and severity. On March 13th, President Trump declared a national emergency, imposed a travel ban from Europe, and encouraged all Americans to return to the United States. On March 14th, I saw a post on social media in Dubai that the airport was going to close and Emirates was going to halt flights. Minutes later, the post was deleted. Typically, posts are removed because they are rumors, and they don't want to create local panic. Too late, I was already there. My heart was racing.

On Sunday, March 15th, I called a member of the government I know and asked if the post on social media was true and if there was any reason I needed to change my flights to leave the country earlier than May. She said to me, "I cannot tell you about any of the government's plans, but if I were you, I would get out before Tuesday, March 17th." My heart sank. That meant I needed to leave tomorrow! OMG. I went into complete turbo mode. I was not going to wait to see how this played out. I decided to do something crazy, even for me.

After living in the Middle East for 23 years, I was going to leave the region and move to the U.S. in 24 hours. This was mission impossible:

1. I didn't have a flight. All the airline websites went down after Trump's declaration, and I couldn't get through to any call centers. I woke up my sister at 4am in the US and told her I needed help finding a flight for the next day. And there was another catch—I couldn't fly through Europe due to the ban, and I needed an airline that allows pets in the cabin. I wasn't going to put Coco (my dog) in the cargo hold. She was too old and recovering from an operation she had the week prior on her leg (she tore a ligament and wasn't even walking). Sigh. It's a 17-hour flight, and that is without layovers.

2. I had to get my dog to the vet for an emergency appointment to get her export papers. This involves taking her to the airport to be seen by the Ministry to secure her paperwork. I called the vet, and they came to pick her up hours later and took her for the day to get her ready to travel the next day. She needed export papers

RULE #3 DON'T BE A WAITER

to leave the UAE and the proper import papers to get her into the U.S.

3. I had a housekeeper who had been my strength and stay for eight years. She was family. Lolita lived in the Philippines, and her passport was being renewed. I didn't even have it, and I needed to pull major strings to get it back because I wasn't leaving her behind—we would all leave together. I also had to get her exit paperwork done as she was employed by me. I dispatched her to the federal office to finalize her procedures while I worked on the other fronts. I would also still need to book her flight too, but I wanted her passport in hand first. She also wanted to be with her family during the pandemic—it was emotional for all of us. I told her when she got back that she needed to pack up. Leave no man (or woman) behind; we were leaving together to each of our respective families and hometowns.

4. I had an apartment to pack up—should I move things into storage, give things to friends, or arrange movers to pack up my entire home? I didn't have time to think—time was ticking. I called a moving company and arranged for them to come the next morning at 7 A.M. and asked them to bring a ton of staff since my goal was to be done by 5 P.M. that same day. I started working on export papers and giving them

an inventory of what we were shipping to the U.S. I gave all electrical appliances to my friends since they wouldn't work in the U.S. due to voltage. I gave my outdoor furniture to my best friend, and everything else was packed up for shipping. I packed three suitcases of things I actually wanted to have on me and personal mementos in my handbag. Shipping these goods by sea would mean it would be months before I would see them, so I had to be very selective about what I needed on me vs. what I could wait for.

5. Lastly, I had a car. I didn't want to put it in storage. A friend suggested going to the mall to the sellanycar.com kiosk and letting them bid to buy it via auction. I literally drove to the mall, and some guy with an iPad did an inspection, uploaded photos, and within 40 minutes my car was sold. That was done!

I got everything in motion on Sunday and was gearing up to leave Monday night. I started texting friends to pass by because I was leaving and wanted to say goodbye. It was 10pm on Sunday night, and I still didn't have a ticket as I couldn't get through to any of the airlines. I finally decided to go to the airport to see if I could buy a ticket from a counter agent. I was at the airport for three hours. It was pure chaos. I left the airport at 1am on Monday with an airline ticket for me, for Lolita, and for my dog. It sank in on the way home. I was leaving.

RULE #3 DON'T BE A WAITER

I didn't have a reason to leave. I loved my life there. But I didn't have a reason to stay; my family was my world, and they were not in Dubai. When I put it into that lens, nothing mattered more. It was time.

At 8 P.M. on Monday, I had packed up my life of 23 years in 24 hours. I didn't wait. I just decided to do it, and if it was meant to be, it would all work out. If it wasn't meant to be, I would face obstacles. But it all worked flawlessly. By the time I landed in the US, the world had shut down—schools went remote, people were ordered to work from home, and lockdown had begun.

During the weeks and months that followed, I rebuilt my life in the US. I opened an office in the US, built an incredible roster of clients, and a remarkable team. And I am closer to my family, which means the world to me. When I look back now, I don't know how I did it. But I am glad that I did. Choosing not to wait to see how it played out, I created a new life and chapter that I am beyond grateful for. After the two-year lockdown ended, I am back in the region monthly, and I picked up where I left off with even better business opportunities, more relationships, and new ways to bring value to others.

RULE #3
DON'T BE A WAITER

How do you put yourself at the top of your priority list and create your dream life? You realize that no one is coming to save you, prepare you or create opportunities for you . . . except yourself.

RULE #3 DON'T BE A WAITER

Cheat Sheet

- **Be curious:** Develop a sense of curiosity about the world around you. Ask questions, explore, and seek out new experiences. The more you learn about the world, the better equipped you will be to leverage new ideas.
- **Get an accountability partner.** When we share our ideas with others, it can help us stay accountable to achieving them and keep you in check.
- **Identify your strengths:** Start by identifying your skills, strengths, and interests. Think about what you enjoy doing, what you're good at, and what kind of work would make you feel fulfilled and seek to spend more time in those areas.
- **Be a dreamer.** Dreams don't magically appear—dream big by manifesting your ideas, journal about them and ideate around them.
- **Be open minded.** Be open to exploring different options and taking on new challenges, even if they're outside of your comfort zone.

How Not to Wait

- Be proactive and take initiative rather than waiting for others to bring you opportunities.
- Rely on yourself, not other people, to measure what is important.
- Don't be afraid to take charge and make decisions.
- Don't stay in your comfort zone.
- Go beyond the status quo and do so bravely.
- Take risks, even if it means putting yourself in vulnerable positions.

RULE #3 DON'T BE A WAITER

Reflection Exercises

1. What would you do if time or money wasn't a limitation for you?

2. If you were to admit something you were "waiting on," what would you write down?

3. How can you drive your future in ways that align more with your passion or purpose?

4. If you were to take charge of one area of your life that would lead to the most happiness, what would that be? It can be personal, financial, health, leisure, work, or relationship based.

5. How can you expand your network to gain access to the opportunities you wish to pursue? And who would be on that wish list?

> Why invest in yourself? Because to give value, *you must be valuable.*

RULE # 4
UNLEARN, RELEARN, AND INVEST IN YOURSELF

Live as if you were to die tomorrow.
Learn as if you were to live forever.

— MAHATMA GANDHI

I'm a big believer in lifelong learning and I truly feel that if I'm not learning, I'm not growing. Being challenged is what makes me tick, and learning new things is paramount to that. Maybe it's because education is in my DNA.

I come from a family of educators. Besides my dad, my aunt Susie, Dr. Seham Moussa, was the head of home economics at Helwan University (she was one of pioneers in her field); and my uncle, Dr. Osama Zaki, is a professor of accounting and finance at Cairo University. And my grandpa was the principal of a school in Mansoura, which is located in Lower Egypt along the Delta banks of the Nile.

At 23-years-old, my dad left Egypt and came to America with his new bride (my mom) to study. He spoke no English, had never been on a plane and had no clue how life was going to play out. But he knew that if he was educated, his chances of success were going to be greater than if he wasn't. My dad worked hard, and he relied on and invested in himself. Not only did he build a family and a good life, but he also built an accomplished one. He excelled at academia. He landed at the University of Michigan in Ann Arbor and went on to get his master's degree and Ph.D. at the University of Illinois. He got his first teaching position as a management professor and worked his way up to become the dean of the business school at Minnesota State University, Mankato, where he accredited the College of Business and oversaw all the faculty, students, and courses. It's also where I had some of my fondest memories as a little girl.

I grew up on that campus. I studied every tree on the grounds; I knew the hall janitors by name and when the candy in the vending machines would change. I remember the clay-colored rubber flooring and when the light box signs were out and needed to be replaced. I knew where each teacher's office was and who held office hours on the weekends and who didn't. I loved going to work with my dad. It was like going to a museum or being in a live science project—every day was different.

On weekends, I'd go with him to his small campus office filled with wall-to-wall books. I'd sit in his big, squeaky, wooden desk chair spinning around in circles while he graded a stack of blue paper exam booklets. My dad also wrote management textbooks that were used on campuses across the country and had research papers published in prestigious academic journals like the *Academy of Management Journal*.

RULE # 4 UNLEARN, RELEARN, AND INVEST IN YOURSELF

He helped international students come to the United States and build a legacy. After he passed away in 2004, we created a scholarship in his name, the Gaber Abouelenein Scholarship. It is awarded to an international student on the basis of academic achievement, demonstrated leadership, and involvement in extracurricular activities.

"People can take many things from you in life," he often told me. "But they can never take your knowledge."

Growing up, I was a very average student, but I came to love the learning process when I was in college. I went to school at Minnesota State University, Mankato. Not only did I enjoy being the daughter of a very popular professor, but I was also invigorated and inspired by the pulse of a college campus. Knowing that universities are where big ideas are born, research is done and lifelong friendships are created, I wanted to learn everything I could from everyone around me. I also loved the concept of "applied academics." I realized that if you put in the hours to study, you can become educated and practically an expert on almost anything. With the advent of the Internet, my interest and ability to sharpen my skills and education exploded. Early in my career, it was clear that if I want to succeed, add value, and stay relevant, I better be well versed in different topics and trends and aware of what's happening in the world around me. To be the voice of what's now and next in culture and advise clients on what they need to know, I need to be IN the know.

Being a lifelong learner means that you continue to focus on new things, gain knowledge and skills, and are culturally aware. It also means that you are curious, and that curiosity doesn't have to be work-related. It can be about anything you're interested in: longevity, watercolors, making TikTok videos, the environment, skiing, building something with your hands. You can focus on learning something new or on getting better at something you already love to do. Yes, learning takes time and effort, but the best investment you can make is in yourself. And the time to start was yesterday! You never know what you'll learn that could turn into a tremendous opportunity. However, as I've said before, nobody is going to put you at the top of their priority list. You have to put yourself at the top.

That's what I did when I was curious about how governments worked. I didn't study foreign policy or foreign relations, but I started to dig into how governments, like companies, need to build and protect their reputations. They need to communicate with their stakeholders (citizens are their consumers); they need to build trust and relationships with their audiences (create websites and social media channels, and host in-person events to meet their constituents), and they need to bring value to keep their stakeholders interested (keep the votes and public support), which companies do by running campaigns and generating excitement. The more I studied this, the more I knew it was an area of business I could get into. I found a tremendous opportunity in doing strategic communications consulting for ministries, government entities, and public affairs offices of embassies. By doing this, I added value to myself.

You don't want to stand still; you want to move forward and grow. Lifelong learning is stimulating, motivating, and inspiring. It's empowering and, as a result, can enhance your confidence. In addition, it can improve your business and income. "A hundred years ago, we were compensated for our brute strength; now it's our brain strength," explained Jim Kwik, a brain performance coach and author of *Limitless: Upgrade Your Brain, Learn Anything Faster and Unlock Your Exceptional Life*. "Today, it's no longer our muscle power. It's our mind power and the faster you can learn, the faster you can earn because knowledge is not only power, knowledge is profit."

Acquiring knowledge is also good for your health. Various studies have shown that it can positively impact your psychological well-being by reducing stress, depression and anxiety. Additional research suggests that lifelong learning can help the brain grow in areas like the hippocampus, which boosts its ability to adapt, and create new neural connections and nerve cells, which are linked to memory, focus, and reasoning. Learning a complex skill—digital photography or sewing, for example—may slow age-related cognitive decline, which refers to changes in your memory, thinking, and brain function that go beyond what is a normal part of the aging process. Last but not least, research reveals that a never-stop-learning mentality can boost self-esteem and a sense of satisfaction with your life.

Investing in Yourself Is More Important Now Than Ever Before

Being proficient in new things has always been beneficial, but more so now as the environment around us changes constantly. Life is moving at a million miles a minute, so the number of things we need to educate ourselves on has grown exponentially. For example, with the rapid innovation and development of transformational digital technologies like generative artificial intelligence (AI), cloud computing, and augmented reality (AR), to name just a few, we need to invest in ourselves in order to keep up. We used to value degrees and which university someone went to and put higher education on a pedestal. Years ago, where you went to school decided who you would become. But that's not the case today and the learning shouldn't stop once we get handed our diploma. In fact, that's where it should begin to accelerate.

In many industries, they don't use that measuring stick anymore. And some companies don't care where you went to school or what your degree is. What matters is your skills and knowledge. What matters is your experiences and failures. What matters is your character and empathy. What matters is the way you treat people and your hunger to learn and contribute, collaborate. What matters is how you are evolving and embracing change and bringing value to it.

Today technology can automate so many jobs and skills. This means you need to continuously sharpen your saw. Yes, it can take time, effort and money, but that is an investment in yourself that is priceless. You need expertise and knowledge that is uniquely yours—that hopefully can't be replicated by machines and robots. "Innovate or die" is a saying attributed to Peter Drucker, one of the most influential experts on management. He said it almost four decades ago and then Bob Iger, CEO of the Walt Disney Company, added, "There's no innovation if you operate out of fear of the new or untested." This is so important, especially if you're an entrepreneur. When it comes to business, you must be a practitioner of the things you are going to talk about and be open to learning what you don't know.

I want to elaborate on what I mean by investing in yourself. Investing in yourself is tied to learning because it's about putting your best foot forward in how you show up in the world. Investing is not about money; it's about putting time, effort, expertise, and love into yourself. I am learning because I want to give myself the best opportunity to be happy and succeed. I don't want to be left behind because I don't know things! And I don't think you want to be left behind either. I am investing in myself because I want to take advantage of what life has to offer and be an active participant *and driver* of living my best life.

Lifelong learning is so important to me that it's in my company's employee handbook that each team member gets on their first day. It says, "Always be hungry for more information, to learn about the business, educate yourself, and study." I encourage everyone to learn new things, even if it's not a core part of their job description. For example, when ChatGPT was getting daily media attention, I had everyone on my team spend 15 minutes researching it. Then we had a staff meeting where each person shared what they'd discovered. Having my team explore this new technology got them in early, gave them confidence, and made it less intimidating. The goal is to make them feel like they can learn anything. Why? Because they can! And so can you.

Think about learning in terms of continuously developing building blocks for your career and life's journey. I started my career in sports marketing and branding, then I shifted to communications and public policy. But I know that communications is not just one thing, so I learned about corporate communications, then internal communications. Then I built on this by learning about branding for CEOs and high-profile figures, which is called personal branding. Constantly think about how you can raise the bar and add to your experience grid by investing in learning and improving your knowledge. Build on what's going to bring value to you.

How to Learn

So far, we've talked a lot about creating value for others. Now it's time to add value to yourself by adopting a lifelong learning mentality. After all, to give value, *you must be valuable*. The good news is that it's never too late—you're never too old or too smart to learn. It's always going to benefit you. Often, we're eager to learn, but struggle with how to go about it. We're unsure where to go first and what to do, but educational opportunities are everywhere. Here are some approaches on how to learn so you can *build this muscle for yourself*.

1. Go online. Lifelong learners seek information from multiple sources and today it's so easy that there is just no excuse. We live in one of the best times to learn. With the Internet and social media, fresh insight is free and available anywhere at any time. (You don't even have to leave your house or get out of your pajamas.) YouTube has more than one billion videos on its platform so you can learn almost anything there from how to tie a tie to how to make the perfect hard-boiled egg to how to pave your driveway. The array of free online courses is incredible, too, and the paid options are endless and available at all price points. Universities, community colleges, libraries, and community centers are just a few of the places that offer in-person classes on so many subjects and provide a social aspect too.

I'm always hungry to absorb the intricacies of how things work, so I try to take a course every few months and they're not always related to my business. Recently, a friend was talking about Photoshop, something I'd never considered. *I wonder if I could do that*, I thought. Then I went online, found a few classes on the subject, and decided that's going to be my next one. There are also workshops, lectures, retreats and bootcamps of varying lengths and locations that allow you to do a deep dive into a subject. (Many are on the weekends so you can learn but not take away from your day job.) Before I joined Google, I spent hours trying to learn about the Google Ads business and how it worked.

RULE # 4 UNLEARN, RELEARN, AND INVEST IN YOURSELF

There were tons of resources online. You just need to put in the time and the opportunities are endless.

2. Learn from people. You can also learn from professional and personal relationships. This is why I have spent money on plane tickets to travel to events not funded or requested by a client and gone out of my way to meet someone just because the insight I gain will reap benefits for me, my clients, or my team in tangible and intangible ways. It's also why I've joined various organizations. Remember the story about me joining AmCham (American Chamber of Commerce) when I first started my company in Egypt? The education I got from that was priceless, not to mention the long-term business and personal relationships I built as a result.

In January of 2020, I met Matt Higgins and his wife, Sarah, at a party at the Super Bowl. It was a quick introduction and we exchanged numbers. I didn't hear from Matt again until June of 2023, when he reached out about a project he was working on. Then Matt's book *Burn the Boats* came out and I wanted to read it to learn more about him. It was a fascinating read. When I finished the book, I texted Matt and asked if he could meet for lunch on my upcoming trip to New York. I could have sat there for hours learning from him and talking to him about his journey, business and how we see the world. He was the press secretary for the mayor of New York City during 9/11 and a caretaker for his mom; we had so much to talk about. He is a guest shark on ABC's hit show *Shark Tank* and an executive fellow at Harvard Business School, where he created an immersive class called "Moving Beyond DTC," which recently featured a busines lecture by SKIMS founder, Kim Kardashian. He also is an investor in more than 150 direct-to-consumer brands, and he works across many industries including food, tech, sports, and entertainment.

When Matt said he'd never been to the UAE, I told him I would be happy to plan a trip for him if we could align on dates. Reminder, Matt is not a client and I don't do work for him. Plus, organizing an executive visit is a lot of work. First, you have to understand their business and what they care about. Then, you have to connect with people in the region who have aligned goals or interests and find a strategic fit. I had to conduct meetings, calls, and briefings with parties in the region to introduce them to Matt and understand their priorities to determine if there was a fit. The process also involved setting up meetings, scheduling pitches to the press, and organizing VIP dinners—not to mention handling logistics such as cars, hotels, and dinner reservations to ensure the visit executed flawlessly. Planning these visits often takes weeks of ongoing work across time zones. It also required me to quickly get up to speed on his business interests, not only to curate the visit but also to free up my schedule and commitments to be in the UAE as well. Despite the challenges, I signed up for it because I wanted to spend time with Matt and discuss a business idea I had with him. I knew that if we could travel together, we would be able to discuss business and break bread—all while I was bringing him value through meetings and learning about the UAE. Matt gave the trip the green light seven days before he wanted to fly. Yikes! Seven days, and three of them were a holiday weekend. So, I really had four business days to work with, all while managing a 10-hour time zone difference. Not easy. I am telling you this story for two reasons. One, I practiced many rules I share in this book. These include:

RULE # 4 UNLEARN, RELEARN, AND INVEST IN YOURSELF

- Be a value creator (Rule # 2). I introduced him to the UAE and business people there and created new relationships and memories for him and his wife.

- Don't be a waiter (Rule #3). I could have waited to get five days of his time in the United States (impossible) or be on a focused trip overseas with his undivided attention. It was a no-brainer for me. Don't wait; create the opportunity!

- Unlearn, relearn, and invest in yourself (Rule #4). This trip was an investment of weeks of my life—one to plan the trip and another to go on it and then all the follow-up—all for a chance to learn and be around Matt and learn.

- Be a long-term player (Rule # 6). I met Matt in January of 2020 and we took that trip to the UAE in October of 2023. That's three months short of a four-year time period. Four years—that is long-term!

I am also telling you this story because learning from people is invaluable. Spending time with someone is the ultimate way to learn. I don't see it as sacrificing time and effort to learn from Matt; I see it as investing—investing in myself, my future, and my future business idea.

Another way to learn from people is to audit your circle of friends and colleagues. "You're the average of the five people you spend the most time with" is a quote by motivational speaker Jim Rohn. In general, this means that the people around you have a huge impact on who you become. This also means that they have an impact on how and what you learn or whether you learn at all. So think about the people you spend the most time with. Are they curious? And interested? Do they seek out new information and knowledge? Do they encourage you to unlearn bad habits and learn healthier ones? If not, try to spend time with people who continue to learn. Not only will they rub off on you in a positive way (and vice-versa), but they're probably more exciting and interesting to be around as well.

Learning also doesn't have to take a lot of time or effort. It can be simple and small. Michelle told a story of a woman she met on a plane years ago who shared her take on lifelong learning. She said that every day she Googles one thing. It's not something she plans; it just comes up from her environment. So, if she's reading the newspaper and there's a word she doesn't know, she looks it up. If it's almost Valentine's Day and she realizes she doesn't know the true meaning behind the holiday, she looks it up. If she drives past a billboard advertising a new TV show, she'll Google that. If she's playing cards with friends, she'll look up the history of the game. It really struck me when she said that it's literally a minute or two out of her day, but by the end of a week, she's learned seven new things. By the end of the month 30, and by the end of the year 365 new tidbits of info. Some of what she learns is just the 'Google of the day' exercise and she may not think about it again, but she said often it leads her down a path toward a new interest. It also makes her a very engaging person to talk to. Michelle said, "Imagine her at a dinner party!"

Learning Includes Unlearning

There are also times when we need to unlearn. Unlearning is the process of taking habits, opinions and behaviors that are now outdated and replacing them with new ones

RULE # 4 UNLEARN, RELEARN, AND INVEST IN YOURSELF

(relearning). This means letting go of old ways of thinking and unlearning certain habits that don't create value or serve us anymore. That's why the word *disruption* is part of our vernacular. We talk about disruption in this industry or that industry. It's getting out of old habits to learn new techniques and skills and allow other ideas in. This keeps you relevant and aware of the world around you. However, it takes a certain amount of humility to unlearn something.

Unlearning is hard. It involves self-awareness and the ability to recognize unhelpful beliefs, replacing them with more relevant or accurate ideas that reflect today's society. Unlearning requires a willingness to be open to change, as well as critical thinking and reflection before transformation can occur. This process is especially difficult when it necessitates a hard reset, as habits are often deeply ingrained over time.

However, the benefits of unlearning are significant. In a world where technological and societal shifts occur daily, unlearning helps individuals and organizations stay relevant and effective. It forces us to be more creative and to problem-solve in new ways. Unlearning also promotes personal growth and learning by making it a habit to question and expand our own thinking, environment, and skills. Most importantly, unlearning stereotypes and biases is crucial for fostering a more inclusive and understanding world, both socially and professionally.

Unlearning means that we understand that we may need to expand our thinking, change the way we view things, and dispel any misinformation we were taught. We need to see the world as a place of opportunities, not obstacles, and adopt the mindset that the way we used to do things isn't the way that things are going to be done today or in the future. For example, how children were parented 10 years ago or more isn't how you can parent them today. Where before we would have done everything for our children and thought that was loving and helpful, experts and research have taught us that might not be for the best. Helicopter parenting, where you constantly hover around your children overseeing every inch of their lives, and lawnmower parenting, where you rush to clear away every potential obstacle so they never experience discomfort, isn't doing our kids any favors. In fact, it can hold them back, making them unable to handle real-world situations like adversity. Today, we know that if you want responsible children, you have to give them responsibility. If you want accountable children, you have to give them things to be accountable for. If you want independent children, you have to give them independence.

One organization that unlearned well during the pandemic was the National Basketball Association (NBA). During COVID, the world shut down with just weeks until the playoffs. To allow this culminating event of the NBA season to occur, they created a bubble in Disney World during the summer. There were no fans in the stands at this secure location, teams played on neutral courts (no more home court advantage), and they were away from their families for weeks and months (depending on how far their team got in the playoffs). After almost four months of no sports, ESPN called it "a return-to-play unlike anything sports fans had seen before."

The NBA and every team had to unlearn everything they knew about the playoffs and recreate this with 22 teams, coaches, and refs living on-site away from their families. (They tried to make this home away from home for the players by having things like on-site barbers, good food, and places for recreation.) This was also the first time there would be no fans in the stands. The NBA had to reimagine ways that people could be part of the game without physically being in attendance. So they worked with Microsoft to come up with technology that would livestream videos of one fan per seat. Fans were chosen after they registered on a special website. This digital attendance was a huge success and they grew the concept by featuring celebrity cameos in the seats to surprise and delight fans.

Unlearn So You Can Relearn

There is so much more serious unlearning that needs to occur—and that ties directly to relearning. Unlearning means breaking old habits or the way we think about something because we have evolved and have new information. Relearning is now learning how to behave and operate in the new framework of that evolution. We must accept new ways of thinking, behaving, and communicating.

Relearning is a term typically used after someone has an accident, such as, "She had to relearn how to play the piano after an injury." That's a simple example. But what I am talking about here is the modern way to evolve as a human. Time and technology are moving too fast. What's old is just that: old. This means that there are times when we need to relearn things as they apply to today's world.

"Relearning involves staying informed about emerging trends and technologies in our fields. It requires a willingness to step outside our comfort zones, seek new learning opportunities, and continuously upgrade our skills," explained Sam Soyombo, a coach dedicated to teaching people to become lifelong learners. "The power of learning, unlearning, and relearning extends beyond personal and professional benefits. It also has broader implications for society as a whole. When individuals embrace these processes, they become catalysts for innovation, collaboration, and progress." Relearning is a mindset shift that can help us make progress that we desperately need in many areas of our lives.

In 2020, we all watched what happened to George Floyd in a state of shock. It was a pivotal moment that changed behaviors, conversations, policies, companies, and the street. And in the months following, it started conversations and pushed our thinking in so many ways. It was the first time I had heard the term *micro-aggression* which refers to "words or actions that appear subtle but have underlying meaning or offense."

I came to learn that people were projecting microaggressions at me, but I didn't know that's what they were at the time. My whole life people would hear my Egyptian name or look at my dark skin and hair and then say, "Wow, your English is so good." That sounds innocent enough but what they meant was, "It's surprising that someone of Arab descent has good English." I only became aware of that term because of George Floyd. I also learned about allyship.

Allyship involves proactively stepping up to support marginalized voices and communities. Allyship is about relearning—re-educating yourself about other communities and their issues—and then determining how you can lend your voice to support them and let them feel seen and heard.

This manifested itself in many ways including on social media where many public figures did a campaign called, "Sharing the Mic." They gave other people their platforms so that their audience could hear from more diverse voices. In the aftermath of George Floyd's murder, companies and businesses had to relearn how to navigate and operate their company culture. Companies across America looked inward at their diversity performance. Was their staff

RULE # 4 UNLEARN, RELEARN, AND INVEST IN YOURSELF

diverse enough? Did they use diverse suppliers or vendors? Were they giving opportunities to everyone or a narrow group? Companies started diversity training and all-hands meetings. In addition, everyone had to relearn the difference between equity and equality.

Equality means each individual or group of people is given the same resources or opportunities. Equity recognizes that each person has different circumstances and allocates the exact resources and opportunities needed to reach an equal outcome. I would have never focused on that, and I had to learn and relearn so much coming out of that time period. One thing I also did was to be more intentional about seeking out new perspectives.

My advice to you is to surround yourself with people with different backgrounds, experiences, and viewpoints; this is an investment in yourself to learn. First, it will help you see things from new angles and challenge your existing beliefs—questioning your thinking is a good thing! Second, it will increase your awareness and appreciation of cultural differences, which is invaluable in our globally connected world. And third, it can foster innovation because a diverse team can offer a wider range of insights into customer needs and preferences, increasing competitive advantage. I really believe in the power of learning from people.

Learning encompasses not only business and knowledge but also behavior, and sometimes it involves discovering more about yourself. It can be hard to admit what you don't know, and I can admit that imposter syndrome—which many female leaders face— is a real thing because I experienced it. Imposter syndrome occurs when you feel incompetent or that your success is due to luck or timing and not your efforts and achievements; or you downplay your role because you feel you're not qualified to do it. When I started my business in Egypt in 2000, I was the managing director of the company. This is a common title in the Middle East and Europe, which signals you are in charge. It wasn't until 20 years later—yes 20 years—that I called myself what I really am ... a CEO.

> **Feedback makes you grow—so embrace it no matter how hard it is to hear.**

Learn on and from Your Job

Part of lifelong learning is assessing your progress and self-reflecting. It's celebrating wins and identifying areas that still need improvement. After we finish a project or assignment, my team and I always do an internal post-game. What did we do well? Where did we fall short? For example, there was a big charity golf event in Las Vegas for the NBPA Foundation, and we didn't get a good turnout from the media. We had invited them to an 8 A.M. breakfast before the golf tournament started and hardly anyone came, despite the fact that several people confirmed their attendance. The point we overlooked is that it was too early in the day and competing events were happening over breakfast. So, we asked ourselves, *What could we have done better?* In hindsight, we realized that we should have given the media two windows of opportunity to attend so that anyone who couldn't make the 8 A.M. breakfast was invited for lunch. This is just one example, but we came up with a whole list of things we could have done differently. What we learned not only helped the NBPA but will also help all our current and future clients. Lifelong learners do checks and balances on themselves so that they hold themselves accountable to do better and innovate rather than repeat mistakes.

What about your role or job do you think you could improve if you took some time to identify what you don't know or feel confident about? Set forth a plan to lean in to closing that vulnerability gap. That is what lifelong learners do: they seek to close those gaps no matter how big or small. I have a member on my team who is a total rock star, but she struggles with giving feedback to her direct reports and external partners. I coach and encourage her and provide resources, but she has to do the work on herself for herself or she will never grow as a people manager. Giving employees feedback is paramount to their growth and performance. Nobody wants to walk around oblivious to their blind spots, so help them by guiding and coaching them. Then everybody wins.

How to Be Your Own Bank

Want to invest in yourself financially? Think about how you can be your own (self-reliant) bank. Ayn Rand said, "Money is only a tool; it will take you wherever you wish, but it will not replace you as the driver."

Nothing keeps people awake at night as much as worrying about money. Now that we are living longer due to advances in health and medicine, we need our money to last us as we live longer. There are no classes in school that teach us how to manage our money, save money, or about compound investing. Being financially literate is challenging, especially for women. Studies show that women are behind when it comes to financial literacy, even though women make most purchase decisions. The disparity is real, according to the Board of Governors of the Federal Reserve System report released in August 2023 on the Survey of Household Economics and Decisionmaking (SHED):

- Women are less financially resilient and face greater risk exposure.
- Women struggle more to pay bills on time and in full.
- Women are less likely (at 79 percent) than men (at 84 percent) to be able to pay all their bills on time and in full.
- Women are less likely (at 52 percent) than men (at 56 percent) to be able to cover three months of expenses with emergency savings.
- Women are more likely (at 15 percent) than men (at 12 percent) to have increased their usage of credit card debt.
- Women are less likely than men to have three months of emergency savings.
- Women accumulated more credit card debt year over year, and have higher rates than men overall.
- Women of color are the least likely to have three months of emergency savings.

Now more than ever everyone needs to empower themselves economically, feel financially secure, and be responsible for their financial well-being. For entrepreneurs, your reality is simple: You quickly come to realize there is no paycheck coming to save you and that you have to build, sustain, and grow the business to generate your personal income. And if you take capital from investors, you need to give them a return on that investment and ensure you don't burn through it.

The other reality for female-led businesses and entrepreneurs is that they receive less funding than male-led

RULE # 4 UNLEARN, RELEARN, AND INVEST IN YOURSELF

businesses: less than 2 percent of investment goes to women-led businesses! Consulting firm McKinsey & Company released a report that found companies with three or more women on their executive committees grow the company revenue by almost 50 percent compared to companies led by men. Another consulting firm affirmed this in their research: when women-led startups do get funded, they're more likely to be successful. They "ultimately deliver higher revenue—more than twice as much per dollar invested," a Boston Consulting Group analysis found.

This is why it's so important we focus on being financially literate and self-reliant. Being financially literate gives you confidence to make your own decisions on your terms and it also gives you freedom and flexibility.

How can you be your own bank? Your goal should be to be better at investing your money, knowing how to transfer less out and build up the right skills (services) to feel more confident and self-reliant about your financial future. There are five key ways you can adopt this mentality:

1. Leverage the gig economy

Have more money in your bank account by spending smarter not harder.

The gig economy is a world we live in today where you can hire someone on a temporary basis for a project or need. The term *gig* is used widely in the music industry to define being hired for a performance. The gig economy now plays a significant role in every business industry, fundamentally changing our society. It has transformed how we work, how we define work, and our working hours, while redefining entrepreneurship. The gig economy offers opportunities for both consumers and businesses to benefit.

This new economy has created a new generation of earners and innovated how we make money. Now, anyone can supplement their income, even with a full-time job, by participating in the gig economy. For entrepreneurs, this shift has brought about a massive change in work culture and expectations, providing more autonomy and flexibility. We now have a generation in the workforce that has never experienced traditional office work, as they can work from home or from anywhere—an enormous societal shift.

Gig workers are independent contractors, online platform workers, contract firm workers, on-call workers, and temporary staff that give businesses much needed support without having to invest in bringing them on full time. Gig workers can support your business on-demand and provide services for you. You can take advantage of hiring contractors and freelancers to save your company or start up money. Hiring full time brings with it many financial obligations: you must insure the workers, pay payroll taxes, invest in buying their work related equipment such as laptops etc. But if you take advantage of the gig workforce, you can get the help you need for the skills you need when you need them. In my company, I have full-time employees and fixed contractors. The contractors have skills that I only need for specific jobs and projects. I have created a "bench" of talent that I use for specialized services and needs and it serves me well. All contractors work with contracts and are treated with as much value as full-time employees.

Think about how you can leverage the gig economy with agility in ways never thought possible.

2. Become a pricing ninja

How you price your product or services can help your financial status.

How you price your services can play a big role in your financial success. Deciding what to charge stresses people out: if you price too high you might not get business;

if you price too low your margins might not sustain your business. Of course you want to cover your costs; you're in business to make a profit but this also goes for your personal bank account as well. Once you know how much you need to cover your expenses, take into consideration market value and prices. Pricing strategies tie directly to resources. You need to evaluate if you have the staff and resources to handle incoming demand. One of the most valuable things I learned with my consulting business is that if clients want your services, they will be willing to pay the prices you set, so I never negotiate my prices or value. I will never be able to sustain or grow my business if I let my customers set my prices. I also don't do business by haggling. It's part of our values and ethical approach that we don't set a high price with the sole purpose of knowing it was fake so that we leave wiggle room for the client to feel good that they negotiated us down for a bargain. It's a bad premise and not something I value in myself or others.

3. Negotiate like a pro
Learn how to negotiate creatively.

All of us have had to negotiate something at one point in our lives, whether a salary or the price of a car, so it's really important to learn how to sharpen your negotiation skills, which can benefit both you and your business—and ultimately your bank account.

If your business uses a service, can you negotiate a longer-term contract for a lower rate? Even if it's something the company doesn't offer, it's worth asking. You would be surprised how often people might take you up on your offer. Look at all your agreements: office leases, subscription services, and even insurance policies. Think about ways you can save money by how you negotiate. Did you ever think of using barter as a negotiation tactic? This includes things like bartering or trading services instead of paying for them. Can you negotiate part payment and part barter? Another negotiation strategy is to share revenue. This pays out revenue when you both succeed and that shows you are willing to invest time and effort and take rewards based on performance.

4. Get professional help
Don't wing it, ask for help.

I have never felt confident with my knowledge of finances or managing money. Sure, I took some accounting classes in college and also completed an executive education class at the London School of Business called "Finance for Non-Finance Executives" but like most entrepreneurs I don't have any formal training in accounting. I am very much learning on the job even 20 years later. An expensive lesson is one you can't recover from financially, so don't skimp on getting help to manage your finances. Financial professionals have extensive knowledge and experience on investment strategies, taxes, and changes to regulations that might impact your business. They also know benefits that you can be eligible for and how you can take advantage of ways to protect your business and reduce financial risks. I never met an entrepreneur who wasn't interested in saving money by learning about new options for small or large businesses that they could be eligible for.

5. Create boundaries and then get educated
Understand your boundaries and level up yourself.

I have never lived on a structured budget, but I know my boundaries for my business and my personal livelihood. Think of boundaries as guardrails that protect you. Knowing what you are willing to lose or not lose and having a system for saving will help you in case of an emergency,

RULE # 4 UNLEARN, RELEARN, AND INVEST IN YOURSELF

recession, pandemic, or economic downturn that puts your livelihood at risk. Be smart about your saving and spending, but most importantly adopt a planning mindset. There are so many applications and tools to help you save and track your finances so take advantage of them.

***

Self-reliance means that we must rely on ourselves to evolve, learn, and unlearn. Learning is an investment that has always paid off for me. At the end of each year to prepare for the new one, I ask myself, *What do I want to learn? What am I going to test? What am I going to try?* Answering those questions was why I launched my *Savvy Talk* podcast in 2019. If you have a sense of curiosity, you will open yourself up to more opportunities. Yes, you are busy, but investing in yourself will lead to more happiness, new ideas, and a greater sense of purpose and power. And that kind of ROI is priceless.

RULE #4
YOU UNLEARN, RELEARN, AND INVEST IN YOURSELF

This is how you stay relevant, be in the know and sharpen your skills, especially with rapid innovations in technology and when you're competing against a global remote talent pool. This is so important because investing in yourself leads to enormous ROI.

RULE # 4 UNLEARN, RELEARN, AND INVEST IN YOURSELF

> **Cheat Sheet**

- **Question your assumptions:** Identify the assumptions you have about yourself, others, and the world around you, and question their validity. Ask yourself, *Why do I believe this?* and *Is this belief serving me?*
- **Seek out new perspectives:** Surround yourself with people who have different backgrounds, experiences, and viewpoints. This can help you see things from a new angle and challenge your existing beliefs.
- **Practice mindfulness:** Mindfulness can help you become more aware of your thoughts and feelings and identify patterns of thinking that may be holding you back. By being present in the moment and observing your thoughts without judgment, you can begin to let go of old ways of thinking and make room for new ones.
- **Try something new:** Engage in activities that challenge you and push you out of your comfort zone. By trying new things, you can discover new talents and interests, and develop a growth mindset.
- **Embrace failure:** Failure can be a powerful teacher. Instead of avoiding failure, embrace it as an opportunity to learn and grow. By reframing failure as a valuable experience, you can let go of the fear of making mistakes and take more risks.

How to Be a Lifelong Learner

- Be curious.
- Seek information from multiple sources including friends, family, your network, managers and work colleagues, the Internet, social media, podcasts, conferences, formal and informal education, and online learning programs.
- Be open to changing your mind and embracing new information.
- Understand that change equals growth, so learning about new things is the key to growth.
- See the world as a place of opportunities not obstacles.

RULE # 4 UNLEARN, RELEARN, AND INVEST IN YOURSELF

Reflection Exercises

1. Where and how do you learn?

2. What are you curious about?

3. What do you want to learn and why?

4. Name three things you think you need to unlearn?

5. Identify the areas where you want to grow and develop and set specific goals for yourself. This could be learning a new language, mastering a new skill, or deepening your understanding of a particular subject.

6. Find one YouTube channel or podcast that you can start following to learn from.

7. What is the reason you are not learning new things? What is truly holding you back?

8. List three ways you can invest in yourself.

9. Name two ways you can be your own bank.

> It takes a lifetime to build a reputation, but only a few seconds to destroy one.

RULE # 5
THINK OF YOUR REPUTATION AS CURRENCY

*Reputation is like fine china:
Once broken it's very hard to repair.*

— ABRAHAM LINCOLN

In June of 2010, a man from Alexandria, Egypt, named Khaled Saeed was beaten to death and tortured by two Egyptian police officers because he posted a video on the Internet that showed officers handling illegal drugs. The police released the results of their investigation saying Saeed had died of suffocation after trying to swallow a packet of drugs he had been carrying, but photographs of his battered face were leaked, casting doubts on the explanation. This led to the creation of a Facebook page called "We Are All Khaled Saeed," which campaigned against police brutality. The Facebook page, which attracted hundreds of thousands of followers, urged people to participate in nationwide anti-government demonstrations in Egypt's Tahrir Square on January 25, 2011, which was a national holiday to mark Egypt's National Police Day. Egyptians took to the streets. Protests, lockdowns, and curfews gripped the country and Egypt came to a complete standstill. It became a global news story with every TV station, news organization, and citizen reporter descending upon Tahrir Square broadcasting live to cover the breaking news.

I had never witnessed anything like this in my life. We were in the middle of a "revolution" unfolding as we watched the nation and the streets come undone. Stores and companies were closed. Everyone was forced to stay home, curfews were issued, and we were all glued to our televisions. It was scary.

The morning of January 25, I made a big decision not knowing that very decision would place me in the middle of this story.

It was the day I accepted the job to become the head of public policy and global communications for Google in the Middle East. This was the very day the nation took to the streets in nationwide protests.

For 18 days there were peaceful protests, and a sense of pride and nationalism, but there was also rage, resistance, violence, fires, and even looting. Neighborhoods organized 24-hour watches to protect themselves. State and local media waged campaigns to calm the nation while social media had another narrative going. The Facebook page was gaining momentum. It was the mouthpiece for the day's activities to organize and mobilize protestors. The activities on the ground started to swell, taking to the streets grew bigger and louder, and the news story was dominating all over the world. Information and disinformation took over. There was talk that the military was going to step in and

RULE #5 THINK OF YOUR REPUTATION AS CURRENCY

take over to force President Mubarak out. The Facebook page pushed harder to keep up pressure.

The day I accepted the job at Google was the same day I found out that the marketing manager of Google was one of the anonymous creators of the Facebook page that was organizing the movement. And just like that, unbeknownst to Google, they were immediately thrust into this global crisis. Now keep in mind, I was not an employee of Google yet. I had just accepted the job. But in the hours and days that followed, everything changed for the company and I was about to take the helm managing their reputation and communications.

Google had nothing to do with the protests, and they weren't aware that their marketing manager had been involved or any of their employees for that matter, yet the public didn't know that. Some naively thought Google was aware, involved, and instrumental because of the actions of one of their employees. This was not true.

As the news story continued to mount, all my employees were forced to stay home and we couldn't work. I got wind that several news organizations were descending into Cairo and they needed help to do their jobs. They needed translators, writers, fixers, and stringers to help them tell this story and they couldn't afford to fly in boatloads of staff; they were going to need to hire freelancers and boots on the ground. I offered to step in and help BBC and CNN by providing staff to do translations and admin work to support their news operations and generate some much-needed income for my company. A friend of mine worked for *CBS Evening News with Katie Couric*. She reached out and asked if I could staff Katie for a few days. I immediately signed up. I would be getting paid and since business was at a standstill, I could really use the income to keep the company afloat. I also wanted to bring value to their efforts because I had local experience and understood what U.S. audiences would be interested in.

My day job was to be on the front lines with CBS News, hitting the streets to support them as they interviewed officials, protesters, field hospital workers and political experts. I helped set up interviews and gave local context. We moved in a convoy clearly marked PRESS so that we didn't get targeted or hit, but it was not safe. The crowds were turbo-charged. We were there when Molotov cocktails were being thrown into crowds.

There were designated hotels for the press that overlooked Tahrir Square. The lobby of our hotel was all boarded up and the hotel implemented a dark policy where lights couldn't be on and windows and blinds always had to be closed. Every network used the hotel balconies for their live shot locations. I was so impressed by how each network would take over a whole floor by leaving all the hotel room doors open, running cables and cords between them, with each room serving as a make-shift newsroom. One room was news gathering, one room was writing and editorial, one room was editing, one room was broadcasting feed operations and so on. I will never forget the day they were working on deciding which story to lead with when Katie got a phone call from Brian Williams, the anchor at NBC News. He was staying at the Ramses Hilton on the other side of Tahrir Square. He called to warn Katie that their hotel was being raided and to be careful because tapes and footage were being confiscated. It was getting so dangerous that I was unable to go home every day after we worked together.

We were on the final day of Katie's assignment and the next morning she would be going home to the States. The environment toward journalists became very hostile—there were deliberate efforts taking place to intimidate, threaten and attack reporters. There was a great deal of anger and

RULE #5 THINK OF YOUR REPUTATION AS CURRENCY

animosity toward the press, the United States specifically. At this point, Katie said to me, "I just want to get home to my daughters and get out of this safely." We were so scared that night that Katie, her producer Nicola, and I all slept in the same bed, *in our street clothes*. They put their passports in their pockets in case they had to flee at a moment's notice. We could hear the violence outside our window all night. We told stories and tried to think of other things to drown out the fear. Thankfully, Katie got home safely the next morning and I went back to work.

Meanwhile, things at Google needed urgent attention.

Google needed communications support and I wasn't employed yet, so they moved quickly to give me a contractor agreement to retain me through my company. My job was to protect Google's reputation, which was front and center—not a small task when I also had to balance my personal emotions as an Egyptian.

The tension between my work duties and moral obligations were being tested. I knew how important it was to stay true to my values and uphold my personal integrity because long after this news story would pass and this company's crisis was over, I would still have to be me and carry on and carry forward in the world. How you operate in a crisis is a true test of who you are as a person and your character, and you want to show respect, integrity, and resilience.

We spent our days and nights trying to figure out what happened to the marketing manager of Google as he went missing after the first day of protests in Egypt. The protests in Egypt lasted 18 days, and at the end of it, Mubarak was forced to resign, ending a 30-year regime as president. The fall of the Egyptian president marked a tipping point for the Arab Spring.

The Internet became a catalyst of change, freedom, expression, and economic prosperity. Two months after the protests had started, I finally became a full-time employee of Google. I stepped into the company at a very difficult time in its history in the Middle East.

Google has taught us that reputation matters just as much internally as externally. The first rule of thumb is to ensure you communicate with your teams. During the events on the streets in Egypt, every employee in every company had an opinion, ranging from pride to frustration, economic turmoil, insecurity, economic freedom, and freedom of expression.

The first thing I did was to get everybody on the same page, ensuring that everybody knew our values as a company. I reinforced the company's purpose and mission. The most effective way to deliver your message is to ensure that all the messengers know what the message is and how to share it authentically. Once we were strong internally, I worked closely with upper management and the legal department on an official statement to explain Google's involvement to the public.

Google understood the importance of being transparent, proactive, and swift to share their position. Rapid response is crucial; it builds strong credibility. On top of that, Google had a business to run. In meetings, people wanted to ask questions about the Arab Spring and we had to bring them back to focus on our primary business objectives. Working with them, I got a front row seat on how Google leads with empathy, demonstrates leadership and what it truly means to engage employees and lean in to support them.

Communication is a gateway to win hearts and minds, so we used it to redefine what Google meant in their eyes. The ties to the streets of Egypt was a strong image in the minds of many. We showed the public and employees that Google cared about the Middle East and demonstrated

RULE # 5 THINK OF YOUR REPUTATION AS CURRENCY

> Communications is a gateway to win hearts and minds.

how Google cared. The company invested in startups and local communities in the region, trained journalists and launched new products in Arabic like Gmail, Google Maps and YouTube. Google put time and effort into building a strong global reputation as the tech darling that so many loved. But Google wasn't a company with underlying geo-political agendas. What looked to be a big crisis for Google became a moment for them to go all in and show the community what they were really about: being a net contributor to the economy, society, and knowledge. They embraced the chance to play a central role in the region and became a catalyst for change. By doing things that people cared about, they turned the crisis around and were able to be a positive force in shaping their reputation.

During much of the Arab Spring, the narrative was consumed by Facebook but Google was effective in using the moment to define themselves and deliver products people love to millions of Arab users. Google was not only able to protect their reputation, but they also understood the value of their reputation currency.

Reputation as Currency

Understand that reputation is the foundation of trust. Oprah Winfrey once said "In the end, all you have is your reputation." Having a strong reputation is essential and I'm not just talking about your reputation as a business or a company. Your personal reputation is priceless too. Your name is all that you have, and you need to own it. It's the only thing that actually and uniquely belongs to you and that you can control through your actions and words. Protecting your reputation is the ultimate act of self-reliance because no one will care about your image more than you do.

RULE # 5 THINK OF YOUR REPUTATION AS CURRENCY

> Own your name and your assets, they are your digital currency.

Your reputation is your most valuable asset. It's how you position yourself in the eyes of the world. Your name is your reputation and there's a lot of equity behind it. That's why brands spend so much money on their names. Think about it: When you put Nike in a conversation, you automatically know what it stands for. The same with Apple. You know what the name Rolex or Cartier represents because each one has an image: a reputation and a name that stands for something. It has a persona. It has a perception.

Because reputations are so valuable, I want you to think of your reputation in terms of currency. What is its value? What is its worth? How do you grow it and protect it? Increasing the value of your reputation opens you up to more opportunities, brings you more business, leads to more success, improves your relationships, and draws more people into your circle and network.

After all, you could have the best business, product, or marketing in the world, but none of that matters if you don't have a good reputation and people don't trust you or what you stand for.

When you think of your reputation in terms of currency, you value it so much more and realize its impact on everything you do: whether it's how you interact with your Uber driver (who can give you a customer rating), how you show up at business events, or how you appear in Zoom meetings with co-workers or clients.

Think about people or brands with powerful reputations that were wiped out because they didn't value their currency. I can think of a number of reputations that got destroyed by their behavior: Elizabeth Holmes, founder of Theranos; or FTX, the crypto currency exchange; and many more. The lesson here is to remind you that nothing matters more than your reputation, so take deliberate steps to build it, protect it and value it like a currency.

RULE #5 THINK OF YOUR REPUTATION AS CURRENCY

Throughout my career, I have invested in fostering strong relationships and building a valuable network. But these are not contacts or relationships that I would compromise. I would never share phone numbers or e-mails of anyone in my network unless they asked me to share these details. Why? Because my name is on the line and my reputation of being loyal and trustworthy is so important to me. I treat my reputation like a currency that I'm not willing to buy, sell, or trade for anything. I have a relationship with a well-known billionaire, who is one of the most powerful people in the world and you couldn't pay me enough money to give out his e-mail or phone number or introduce people to him for their sole benefit. I value these relationships and my integrity is on the line. I wouldn't reduce the value of my reputation for a transaction—ever.

But reputation goes beyond trust. There are so many other key attributes that impact reputation. Let's start by exploring consistency. Having consistency—the ability to maintain a stable and predictable pattern of behavior over time—reinforces trust and reliability in a brand. An airline for example, must deliver consistently to have a strong reputation. And for you, your personal brand, or your personal reputation, you have to act consistently too. Are you a leader of a company who has a reputation for being an empathic leader? Your consistency in being empathetic is what drives that.

Cancel Culture

Reputation has had to deal with a new kid on the block called "cancel culture." Being canceled is the act of being called out by the public, and then boycotted or excluded by society for your behaviors. Cancel culture came into the collective consciousness around 2017, after the idea of "canceling" celebrities for problematic actions or statements became popular. The term was once thought to be coined by Kanye West, but it was not, although he has been canceled many times for various things he has said and done. But it's not just people that are being cancelled; companies can be cancelled too, significantly affecting reputations.

Driven by a growing demand for public accountability, cancel culture is fueled by our constant access to information. It poses a serious threat to reputation management because being "canceled" can lead to immediate and severe consequences that are often challenging to recover from. Individuals have lost their jobs, companies have experienced declines in sales and customers, and their public image has been tarnished, sometimes irreparably.

Building and protecting your reputation today requires considering your impact and behavior beyond social media. With everyone having the power to film and broadcast, whether you're ordering coffee, attending a public event, or simply at the office, you must operate as if the camera is always on. Acting ethically and holding yourself to high standards of accountability can help you avoid being canceled.

The challenge with cancel culture and reputation management lies in the constantly shifting and evolving cultural and societal norms. What was acceptable in the past may now be considered taboo. The public tends to be quick to cancel, rather than taking a more inclusive, long-term view.

To master reputation management, you must be nimble and agile, ensuring that you are consistently building and protecting yourself in ways that are culturally relevant, authentic to you, and aligned with your values.

RULE #5 THINK OF YOUR REPUTATION AS CURRENCY

Being on the receiving end of cancel culture is not only stressful but costly. And many reputations find it difficult to crawl out of the mess and deal with the sometimes heavy aftermath. But there are some steps you can take if you find yourself in the crosshairs:

- **Apologize:** It's the first step and best step to being accountable. Your apology should be direct, with no excuses; express remorse and certainly do not be defensive.

- **Pause:** Stepping away from the public eye temporarily can be beneficial. This allows for the situation to de-escalate and gives you time to reflect and plan your next steps. Don't fuel the fire by putting out confusing statements and being defensive.

- **Rebuild:** Focus on rebuilding your reputation and relationships. This can be a slow process, and it's important to stay consistent in your efforts to show that you have learned and grown from the experience. Address policy changes and actually implement them. Make systemic or operational changes and train everyone on the new policy to ensure it doesn't happen again.

Not all cancellations are created equal so exercise self-awareness. If you need professional crisis communications guidance, get help. Your reputation depends on it. Ask Starbucks in the Middle East. The Starbucks Middle East franchisee laid off roughly 2,000 workers at its restaurants throughout the region in the face of ongoing boycotts of the brand over the Israel-Hamas war. And the fast fashion brand Zara was canceled after it was forced to withdraw an ad campaign featuring statues wrapped in white resembling photos of corpses in white shrouds in Gaza. "#BoycottZara" trended on the messaging platform X, and the company had to issue a statement saying that it regretted the "misunderstanding."

> ### Reputation Management Is Everyone's Business
>
> When I was working with the Uber of the Middle East, a company called Careem, I was in a meeting with a team of employees.
> "Who's in charge of Careem's reputation?" I asked. Only a handful of people raised their hands.
> "The CEO," said one employee.
> "No, it's the PR manager's job," said another.
> They were both right AND wrong. Reputation management is not the responsibility of one person: it's everyone's business. Every employee, every leader, every shareholder has a stake in ensuring a company's reputation is a strong one. An organization is made of people and all the employees are the front line and the ambassadors. Every interaction and touchpoint is an opportunity to build and protect the reputation, which means that everyone has a chance to make a real impact.
> A perfect example of this was a few years ago when two friends and I were standing in a really, REALLY long line to visit the 124th floor for the "Top of the Burj" experience at Dubai's Burj Khalifa, the world's tallest building. The line twisted and turned around several velvet ropes and a sign told us to expect a 45-minute wait. My friends and I didn't mind because we were just talking and catching up. But that wasn't the case for the young couple in front of us and their toddler,

RULE # 5 THINK OF YOUR REPUTATION AS CURRENCY

who was having a hard time containing his frustration and his lungs. He just couldn't stop wailing.

After what seemed like forever (but was probably 10 minutes), one of the floor supervisors happened to walk by. The second she heard a high-pitched scream coming from the toddler, she walked right over to the family and opened five hooks of the velvet ropes. Then she escorted the three of them to the front of the line and made sure they got on the next elevator up. (The rest of us seemed to let out a collective sigh of relief.) It was such an impressive act of customer service and reputation protection. Why? The floor supervisor saw a situation that could potentially damage the reputation of the Top of the Burj experience and took control to solve a problem that ultimately protected their reputation and improved the experience for everyone. She made the parents happy because their son stopped crying, thus their experience was no longer compromised. She made the guests who were patiently waiting happy because they no longer had to endure a screaming child. She instantly won everyone over. And not only that; I am sure that story spread like wildfire—I know I told at least two dozen people and now I'm telling you. In other words, that floor supervisor had a profound impact on the reputation of the Top of the Burj experience.

Reputation Is an Inside Job

In 1961, when John F. Kennedy was touring NASA headquarters, he met a janitor in the hallway who was mopping the floor. When Kennedy asked him what he did, the janitor said, "I'm helping to put a man on the moon." He knew exactly what he was there to do because that was the mission and essence of the reputation of the company and he understood his role in shaping and contributing to it. No matter what the job—big or small—everyone matters and everyone contributes.

Reputation is the same way. Exceptional employees and a fabulous CEO can help a reputation, while disgruntled employees or a scandalous CEO can ruin one. Even an employee who trashes their employer on their personal social media pages will have an impact on the company's reputation. That's why everyone needs to pay attention to it.

This is also why you need to lean in to internal communications. Most companies spend a lot of time working with PR teams and communicating with the media, stakeholders, and customers, but they don't put the same effort into internal communications. They don't spend enough time talking to their employees and team members, who are the ambassadors of the business. Internal communication with employees is one of the most overlooked areas.

I consider internal communication the unsung hero of communications! I strongly believe that the effort companies and brands put into external communication should be matched by investing in their teams and employees first. Employees and team members are the front lines of any company; they have friends and family members who often inquire about their work or may be familiar with the company or brand they represent. Wouldn't it be smart to arm them with all the information they need to advocate and promote your brand?

People trust people more than they trust companies. Therefore, I believe that we should prioritize a robust internal communications practice. This goes beyond a company newsletter or Slack channel; it means finding new and

RULE #5 THINK OF YOUR REPUTATION AS CURRENCY

meaningful ways to engage employees and inspire them by sharing more information with them.

Sharing information builds trust and loyalty and can be an effective tool for employee retention and recruitment. When employees understand the story behind the purpose—driven from the top—they are more likely to see themselves as part of that journey.

How companies treat and value their employees can have a profoundly positive impact on both the employees and their external reputation. It's a win-win scenario. Additionally, it can lead to better results and long-term performance. Companies with highly effective communication practices enjoy 47 percent higher total returns to shareholders (Tower Watson), and companies with engaged employees outperform the competition by as much as 202 percent (Gallup). People find employees to be the most reliable source of information about a company since they work there, trusting them more than the PR department or even the CEO, as they bring a strong sense of credibility. These employees are priceless brand ambassadors.

A few years ago, I was working with this really big company and told the CEO that we needed to train all their employees on the company's key messages, such as their mission and values.

"We don't need to do that," the CEO said, shaking his head. "They don't talk to the press."

"True, but they have friends and families. They go out to dinner and to parties and when they tell people where they work, they're asked questions about things that the company is doing," I told him. "We need to make sure that they know the right answers to give." In other words, an investment in the internal piece is crucial when it comes to reputation.

Imagine working for a company and you learn that the owners decided to sell the company; it would be critical to share this with internal employees first to reassure them what the change in ownership means and how it impacts their jobs, the company's future and the overall business in the industry.

Some of the most rewarding work I've done in my career has been internal communications because it means engaging with employees and winning on internal culture. Leadership requires better communications internally, not just to prevent miscommunication, but also to support crucial bottom-up conversations. This helps build stronger connections within and between teams. With remote working, employees have more choices than ever before, so a company must deliver more than a paycheck. If you want to build loyalty and retain employees, creating and protecting the culture of an organization is one of the most important things you can do, and internal communications plays a role in that. Not only will it enhance collaboration and productivity, it will also boost employee engagement within the organization.

First, ask yourself, *Is there infrastructure in place that promotes dialogue and two-way communication?* Then think about how you communicate with your employees in a way that is effective and will resonate. How many HR e-mails can one read (or archive)? Use modern communications to connect with your teams, formally and informally. Some companies use Slack or WhatsApp groups, virtual events, or interactive newsletters.

However, connecting internally shouldn't just be about communicating your business objectives, vision, and purpose. Find ways to build loyalty and awareness around what the company stands for and foster connective tissue

RULE #5 THINK OF YOUR REPUTATION AS CURRENCY

between teams. Be timely when it comes to communications too. During a tough time or a crisis, an absence of information makes people nervous. You may be busy working as fast as you can to try to put out the fire, and employees need to see what's happening. Keeping them in the dark too long leads to rumors, uncertainty, and anxiety. Think about what employees want to know and what employees need to know and make sure you're filling both of those buckets.

> **Say the right thing to the right people—and say it well.**

Be Crisis Ready

I've dealt with some pretty big crises in my career and I've learned a lot from each and every one of them. One thing is for sure: a crisis is a moment that can define you, your brand, or your company. If it's handled well, it can turn into an opportunity, as with Google in the Middle East, as I described earlier; if it's not, it can damage not only your business and revenue but also your reputation and sometimes that damage is irreparable. The worst time to prepare for a crisis is when you're in one. It's sort of like doing maintenance on a car while you're driving full speed on the highway. This is always a bad idea, and it's even worse in today's digital environment, when the whole world is watching in real time.

To protect your reputation and avoid putting yourself in a vulnerable position, it's crucial to understand your crisis risks and challenges. This requires a risk assessment. First, identify all the worst-case scenarios and issues that could impact your business. Think it through, focusing on everything from operations to people. Then plan for each scenario as if it were real. This includes but isn't limited to how to handle the crisis on social media, with employees and key stakeholders plus dealing with the press, any authorities or the government.

With my company, before any big event—like VeeCon—I put everyone through training about what to expect and the different types of crises we could potentially face. These include an active shooter, electrical problems, a death at the event, a missing child, a fire, etc. We think of all the worst things that could happen and then we go over what we would do in each and every situation so we are prepared and have detailed procedures in place. What crises could you or your business face and how are you preparing for them? Bring your leaders together and have this conversation. Your reputation depends on it.

Not all crises are created equal, so it's important to identify the various types of crises and what kind of response is appropriate for each one. Not all crises require the CEO of the company to come forward. Certain types of crises can elicit a response on one social network but cannot work on another. Identifying the type of crisis gives you lead time to produce customized content that best suits the platform of choice. In preparing, you also need a checklist of what to do internally and externally. You need to gather relevant information for each crisis, including identifying the key stakeholders, messages and people who need to know. Certain people—like the customer service phone line in the above example—need to be trained on readiness exercises. Your readiness will reflect on your reputation.

RULE # 5 THINK OF YOUR REPUTATION AS CURRENCY

| You cannot edit a blank page.

Crisis Response

The biggest thing that impacts the reputation of the company is not usually the crisis itself but how it was handled.

This is a very real problem thanks to the lightning-fast dynamics of 24-hour social media and real-time news. Something going viral can cause tremendous reputational damage in mere minutes. Rapid response is key. The time that lags between when the crisis hits and a company responds is critical.

The larger the vacuum of time and space with no response, the more room there is for rumors, misinformation, and speculation; and that gives you more problems to deal with.

The first thing you should do is show empathy. The second thing you should do if you made a mistake is to apologize. Third, figure out what you are going to do next. Your response has to have some meat on the bones. You can't just come out and say, "We don't always get it right. We're sorry." You have to say you are taking active steps and then outline them clearly for everyone to understand.

United Airlines didn't do any of these things in 2017 when a man was forcibly dragged off a flight. Apparently, passengers were asked to volunteer to take another flight because the flight was overbooked. When this didn't happen, the airlines chose to randomly bump passengers. David Dao refused to give up his seat, so officers came and pulled him off the plane, something that's clear in the disturbing video that went viral. It took almost a day for United Airlines to issue a statement about this incident and when they did, they took no responsibility. They called the passenger belligerent and disruptive, claiming that they had no choice. None of it made sense, especially since the video showed Dao's rough handling—and the backlash was huge,

RULE # 5 THINK OF YOUR REPUTATION AS CURRENCY

with people posting negative comments about United on social media and calling for the CEO to step down. More than a week after the incident, the company issued an apology. Life happens in real time and consumers expect a rapid response for any crisis that happens. The longer you leave a vacuum or don't respond, the worse it can impact your reputation.

In dealing with any crisis, it's crucial to gather the facts as quickly as you can. Find out what happened—the good, the bad and the ugly—and the key people who are involved. Figure out if you need to deal with local, regional, or international media and determine your messaging strategy. Then communicate early and often. Apologize immediately and show that you care that you messed up and hurt your customers. This is crucial. Put yourself in the shoes of the people affected in the crisis. If you don't, you can appear insensitive or out of touch. For example, if your customers have a lot of anxiety and uncertainty, try and calm those fears. Don't talk about things that are not useful at the time. You can mitigate a lot of damage with empathy, so if appropriate, apologize and take accountability. Saying sorry goes a long way.

An example of this was KFC. In early 2018, the UK unit of KFC ran out of chicken. This forced more than 600 KFC restaurants to close and created a PR nightmare, but how the company responded was simply brilliant. KFC immediately apologized to customers, running a newspaper ad showing a photo of a chicken bucket with the KFC logo letters rearranged to read "FCK." The ad text read: "WE'RE SORRY. A chicken restaurant without any chicken. It's not ideal . . . Thank you for bearing with us." The ads went viral on social media, helping KFC recover from its disaster in a very clever way.

In 2021, VeeCon was being held at U.S. Bank Stadium in Minneapolis. This is a superconference for all things Web3, tech, culture, and marketing. One long-standing criticism of the Web 3 and NFT space is that it's predominantly male. During VeeCon, a tweet of a photo of one of the U.S. Bank Stadium's bathrooms went viral. Somebody posted a picture of the men's and women's bathrooms with the *wo* of the women's bathroom crossed out so it just said *men*. In other words, there were two bathrooms designated for men and none for women. The photo's caption read, "We support women in the NFT space," implying that this was done on purpose by the conference organizers. People on social media started bashing the event organizers, which is our client, saying that they were only focused on men.

First, we had to determine whether this was a real photo or was Photoshopped to hurt our client, so we sent someone to check every bathroom in the stadium. Keep in mind this is a seven-level venue with 979 bathrooms, so it took us some time to get to the truth. It turns out the photo was real. The bathroom was on the third floor of the stadium, which was a level we weren't even using for the event. Once we knew the facts, we escalated to all the key members of the executive leadership team, the event producers, and my press team to make sure they were all aware of this situation.

We didn't change the bathroom sign and we wondered why someone would go out of their way to modify a stadium bathroom on a level we weren't using—that would certainly appear to be real malicious intent. But the whole beauty of the VeeFriends community, which was on display 10X during this event, is that the community is kind and empathetic; it's what makes them distinctive actually.

My gut told me to check with U.S. Bank Stadium to investigate. That is where we uncovered the truth.

RULE # 5 THINK OF YOUR REPUTATION AS CURRENCY

In 2019, U.S. Bank Stadium changed the bathroom signage because there were more men attending their events than women, and they didn't have enough bathrooms. They had received complaints from male visitors that the venue didn't accommodate them enough. This was great news because it meant that the sign had nothing to do with us. However, the photo had already gone viral by that point and everyone was saying that the event didn't care about women linking us to a photo and move done by the stadium many years prior. And this tweet was picking up viral steam and soon *The Verge* media outlet was writing a story about it and asking for our response. Urgh.

Everyone said we should put out a statement explaining that the stadium had changed the sign in 2019. I said no. It would be more credible if the stadium issued the statement and we shared it. I wanted a statement out on their letterhead with their own spokesperson named because it would be far more credible to have the source explain their actions than to have us, a third party, explain their actions.

I now had to convince the venue to get involved in a PR crisis they didn't really want to be involved in. But they understood the situation and they were professional. They had to get internal approvals and alignment, but within 30 minutes they sent me a statement, they posted it, and we then shared their official response.

The official response said that U.S. Bank Stadium changed the bathroom signage in 2019 and VeeCon had nothing to do with the photo circulating online. And they put it on their official letterhead.

Within seconds the online swirl and viral tweet came to a screeching halt. Whew. The facts remained that VeeCon had more female speakers and participants than other Web3 conferences. That was an intentional standard they were setting for the industry, but one viral moment could have erased it if we hadn't been quick to act and engage.

That said, you can also react too quickly in a crisis, so don't jump in too soon. Oftentimes CEOs and founders get emotional and tend to overreact in a crisis to protect their reputations, but this depends on the situation of course. I often have to walk leaders back from the cliff and ask them to pause and let the dust settle. Let the truth come out. Let the facts reveal themselves. Don't insert yourself into a story that might end up harming your business because you reacted too quickly.

Determining how and when to react is why having someone on your team with communications expertise is important. They have that strategic thinking on timing and message. They know when to throw your hat in the ring and when to step back and hold on. It is hard when you're in it to think strategy, but it's essential in order to have the result play out in your favor and protect your reputation.

Crisis Recovery

Once a crisis passes, you enter recovery mode. How do you recover from a crisis or cancel culture? By taking deliberate action. Listen and take the feedback that you received from that experience and improve. Next, demonstrate how you are changing your behavior and your policies. Articulate your values authentically and consistently. If you're part of an organization, evaluate what new training is required and how you will cascade your new ways of working with your employees. Think about your customers: Do you need to push out a communication to them explaining what happened or what your next steps are?

RULE #5 THINK OF YOUR REPUTATION AS CURRENCY

In 2023, Delta Airlines announced sweeping changes to their Sky Miles loyalty program. They had too many customers at the highest tiers. The airline announced new policies on how to earn miles, including who could access their coveted airport lounges. Instead of earning benefits by number of miles flown, they were now going to tally based on how much money was being spent with the airline. This move would make it more difficult to earn benefits of elite status, such as complimentary seat upgrades or waived baggage fees.

Customers were angry. They flooded the call centers, vowed to stop using their SkyMiles credit cards, and felt flying Delta was no longer beneficial. Headlines read, "Delta changed its frequent flyer program—and customers are truly furious." In the weeks that followed, the company listened. The response was so overwhelmingly negative they had to do something to protect their reputation. The CEO, Ed Bastian, came out and said, "We went too far," and announced they were modifying their initial plans to ensure customer satisfaction. Bastian went on to explain the reason why they wanted to make sweeping changes—something they failed to clarify when they announced the stricter policies.

"It's gotten to the point, honestly, where we have so much demand for our premium product and services that are far in excess of our ability to serve it effectively in terms of our assets," Bastian said. He cited a surge in travel during the Covid-19 pandemic that doubled the number of Diamond Medallion status members. He added "If everyone's special, no one feels special," and the move was done to ensure service levels could be met for their customers.

By explaining their policies and sharing the WHY and not just the WHAT was important; it gave customers insight they didn't initially have. Giving people context can go a long way, and as a Delta customer I was satisfied with this answer because he let us inside their decision making and thought processes.

I love this example of making a public mistake, listening to the feedback, and then making a change based on the public's response. Delta turned around a public backlash that was having a major impact on their bottom line and reputation. Owning your mistakes and doing it publicly can build consumer confidence and trust in your business.

If an apology can come with a bit of humor, even better. When Netflix launched in France, they started dubbing their shows. Can you imagine watching *Friends* dubbed in French? To make matters worse, the dubbing was poorly done. Initially, French viewers were offended and criticized Netflix, but the PR team in France mastered a rapid response. The minute they saw things going horribly wrong, they created a terribly dubbed video of their CEO apologizing. It was their way of saying, "We made a mistake. We're sorry." The video showed that the CEO and company had a sense of humor and that they were taking accountability. The response was overwhelmingly positive because it was clear that Netflix understood the problem, admitted it, and made a bad situation better. In fact, they got a lot of positive PR coverage: people loved Netflix and thought the CEO apology was cool, and they were even featured in stories as an example of how a company should respond to a mistake.

Netflix apologized, they took accountability, and used the moment to point the finger at themselves instead of others.

Of course, Netflix changed how they did their dubbing and translation and the company learned a lot too. They took it as an opportunity and used it to train all the PR

RULE # 5 THINK OF YOUR REPUTATION AS CURRENCY

people around the world. Now, when people remember that incident they remember that there was a problem, but they also remember how well it was handled. There are a lot of positive repercussions that can come from a crisis because you can improve your operations, motivate employees, and really show your team how to step out of a crisis. Today Netflix is hailed as one of the case studies on how to build a global business through the power of localization. Just read the headline of this story that appeared on Rask: "Dubbing: The Secret Weapon Behind Netflix's International Popularity." That crisis turned into a big business win for them.

> **Personal branding is the practice of marketing yourself as a brand.**

Build Your Personal Brand Now

The best way to protect your reputation and increase the "value" of your currency is to invest in your personal brand. Years ago, I thought people who had their own personal brands were driven by ego. I thought it was sort of an arrogant, pushy thing to put yourself out there and say, "Hey look at me. I know stuff!" It seemed self-serving.

There is a big difference between self-promotion and idea promotion. Self-promotion is "look at me, I know stuff, I am the coolest and you should listen to me." Idea promotion is about the ideas, the expertise, the knowledge, and experience of your ideas that you want to share, and you are the vessel and conduit to share it.

Today, I have a very different point of view.

The more I thought about the role of having a strong personal brand, the more I understood its importance.

Personal branding is not about self-promotion; it's about leadership. It's about reputation management because it builds your authority and influence. Establishing a strong personal brand is vital because to master self-reliance, you must master yourself, and that includes what you stand for as a personal brand.

When I first started my career in communications, I worked with companies and governments to build their reputations and brands. Today, my work has expanded to include helping several CEOs shape and build their personal brands. And sometimes, people, like brands, want to rebrand themselves, whether it is about changing perception or reintroducing themselves to new audiences. I also help with that.

Understanding how to build a strong personal brand is something I want everyone to learn how to master. It's the fundamental way to build and protect your reputation and creates the foundation for opportunities, growth, influence and effective communications. Take ownership of your personal brand; don't outsource it to someone else or ignore it because you think you're not a "brand." You most certainly are.

But What Is a Personal Brand, Exactly?

Personal brand = reputation

Your personal brand is what you intentionally communicate about yourself to define who you are and the value you are bringing to the world. The founder of Amazon, Jeff Bezos, said, "Your brand is what people say about you when you're not in the room."

This is all about reputation and underscores the idea that a brand's true essence and reputation are determined

RULE #5 THINK OF YOUR REPUTATION AS CURRENCY

> Your personal brand is the unique combination of skills, experience, and personality that you want the world to see.

by the perceptions, feelings, and talk among its customers or audience outside of its direct control or marketing efforts. It highlights the importance of the public's opinion and experiences with the brand, rather than just the image the brand tries to project through advertising or targeted PR. This perspective emphasizes that genuine brand reputation is built over time through consistent customer experiences, trust, and the value delivered by the brand, rather than just through crafted marketing messages or smart advertising.

Your personal brand embodies a combination of three things: your skills, your experience, and your personality. You may think, *I'm not a company, so I am not a brand—only companies are brands.* But whether you like it or not, if you have a website, an Instagram account, or a TikTok or LinkedIn page, then you're a personal brand and everything you share reveals something about who you are. It defines how people see you. And this isn't just about your social media presence; in fact, your real life and offline brand matters even more. As a result, you need to consider your reputation—both online and offline. Personal branding is essentially about your reputation—how you treat others, including suppliers, vendors, partners, employees, baristas, and colleagues. Let me reiterate—personal branding is not about being a social media influencer! It's about how you want to present yourself to the world, both online and offline, and how you want to be perceived by others.

When we think of people who have strong personal brands, people like Oprah Winfrey; the Ruler of Dubai, his Highness Sheikh Mohammed Bin Rashid; and Richard Branson might come to mind. What makes them strong personal brands? They are consistent in how they show up. They are relatable even though they are very powerful. And they are also transparent—what we see is what we get. These individuals have built strong personal brands by

RULE # 5 THINK OF YOUR REPUTATION AS CURRENCY

leveraging their unique strengths, values, and expertise, allowing them to connect deeply with their audiences and achieve significant influence in their respective fields.

They transcend generations and geographies, age groups and races. They are visionary yet approachable. They are leaders yet are welcoming and not intimidating. We feel like we know them, but we have never actually met them.

Now I want you to think of people who don't have strong personal brands. They might have some controversy around them or you aren't sure where they stand on any given day. For example, Donald Trump or Elon Musk. They are powerful, but they aren't consistent and often spark debate due to their actions, opinions, or roles in significant events.

Three Qualities that Make for a Strong Personal Brand

1. Authenticity. You have to be who you are online and offline in a way that is not fabricated, made up or produced. Authenticity is key—people want the real you. A personal brand is personal, so they need to connect with you. The only way to do that is if they get to see your authentic self. This is not the time or place to fake it until you make it. The real you is not perfect and the more you can be yourself and express yourself authentically the better. However, being authentic doesn't mean you have to reveal your personal life—it's to show your character, your values and what you believe in.

2. Consistency. You need to be consistent with your message and narrative and what you stand for. It's just like with a jingle or an ad: the more you hear it the more it sinks in. You need to be consistent in what you say so your audience understands what you stand for. Consistency also allows you to build trust with your audience and create a cohesive relationship with them. In today's world, you need to be consistent; and this is not about social media, this is about being consistent in how you show up in the real world too. This means be consistent in how you conduct yourself at work, with friends, on stages, or in classrooms or within your community.

3. Purpose. One of the easiest ways to be consistent with your personal brand is knowing what your purpose is and what you stand for. This is also called your narrative. What do you want to be known for? You need to define what you want others to know about you. One way to define your purpose or narrative is to evaluate what you are doing consistently already. Are you avidly posting about something you're passionate about? Ask yourself what is most important to you and what you want your brand to be about. That is your purpose; a narrative is one sentence that articulates that. For example, my purpose is to *help people communicate better*.

Finding my WHY and boiling it down to four words took me nearly a lifetime to discover and articulate but it was there all along, I just never put it in a mission statement before. Helping people communicate better embodies not just my values but my purpose and intention. I want to help others communicate better whether it's through crisis communications, internal communications, media relations, external communications, personal branding, communicating online, or in real life through networking and more.

I am always checking myself at the door: Am I consistently and authentically sticking to my purpose and bringing value to my audience? This is what I want my personal brand to be about and what I want my audience to authentically and consistently see.

RULE #5 THINK OF YOUR REPUTATION AS CURRENCY

> Personal branding is not about SELF-PROMOTION, it's about LEADERSHIP.

Why Your Personal Brand Matters

You might ask yourself why it is important to build your personal brand. First, you have expertise to share with the world and you should share it. Your brand value goes beyond your digital currency—having a strong personal brand has nothing to do with being a social media influencer. In today's world, when you meet someone they will google you, they will check your LinkedIn or Instagram profiles, and you have to control your narrative, your image, and your reputation. People who master self-reliance know how important this is, especially with the world we are about to enter with AI and deep fakes. Building and owning your personal brand is more urgent now than ever.

Your personal brand is your reputation. I never met anyone who didn't care about their reputation. Have you?

No matter what your profession, think about setting yourself up for success and protecting yourself *(self-reliance in action)*. You are no longer competing with people in your city. Thanks to the pandemic and virtual work environments, you're competing with anyone with an Internet connection and skills—and they can potentially vie for your job.

Put yourself in a position to own everything about yourself. Your accomplishments and achievements at work are not public unless you share them. Nobody knows them better than you. Put yourself in position to win by being on the front foot; don't rely on your job title or your manager to carry you forward. Build a robust brand. Again your brand is not just skills and experience; it's also your personality. My relationships with people are what get me far. I have credentials and skills and expertise but why people work with me is because of who I am, not just because of what I do. This is the combination that makes for a powerful personal brand and why I invest so much time in it. Building your personal brand gives you a chance to learn about yourself. What is your purpose? That is such a hard question, but wouldn't you love to explore that?

Five Key Benefits to Building Your Personal Brand

1. **Raise awareness and visibility for your business, company, expertise, or side hustle.** Your personal brand does not have to be your full-time job. For example, if you love to bake cakes as a side hustle and want to share that with your audience to get orders, you can start to raise awareness that baking is your passion and you would love to create something for future customers' special occasions.

2. **Expand your network with key industries and stakeholders, connecting with new audiences online and offline (in real life thorough networking).** You don't know everyone and the market is vast. I just did a personal brand training workshop for a CEO who specializes in helping people understand AI and Web3. He tends to talk at tech conferences and summits, but I recommended that he take his message to other industries that don't know about AI and Web3 like the hospitality and retail industries. This way he can bring them knowledge and insight as an expert and expand his network to new industries and create new relationships.

3. **Attract new opportunities for your brand or business.** I work with a client who runs a foundation and a majority of the work they do focuses on the impact of the foundation on the community. Because we are consistent with the personal brand of the executive director of the

foundation, we are able to attract new opportunities like strategic partners, foundation donors and even speaking opportunities.

4. Showcase the credentials of your brand, your impact, and your vision. Your personal brand is all about you; you should drive your reputation and narrative. If you don't do it, who will? That is why you need a strong LinkedIn page and consistent bios on your social media pages. Be religious about it; your credentials are what you worked so hard for. Define it, share it and be loud about it.

5. Leverage the power of storytelling to your audience. We live in an era where everyone has a story and must share it. Today's competitive landscape almost requires it. Powerful storytelling can set you apart from everyone else and with the tools available today, it's easier than ever to create, share, and bring your authentic story to the world. Everyone has an audience, you just haven't found yours yet. Keep telling your story and it will eventually resonate with them.

Online and Offline Personal Brand

Building your personal brand is not about being a content creator. It's about being an effective leader, a mindful communicator and having a presence so you can advocate for yourself. A personal brand is about owning how you represent yourself in order to build and protect your reputation. You should focus on both your online brand and your offline brand because your reputation is shaped by interactions, both digital and in person. Let's start by talking about your digital reputation and how to protect it.

RULE # 5 THINK OF YOUR REPUTATION AS CURRENCY

> Everyone has an audience, you just haven't found yours yet. Keep telling your story.

Protecting Your Online Digital Reputation

Your digital reputation is the digital footprint of everything about you online. It encompasses everything you say and do, whether *you* posted it or others shared it. When you post something online, it's out there and you can't really remove it. That is why you need to be in control. But what can you actually control? You can only control what you share and your actions (that might get filmed, documented or written about). I suggest you conduct a digital audit of yourself to see what you find and make sure you're as strong as you want to be represented. Google yourself and check your bios and profile photos. Look for inconsistencies and any red flags. Look at what is being said about you in all formats of content. You don't want someone to find something you're not proud of or that you are not aware of. Reviews, comments, social media profiles, photos, and posts all shape search results. But the impacts of these results don't end up on the first page of Google. Therefore, you must learn how to own your reputation in the digital space. New content does not erase negative past news, but it is essential to building your online presence and maintaining a positive online reputation.

Three Ways to Protect Your Digital Reputation

1. Participate. You must be proactive in participating and building your brand and online presence. This means setting up your social media pages and having clean profile photos (clear visuals that easily identify you). Don't just be present; push content consistently and regularly.

2. Know your audience. As you gather the data, cater your content to your followers, influencers, and target markets. Not all content is created equal. If you want to own your online reputation, first take control of what you are saying, how you're saying it and who you're saying it to. Go beyond advertising yourself or your business. Share content on a broad range of topics that are of interest and value to your audience. As you continuously engage with them and build positive relationships, you'll see your presence on these platforms improve and so too will your presence in search results.

3. Stay vigilant and stay informed. The world is constantly changing so you must stay vigilant and informed. Monitor open source platforms and own all of your online accounts. Sadly, you cannot opt out, so instead be proactive and remember it's never too late or too early to take control.

My Top Four Ways to Build Your Brand Offline

1. Build genuine relationships. Nothing beats being genuine, and if you focus on creating genuine relationships based on listening and reciprocity with shared interests and goals, you will win. When you initiate a connection that is genuine for your personal brand, it lays the foundation for conversations where you're bound to find further common interests.

2. Help your network. The biggest way to win as a personal brand is to be of service to others. A cornerstone of my brand is this sentence: "How can I help?" In fact, my employees said if we made team T-shirts with our most used sayings that's what mine would say. Always offer to help before you ask for something and then give with generosity. And if you don't have the knowledge, offer a contact who does; remember relationships are a two-way street. And if you have an ask, be specific and always say thank you and follow up.

3. Diversify your events. Attending industry-relevant conferences or summits allows you to meet people with similar interests and provides opportunities to brainstorm and connect with them on a personal level. You can take your event networking to the next level by showcasing your expertise as a speaker instead of an attendee. Then go one step further and attend events you wouldn't normally consider to reach new audiences, gain new insights and develop new relationships.

4. Create a personal board of directors. Pick two or three people who will hold you accountable when it comes to reaching your goals. This is going to be your personal board of directors. Your personal board of directors is a group of individuals you select to act as your accountability team. They are there to support you, offer advice, provide tough love when necessary, and serve as a sounding board to help you achieve your goals. These are people who will keep you honest and who care about what's in your best interest. My sister is on my personal board of directors because she tells me like it is, but she also wants me to be successful. I have a mentor that I worked with many years ago who's also on my personal board of directors. Meet with your board of directors regularly—every quarter or annually. Have lunch or a call to talk about some of the things you're working on and how you're doing. It could be personal, or it could be professional. The other thing I do is write an annual report or letter at the beginning of the year saying these are my missions or objectives for the year. This helps me hold myself accountable. I also put a report together for my personal board of directors at the end of the year on how I did against my personal goals. Your personal board of directors can also help you unlock or solve problems through their experiences or networks. A lot of people are afraid to ask for help. I was one of those people, but I've worked on that and learned that it's important just to ask. The worst thing they can say is no and then you just move on and ask somebody else. But more often than not, they'll say yes.

Personal brand does not mean personal life.

How Personal Should Your Personal Brand Be?

So how personal should your brand be and what lies between personal and professional? I often get this question. You don't have to reveal everything; remember you own and control your brand narrative. Don't feel the need to reveal all. You can always develop your personal brand and organize yourself by the roles you play.

How many platforms should you be on? This depends on what your message is and who your audience is. You want to be on the platforms that allow you to connect with your audience (so you need to know where they are) and you want to be on the number of platforms that you can consistently manage and support with content. You don't need to be everywhere; focus on what you can do well and consistently. If public speaking comes naturally to you, you might want to host X (Twitter) spaces or start your own podcast. If you love video, make content in video format. If you love to read articles, use the green screen feature and comment on news you have seen and give your "hot take" on it.

When it comes to content, try to customize what you post native to that platform, meaning don't copy and paste across platforms. Try to leverage the unique features that each platform has to offer. TikTok has native features that are really valuable if you create the content on their platform. A reel on Instagram doesn't work the same on LinkedIn. Be intentional and take the time to understand how audiences consume content on each platform.

Your profile for your personal brand should be your name, making it easy for people to find you. I learned this the hard way. My name is Maha Abouelenein, so why are my X (Twitter) and Instagram handles @mahagaber? Maha Gaber is my first name and middle name. Let me be honest: when I started on Twitter around 2008 I didn't really want people to know who I was. What if I tweeted something stupid? What if I didn't want to be seen? I just wanted to look around and see other people's tweets until I could get comfortable with the platform and find my voice. Fast forward to 2024, and now I have a big audience on the platform but my name is @mahagaber. I also did that for Instagram to be consistent. Don't do what I did; use your full name so people can find you easily or have your handle be directly related to your personal brand like @TheHotelBoss or @ThePointsGuy. This shows what brand you represent and who you are.

Protecting your name and reputation is priceless so I advise my clients to register their names on every platform that exists—Facebook, YouTube, TikTok, Linkedin—whether they use them or not. This way no one can take your name even if you don't plan to use that platform or create content on it. The most important thing is that you own your name online. I bought mahaabouelenein.com and every handle of my full name and first name/middle name . . . everything. I own my name and my assets; they're my digital currency.

RULE #5 THINK OF YOUR REPUTATION AS CURRENCY

What if you have a full-time job and want your personal brand on social media to be your side hustle so you can eventually quit your job and build your own business? I get this question a lot. My advice is to make it very clear on your personal brand platforms, such as websites and social media, that your bio has nothing to do with your job, your company or your title. This way it's clear that you are not using your job title or your position to misrepresent your purpose; in fact, you are adding to your purpose or role and showing you have interests and activities outside of work.

I know a CMO of a global bank. She is one of the smartest, most accomplished women I know and her credentials and pedigree are impressive. Her social media account is not about her job or her full-time role; it's about her and who she is as a mother, wife, and all-around fun human. She does TikTok dances, takes us behind the scenes in her local community, and shows us her travels. I feel connected to her and her brand without knowing what she does as a job. She is authentic, consistently shows up in the same manner, and she is the person in her personal brand.

I have a friend who works full-time at a major company and absolutely loves her job. Like most people, she seeks fulfillment and has other interests outside of work that enrich her life. These interests can include sports, hobbies, or learning new skills. She has always been passionate about people's origin stories, although this passion wasn't related to her job. Additionally, she enjoys listening to podcasts and experimenting with video editing in her spare time. So, she decided to start her own podcast on a topic she was passionate about.

She purchased some microphones from Amazon and used Canva to design a show poster for her podcast brand.

Then, she reached out to her network of friends and asked if she could interview them to practice and improve her interviewing skills. These interviews served as 'practice content,' allowing her to test the entire process. She found the experience rewarding, fun, and creative.

After interviewing several friends, she felt ready to produce a full show. She decided to find eight people to interview for the first season of her podcast. For her, it was a creative outlet that helped her learn new skills, such as communication in an interview format, content editing, and distribution across platforms. She also found the stories she heard to be enriching. She was learning and building her personal brand around a topic she was passionate about.

She also took a smart step by informing her employer about her new hobby. She wanted to ensure they didn't feel threatened by the possibility of her leaving her job to become a content creator, as many people do. Her employer was impressed with her initiative and supportive of her podcasting venture. They even expressed willingness to support her and possibly become one of her sponsors if her podcast grew and she decided to continue with it.

***

If you want to build your brand, I invite you to join my community where I will share playbooks, workshops, and practical tips on how to build your personal brand effectively with step-by-step pro tips and the latest updates and trends. I can help you build your personal brand and then give you the keys on how to grow and build your audience to scale it. Visit mahaabouelenein.com to learn more.

RULE #5
THINK OF YOUR REPUTATION AS CURRENCY

This is how you position yourself and your company in the eyes of the world. You think "reputation first" and understand what it takes to build and protect it.

> **Cheat Sheet**

- **Put yourself first:** If not you, who? Nobody will put you at the top of your priority list and care about your image, reputation, and brand more than you.
- **We live online and offline:** How you treat people in real life, the relationships you have, and the way you conduct yourself must reflect and be consistent with your online personal brand.
- **Know your stuff:** Lead with the intent to add value to others and make sure you know your stuff to build trust with your audience.
- **Passion over profit:** Prioritize your brand reputation over sales.
- **Be authentic:** Make deposits in the trust bank and be truly authentic.
- **Show *and* tell:** Document vs. create content when you storytell.
- **Be consistent:** Having a clear and consistent personal brand will help you create a recognizable and memorable brand.
- **Demonstrate authority:** A strong personal brand can help you establish credibility in your field and demonstrate thought leadership and authority. By sharing your knowledge and insights through your personal brand, you can demonstrate your expertise and build credibility with your audience.

RULE #5 THINK OF YOUR REPUTATION AS CURRENCY

- **Create differentiation:** In a crowded market, a strong personal brand can help you stand out from the competition. By developing a unique brand identity and showcasing your unique skills and perspective, you can differentiate yourself and attract the attention of potential clients or employers.
- **Increase visibility:** A strong personal brand can help you increase your visibility and reach a wider audience. By building a strong online presence through social media, blogging, or other platforms, you can reach people who may not have otherwise known about your work or your passions/skills.
- **Build relationships:** A strong personal brand can help you build relationships with people in your industry or community. By sharing your knowledge and expertise, you can connect with like-minded individuals and develop a network of contacts that can support your career or business.
- **Create opportunities:** A strong personal brand can open up new opportunities for you, such as speaking engagements, media interviews, or job offers. By establishing yourself as an expert in your field, you can attract new opportunities that can help you grow and develop your career.

Reputation Building Relies On

- Having a strong narrative (purpose) that is clear and easy to understand (internally and externally)
- Deep relationships with the community, partnerships, and key stakeholders like employees, media, and investors
- A reliable product or service that people trust

Why Build Your Personal Brand?

- You have expertise to share with the world.
- You need to own your name and your reputation.
- People will google you.
- You will learn more about yourself.
- It will bring new opportunities.
- Investing in your personal brand is investing in you!
- Personal branding isn't about self promotion; it's about idea promotion and thought leadership.
- Think of your brand in terms of currency. What's it worth? How can you grow it and protect it?
- Reputation is your new currency and the only currency that matters.

RULE #5 THINK OF YOUR REPUTATION AS CURRENCY

Reflection Exercises

1. Personal brand audit: What are your social media handles? When you look at your content, what are the key themes that emerge?

2. What is your digital reputation? What comes up when you google yourself?

3. What are your brand values?
   - What do you want others to know about you?
   - What are you consistently doing in your behavior?
   - What is most important to you?
   - What do you want your brand to be about?

4. What is your narrative?
   - Write down what you are passionate about.
   - Write down what you stand for and what is important to you.
   - Write down three things you are *currently* known for.
   - Write down what you *want* to be known for.
   - Draft your personal mission statement.

5. Develop a personal board of directors. This is a list of people you trust and can share your goals with but who will hold you accountable and deploy tough love when you need it. Check with your personal board of directors quarterly to see how you are doing on your personal brand goals.

Make deposits in other people's trust banks.

RULE # 6
BE A LONG-TERM PLAYER

You don't try to get it all done in one day. In one week. In one year. It's the process of getting better every day. And doing that for a period of years. Then that creates the masterpiece.

— KOBE BRYANT

Approaching business by thinking long term is not an easy concept when we live in a world that values speed. Speed drives results, and we tend to reward those who work harder, faster, and longer. We very much live in a "now" culture.

Now culture is all about instant gratification, immediate access to information, and even fast delivery. We want to watch a whole season on Netflix now, not week by week; we want digital banking and 'tap to pay' speed at checkout. We value 'quick wins' and self-serve checkouts. We certainly don't want to wait in line—it's more efficient to do it ourselves!

And we also have become incredibly impatient. We don't like waiting for pages on the Internet to load and we certainly don't like waiting for success. We don't even have the patience to lose weight the good old-fashioned way by moving more and eating clean—we want to magic pills or weight loss shots to look good. And when it comes to consuming content and information on social media, it's even worse. Research shows that if you don't hook the consumer in the first three seconds of the video, they will keep scrolling—three SECONDS! Our relationship with time has really changed. Everything is accelerated and even managers expect their employees to be "always on" to stay competitive.

Throw work-life balance out the door. You are expected to be reachable and available across working hours and time zones. And if you have WhatsApp, it can tell others if you're online or read their message with those two blue ticks (and you feel the pressure if you read the message and don't reply because they will know you saw it!).

But what I believe is essential to self-reliance is understanding the benefits of being a long-term player. Knowing when to play the long game and most importantly *how* is what I want to share with you.

I define a long-term player as someone who is strategic and makes deliberate decisions based on delayed gratification or delayed outcomes. Have confidence that if you choose to operate differently in specific business situations and show your commitment to the big picture, you will reap tremendous rewards. Sometimes I play such a long game that people think I am crazy, but it's such an essential tool in my self-reliance toolbox that I don't think twice about it.

Remember, I worked for GaryVee for nearly a year for free before we signed a contract. I organized an entire international business trip for Matt Higgins and introduced him to some of my most valuable contacts before we decided to do business together, and I volunteered to work for Dr.

RULE # 6 BE A LONG-TERM PLAYER

Deepak Chopra long before we discussed any business collaborations. I became a speech writer for the prime minister of Egypt and worked for months for free before I got a contract. Every time I chose to give first and receive later, I knew who and what I was doing it for. I have had hundreds of clients, but these are only a handful of times I chose to do the opposite of what I normally do because these individuals presented important opportunities that I knew were valuable for me. That is how a long-term player thinks. And how does it tie to self-reliance? It's all about betting on yourself.

A long-term player bets on themselves, their skills, and their potential. Remember when I took the job as the office manager when I really didn't want that job? I remembered who I was and what I was capable of doing, and I relied on my values to help me get through to the other side. There was so much uncertainty on how that could have played out, but I relied on myself, took initiative, adopted a long-term view; in short, I bet on myself. I took responsibility for my actions, my own life, and my decisions and you can too.

I want to encourage you to be your own advocate and not succumb to self-doubt. You will naturally ask yourself whether you're doing the right thing, but if you make a mistake know that it's a natural part of the journey and be willing to learn from your experience and bounce back.

So how do you become an effective long-term player? Adopt these principles and make them your own.

Make Short-Term Sacrifices

Thinking and acting long term means that you are willing to make some sacrifices in the short term in order to see whether an opportunity or relationship can bear fruit. For example, I am willing to sacrifice fees for a client if it's someone I really want to work with because I see the long-term benefit of having that client on my roster. It may attract other clients and allow me to create new relationships. It can help attract new employees and enhance my company's reputation. Other times, I might take on a client and charge them less than I normally do because they are in an industry I want to crack and learn more about. Not all value is created equal. Not all value is monetary.

For example, a bootstrapped startup that makes expensive sunglasses might sacrifice revenue to get some influencers to wear their products because they need the publicity to boost sales. Although the company sacrifices the money it would receive if they sold those sunglasses, the long-term benefits of the celebrity wearing them is more valuable. When a photo of that celebrity wearing those sunglasses goes viral, it makes fans of that celebrity want to buy the same glasses. Plus, that image is something the sunglasses company can use for marketing purposes. If you want to be a long-term player, you have to know what short-term sacrifices you are willing to make in order to achieve a long-term benefit.

People over Profit

Long-term players value their team members more than their customers. I know it's a hard concept to understand because you need customers to make money, but you can't do that if you don't have people: happy people. Investing in your team and your culture matters more than anything. If your employees believe in your mission and feel connected to the company's culture and purpose, they will be unstoppable, and that will bring you all the customers, sales, and performance you want and need in the long term. In contrast, burning employees to the ground is the fastest way to disrupt your business. A stable team is a high-performing

RULE # 6 BE A LONG-TERM PLAYER

> A stable team is a high-performing team, and a happy team is a productive team.

team, and a happy team is a productive team. Be willing to say no to business or opportunities that might tax your team or your culture. Never sacrifice culture or your people for profits. I wouldn't accept a client with big checks that was going to abuse my team, drain our energy or be unreasonably demanding or unethical.

Reputational Risk vs. Financial Reward

Never risk your reputation for a financial reward or a business opportunity that might pose a threat to your company. It's so tempting to step onto a big stage and grab an opportunity, but if it might hurt your reputation either by association or direct involvement, then you need to walk away. I have been asked to work on some very high-profile PR crises that would have certainly put me and my company on the national or international stage. And they would have benefited the company with a tremendous financial windfall. But I declined. It was never worth the potential reputational risk. When you evaluate your business in terms of reputation, you understand the implications of what comes after that opportunity. You have to think it through and put things into a long-term perspective for the consequences of your decisions.

Reputational risk involves anything that can impact customer trust, brand value or your public perception. It can also involve jeopardizing your reputation with employees. Prioritizing ethical and responsible practices should be your default mode over increased revenue, higher profits, improved market share, investment returns, or even cost savings. By prioritizing your reputation, you might be making short-term financial sacrifices, but a stellar reputation can lead to stronger brand loyalty, customer trust, and sustainable growth over time.

RULE # 6 BE A LONG-TERM PLAYER

Make Deposits in the Trust Bank

One of the most important lessons I learned while working at Weber Shandwick was the importance of making deposits in other people's trust banks. The concept is simple: Build goodwill and trust in others over the long term; these are your deposits. Be genuine, treat people with respect, and do things to bring value to others consistently. Rather than investing money (bank deposits), you are investing deposits made up of time, energy, and effort into a relationship. Over time, after making deposits in other people's trust banks, you earn the right to make a withdrawal *if you need it* because you have built so much trust and goodwill.

For example, I spent nine years developing and investing in a relationship with Ahmed, who was well versed in doing business in Morocco. Many years into our friendship, I ran into a tricky situation with a client who was on a business trip to Morocco. I had developed such a rapport and relationship with Ahmed (by making significant deposits over time) that I didn't hesitate to ask him for help (make a withdrawal) even though it had nothing to do with him or his business. Keep making deposits in the trust bank. Building equity and trust with others not only builds your reputation, but it also gives you an army of supporters who will have your back if and when you need them.

Serve Your Relationships

Long-term players understand the importance of serving their relationships. They don't use their relationships for their own gain, and they don't reach out only when they need something. Abusing your contacts for favors or access is the fastest way to lose them. Think of how you can pull people into your network by attracting them with your genuine behaviors and actions. I really believe the best way to attract and keep anyone in your life is by being a person of substance and value and serving them. I've been practicing this approach for more than 30 years and it consistently works because I don't start any relationship by asking for something. Instead, I think about what I can offer and how I can help create value. I think carefully about what the other person is trying to achieve, what's important to them, and where or how I can add value.

Being intentional and strategic like this requires time. First, you must seek to understand them and then be a very good listener and pay attention. For me, it's the simple things you can do: send a thoughtful article or an idea that might be interesting for them. Think about introducing them to someone or nominating them to speak at an event you have access to. You can also serve your relationships by anticipating needs and doing something before they ask for it. We do this all the time in communications; we think through what journalists might need to build a strong story and we provide it in advance. If we organize an interview and they mention they want follow up information about a topic, we not only go fetch that info for them but also gather photos, videos and other relevant information to make their jobs easier. By packaging the news for them, we create value and get the story to come out the way we want it to land.

Finding ways to serve your relationships may also include personal touches that show you support them. I have the mentality that no job is beneath me. When a client was launching a new brand, the team worked around the clock for three weeks straight—literally 24/7. Of course, I did what I needed to in terms of the work they hired me for, but I also went beyond that. When I noticed that some of the key executives hadn't eaten or taken a sip of water in hours, I made sure to order in meals and drinks to support them and keep them fueled for their mission. This may sound like a small thing, but you can't focus, think, or excel if you're running out of energy. Find ways to serve your relationships no matter how big or small.

Give and Expect Nothing in Return

A long-term player approaches every relationship by giving something of value and expecting nothing in return. When there is a gap between what you expect and what actually happens, it can lead to feelings of disillusionment and disappointment. Unspoken or unmet expectations can also strain relationships leading to misunderstandings, conflict, and even breakdown of the relationship.

For example, remember the story from Chapter 4 about Matt Higgins and the four-day business trip I set up for him and his wife in Dubai? Matt wasn't a client of mine. I organized the trip knowing that. I worked hard to create value for him—introducing him to the market and setting up strategic meetings and high-profile press—and I expected nothing in return. I genuinely wanted to help Matt and show him and his wife a part of the world that I love. The trip allowed us a chance to get to know each other really well and establish a relationship, and as a result we both realized we have aligned values and goals that we wanted to build into a business relationship. Today, we are working together across several business initiatives, and we have even gone back to the region several times building off on the opportunities we created together. When you give and expect nothing in return you will be surprised how that can work to your advantage. It takes off the pressure of expectations and obligations and allows relationships and opportunities to grow organically.

Part of my job is to go to high-profile events. I go to these events to meet people, build new relationships and network. I kept running into a very high-profile CEO at nearly every private event I was attending. After seeing me over and over at the same exclusive events, she probably thought, *Hmm, this girl must be somebody if she has access to the places I have access to.* I finally went over and introduced myself. Then I made a point to talk to her every time I saw her at an event and eventually, we exchanged numbers. Not long after that, she was sending me family photos from her vacation and the relationship grew from there. Next, I started to introduce her to my network to bring her value. And I never asked for anything. This made her see my authenticity because most people she meets ask for something. Once she understood this, I noticed she started to introduce me to her network. Today, we have created so many connections for one another—personally and professionally—all while forming a very genuine friendship. That's what being a long-term player is about: authentically putting in the effort without having expectations or knowing what the end result will be.

Have Patience

Long-term players understand that success doesn't happen overnight. They are willing to invest time and effort into achieving their goals. There is no such thing as overnight success, especially for entrepreneurs. You don't see the stress, the sleepless nights, the hidden effort and preparation, the accumulated failures, the bad timing, the good luck and then that breakthrough moment when everyone finally notices you. The ultimate long-term players are Olympic athletes. They train for years and years without knowing if they're going to qualify for the Olympics. And even after all

RULE # 6 BE A LONG-TERM PLAYER

that time and effort, they don't automatically get into the Olympics. They have to make the Olympic trials. The same long-term effort and patience has to go into your business, your relationships, and your goals. It's not about instant gratification. It's understanding the difference between a marathon and a sprint. If you think long term, everything will change for you. Don't sweat the small failures and setbacks; learn from them and exercise patience.

When a client comes to us for a short-term project, we think with a long-term vision in how we approach and how we execute. We think beyond the scope and timing of our agreement even if we won't be working with them because that is what will serve them best. We have patience and faith in our abilities - that if we do a good job they will come back or even possibly extend the relationship. But it always starts with patience. We know gaining understanding of their business gives us an advantage, and this mindset can help you too. Being patient gives you so many advantages: better decision-making, strong relationships, team development, and more time to innovate and explore new ideas.

Make Networking Your Superpower

I love going into an event and making it my mission to walk into a room and walk out with new relationships and a 'rolodex' of fresh contacts. It's so fun for me, and I love meeting new people. I never think of networking as something I need to do; it's something I love to do. It's just as important to me as managing my team, building my business, and executing powerful marketing. Effective and smart relationship building is the cornerstone of being a long-term player. Building a network and nurturing it happens over time. Relationships take time to build and time to maintain. That's why it's the cornerstone of being a long-term player.

But that's only the case if you give up the biggest misconception about the purpose of networking, and that is that your network is there to serve you.

Most people think a network is a group of people you tap into when you need a favor. You may have done that before: tap into your network for a job search or a connection you need for a reservation or tickets to a game. Some people tap into their network for professional reasons that are valid, like business introductions or professional references.

However, the reason why you need to be very good at networking is for you to rely on yourself, you're going to need your own resources to support yourself. And you're going to need to have your own network to be valuable to yourself or your employer. It gives you an incredible advantage; you know the saying, It's not what you know but who you know! Have all the cards in your hand—and by cards I mean resources, relationships, and supporters that you have spent time fostering, delivering for and doing so genuinely and consistently. If I don't own relationships myself and I need others to activate them, I am not relying on myself. So you need to take the time to invest in building your very own network.

Like everything else, the ways of modern networking have evolved; you need to make this one of your superpowers.

Long-term players adopt networking with an always-on mindset and recognize that the opportunity to network is everywhere. I love how networking is no longer about mingling at events, conferences, and conventions, on golf courses, and at holiday parties. Yes, those traditional settings are important but modern networking means you

RULE #6 BE A LONG-TERM PLAYER

have to be even more savvy. Just as our world operates in real time—you have to be good at networking in real time across the various touch points throughout your day. That means on social media, through platforms like WhatsApp and through virtual work environments such as Zoom. At the end of this chapter, I give you practical tips for networking at events and through social media.

Networking is not a zero-sum game. A zero-sum game is when total gains and losses are equal or balanced, meaning one person wins and one person loses. When I was in Sweden at Brilliant Minds, I met Simon Sinek, the best-selling author and inspirational speaker. I've read all his books and follow him on social media. When we ran into each other at this event, I introduced myself. I didn't want anything from him and I didn't have anything to offer him. I just wanted to connect. I told him how something he said on stage really touched me and we talked briefly. Then we shared contact info, and I said he should reach out if he ever needed anything. I gave him enough information about me and what I do so that if there were a need he could contact me later. That's what networking is about: planting that seed for future good things to happen. And those aren't just things for yourself. In this example, maybe one of my clients or someone in my network will want to connect with Simon. Or maybe I'll be able to bring him value in the future. Don't worry about cashing in today, tomorrow, or the next day; just continue to be consistent creating value for the other person. In the beginning, networking is not about you. It may be eventually, but it also may not be. To me, networking is not about keeping score. It's about relationships.

Be a Superconnector

There are people who introduce people to each other and then there are superconnectors. The difference is that a superconnector finds a strategic reason and purpose for bringing two parties together, and it stems from them knowing both parties really well and what they value deeply. Being a superconnector is a skill and a gift, because when you are able to make those linkages and connections you also win; you boost your reputation and your credibility. I personally get so much satisfaction from it. This requires you to be a good listener and study other people's businesses. You also need to value their needs and be generous with your time. Being a superconnector takes time, but once you do it, the results can be rewarding and meaningful. A lot of people don't want to share their contacts or they think, *If I connect them together they're going to cut me out of the value equation.* But if you've created value for them, both of them are going to remember and recognize that. Also, if you're a good person—both in business and in life—they're not going to want to cut you out of the value chain.

I worked with a client who came to me and said, "Can you just give me your contacts' phone numbers and I'll reach out myself?" That's textbook "transaction" thinking, and that's not how I work. I would never do that. I would never compromise my reputation or loyalty. Also, be careful about who you connect without first knowing whether their intentions are good. Who you connect with is a reflection of you. Don't try to "win points" by making an intro; be deliberate and have a reason. The power of your network becomes strong when you make a connection with someone and bring them so much value that they pull you into their network. You enter their inner circle. That's a full circle moment.

RULE # 6 BE A LONG-TERM PLAYER

Networking Playbook: Practical Tips for Networking at Events

Events of all kinds—conferences, conventions and seminars of all sizes—are great ways to meet people. But if you're going to an event, don't just register and show up, especially if you paid for an airline ticket and a hotel room to be there. Never walk in cold and hope to get something out of it. Instead, follow these strategies:

1. **Post that you are going to the event on your social media pages.** This sends a signal to your network that you will be there, and you will quickly find out what mutual relationships may also be there that you want to connect with.

2. **Study the event program and agenda.** Look at the topics and the speakers. Start to highlight which sessions you want to attend and which speakers you want to meet. Also, don't forget to time the distance between sessions if there are multiple locations; the worst thing is to miss something important because you didn't plan accordingly and account for acquaintances stopping to say hello or being clogged by crowds. I always build a schedule and plan of attack and modify on the ground as needed. I learned the hard way—don't wing it! Always plan in advance.

3. **Develop a list of the key people you want to meet among the attendees and the speakers.** Follow them on social media and make sure the week before the event you are following closely what they are up to. You might need this information for your conversation starters.

Having context is very important and allows you to get personal by showing you are intently following them and their careers. Sometimes speakers host meetups on the sidelines of events and you will know that if you follow them closely.

4. **Know your stuff.** I go to great lengths to build relationships by really studying the other person. There are so many ways to educate yourself. Listen to recent podcast interviews they have done. If they wrote a book, buy it and read it. Go through their social media. Most importantly, google them and hit the "News" button to understand any recent headlines about them or their company. You never want to go in unprepared. Give yourself a leg up. And bonus benefit for doing it: you want them to see your commitment.

5. **DM speakers or attendees on social media that you are going to the event.** You will be surprised at how effective this can be. I do this all the time. Especially if we are fellow speakers, I make sure to highlight for them that I am speaking (gives me credibility) and I always suggest we meet *after* their talk so they are not stressed or distracted. Bonus tip: go attend their session so you have context and can refer to it when you meet them.

6. **Try to meet the event organizers.** Find out who is in charge of programming and sponsors. Why? Because if you're an attendee, maybe you want to be a speaker next year and you need to know who to contact to pitch yourself to speak. And the reason you need to know who is in charge

RULE # 6 BE A LONG-TERM PLAYER

of sponsors is that sponsors are the ones with budgets and you might want to get in touch with them for future work.

7. **Hang out in the green room.** If you're a speaker, live in the green room so you can meet fellow speakers. I was at the NBA Tech Summit in Salt Lake City and a friend of mine was speaking, so she invited me into the green room. The green room is where all the magic happens, where speakers wait and socialize before their events; it's where I met Bob Iger of Disney and NBA player Chris Paul.

8. **Have your business card loaded on a QR code.** Manifest that you will be meeting lots of people and exchanging information and make it easy for them to do it. Have a QR code loaded with your contact information. This takes seconds and makes giving your information quick and easy.

9. **Follow up fast.** Once I meet someone and exchange contacts, I follow up right away by asking them to take a selfie and explain that this is to help my memory (putting the burden on me). I then text them our photo and my name so they have it for recall. I am terrible at saving contacts on the spot, so I started this habit to help me. Sometimes you're collecting so many numbers and meeting so many people at an event that it's hard to keep track.

10. **If there is press at the event, volunteer to speak to them.** Events are usually attended by the press and they usually need to speak to attendees. Volunteer to speak to them to get free publicity and deliver your key messages!

And to all my introverted friends and colleagues: rejoice! You can practice these tips too. Design your networking around how you can best succeed—does that mean small gatherings, one-on-one meetings, or virtual connections? When following up after meeting someone, offer options that cater to your levels of social energy, such as a quiet coffee shop, a walk in the park, or an online chat. Introverts shouldn't aim to meet as many people as possible at events but rather focus on making one or two meaningful connections. Here are some another tips for connecting at events:

1. **Arm yourself.** Prepare a few conversation starters that you can use. Thinking ahead will help alleviate any anxiety you might feel. This can be as simple as planning how you'll introduce yourself or having a few stories ready to share. Prepare some icebreakers such as "what brought you to this event?" or "what do you enjoy most about your work?" or "what projects are you excited about working on next?"

2. **Go with a friend.** Having a familiar face and someone to sit with can make everything easier. If you decide to mingle and talk to others, you'll have someone to come back to and regroup with before venturing out to make another connection or meet new people. Having a buddy can also be comforting during lunch or networking breaks.

3. **Choose the right environment.** Look for smaller, focused groups or clubs related to your interests. These settings are often less intimidating and can provide a more

RULE # 6 BE A LONG-TERM PLAYER

> **Networking is not a zero-sum game.**

comfortable environment for networking. Consider participating in workshops or classes related to your field, as they can offer networking opportunities in a structured environment that suits you better.

4. **Focus on listening.** People appreciate good listeners. Ask open-ended questions and show genuine interest in others. This takes the pressure off you to do all the talking and can lead to more meaningful connections.

Networking Playbook: Practical Tips for Networking on Social Media

It's hard enough knowing how to network in real life and now we have to master it on social media. I know I am not alone in being bombarded by messages on LinkedIn with DMs of people selling me services or asking for jobs. There must be a better way, right? There is. How you use social media for networking must be thoughtful.

1. **Master DMs.** Use direct messaging but be smart about it. You shouldn't hold a detailed networking conversation through DMs. Instead, use DMs as a hook and take the conversation offline. Tell them what you want and ask how to connect with them off social media. For example, Nate Burleson is an anchor for *CBS Mornings* and *CBS Sports*. We first met in 2023 at the Super Bowl in Arizona. I saw a post he did about the 2024 Super Bowl in Las Vegas and I simply wrote over DM, "I

RULE # 6 BE A LONG-TERM PLAYER

want to catch up next week about the Super Bowl. I will reach out to get time, have a great weekend." I kept it short. And he replied "Okay, let's talk next week." So now he knows I will get in touch and I told him the reason. Another simple approach is to DM someone, "I want to touch base with you offline. Is there a best way to connect with you over e-mail?" Then offer your contact info first before asking for theirs. This way if they want to contact you first, you're giving them the opportunity to do so while being respectful and mindful.

2. **Engage consistently.** If the person you want to reach has a social media account, follow them and pay attention to what they are excited about. Comment, like, and share their posts on your social media. Over time, they'll see you consistently engaging with their posts. Nine times out of 10 if you show up and are sincere about it, they will respond and appreciate your commitment. Don't be afraid to tell them you're a fan of their work. Speak up and stand out.

3. **Understand that companies recruit through DM.** Did you know that manycompanies recruit using DM? This is especially true on X (formerly known as Twitter). Keep an eye on your inbox and, more importantly, be mindful about what you post because recruiters and companies study your social media just as much as they study your résumé and credentials.

4. **Maintain relationships.** You can use social media to maintain relationships with low-lift

effort. Maintaining connections is easy if you're active online and helps you stay in touch if you switch jobs or move. One way to reconnect is to reach out via LinkedIn or other social media and congratulate the person on a new job.

5. **Share valuable content.** My social media pages are a true reflection of things I value: my job, my family, my dog, communications, tennis, and all my travels. For years, I consistently built my brand and I feel that my followers have a good idea of who I am and what I value. One day, I posted that I was looking to hire an account executive and I shared a link for people to apply. I got an application from a woman who had seen a post about the job on my Instagram account. When I interviewed her, she said she'd been following me for seven years so she knew all about my brand, clients, and projects. In other words, she invested seven years in a relationship with me before I even met her. I hired her and not only is she a rock star and doing great, she is my deputy at my company and also head of client relations. This is why it's important to share valuable content and stay consistent with how you present yourself. Any post can spark an opportunity.

RULE # 6 BE A LONG-TERM PLAYER

How I Learned about Networking

I first learned about networking when I was just 14 years old, although I didn't know it was called networking at the time. My dad was a professor at Minnesota State University, Mankato. As he rose through the ranks, he became dean of the business school, so he did less teaching and grading papers and more administrative work like creating academic programs, faculty development, and research. He was also responsible for representing the college at official functions like fundraisers, graduations, and student events. By this point, my mom was confined to a wheelchair because she suffered from MS and was self-conscious about it. She didn't want to go out and have people look at her, but she also didn't want my dad to walk into these work functions alone. So, although I was just a teenager, she asked me to accompany him in her place. At those first few events, I was in awe as I watched my dad work the room. With his big bold laugh and firm handshake, he interacted so effortlessly with everyone. You could see the genuine interest he had in each conversation, the way he put people at ease and how much he loved connecting two people who didn't know each other.

But I wasn't there just to watch my father. He used these events to teach me skills and build my character. He wanted me to feel comfortable handling any situation and talking to anyone. This is why he would leave me once we arrived. It was daunting to be a teenager wearing uncomfortable tights and dress-up clothes, forced to mingle in a massive room with a bunch of adults. Initially, I thought I needed something to do as a safety net, so I spent a lot of time getting 7-Up at the bar or hitting the buffet. But after too many mini hot dogs and boredom, I summoned the courage to wander the room and approach some of these adult strangers. It was hard to find enough substance to carry a conversation, but the more I did it the easier it got. And the easier it got, the more confident I became. I learned how to work a room, mingle, and make conversation that went beyond small talk. I figured out how to bring value to any interaction. These moments were my training ground and, over time, I was unafraid to approach people, even those who seemed out of my league.

This foundation really helped when I began my professional life after college, and especially when I moved to the Middle East in my 20s. My family didn't have social or business connections there, so I had to build a name and network for myself from scratch. Walking into a room full of strangers was never intimidating for me again. In time, I developed my own approach to networking and it's become the secret to my success. After being thrown into the deep end of the swimming pool at such a young age and honing the skills I learned, networking became my superpower. You can make it yours as well.

***

Being a long-term player is about relationships. This is so important to me that my company's employee handbook says, "Having the best relationships is how we win. Period." It doesn't have to be a lot of work. In fact, it's really fun.

RULE #6
BE A LONG-TERM PLAYER

This is how you cement and create real, enduring connections—personally and professionally—and have emotional intelligence in life.

> **Cheat Sheet**

- **Build genuine relationships:** Focus on creating genuine relationships based on listening, reciprocity and shared interests and goals.
- **Build connections:** Initiate connections that lay the foundation for conversations and common interests to grow. Be a connector openly and often.
- **Help your network:** Always offer before you ask and give with generosity. If you don't have the knowledge, offer a contact who does. Relationships are a two-way street.
- **Express gratitude:** If you have an ask, be specific and always say thank you (follow up).
- **Stay in touch:** Communication can help strengthen relationships.

RULE # 6 BE A LONG-TERM PLAYER

How to Be a Long-Term Player

1. Don't lead by asking; lead by giving first and doing first.
2. Seek to know what others value and focus on delivering on that.
3. Create value behind the scenes.
4. Be patient and understand that success doesn't happen overnight. Be willing to invest time and effort into achieving your goals.
5. Do not seek instant gratification, and understand the difference between marathons and sprints.
6. Understand that performance is the key to independence.

Reflection Exercises

1. Identify a time when you witnessed something good happen when you waited to see how things played out.

2. Think about a project or person you want to work with. What value do you think you can bring to them if you had time to plan and execute it?

3. Recall a time when you weren't patient. What would you have done differently to change the outcome?

4. What areas of your life do you think you can level up because you feel that would help advance you in a key area of your life that would lead to greater happiness?

5. Think about your network. When was the last time you served them? Can you list three examples?

6. What is one networking tip from this chapter that you will start implementing today?

> The goal for you is to take your struggles and turn them into strengths.

RULE # 7
LIVE WITH NO REGRETS

*I don't have regrets. I don't live in the past.
I live in the present and learn not to make
the same mistakes in the future.*

— SERENA WILLIAMS

I have a tattoo on my back right shoulder that says "no regrets" in Arabic. I feel so strongly about it as a principle for my life that it's permanently etched into my skin.

It's easy to say "live with no regrets," but it's very hard to do. I am the first to admit that. We all have regrets for decisions we made and decisions we didn't make. To me, regret means that you are dwelling on the past and hanging on to negative feelings and energy associated with it. Regret takes up a lot of bandwidth that can lead to unhappiness and weigh you down, which keeps you from moving forward. No regrets for me means one thing: I don't feel sorry for myself. Instead, I accept what has happened, reflect on it, find the lesson, and file it under "valuable experience." It's what made me who I am today.

This doesn't mean I belittle elements of my life; in fact, it's the opposite. I give them meaning by letting them go. Reminding myself of all the wonderful things I have to be grateful for overpowers the regret of what never was.

Rather than look at your circumstances and ask, "Why me?," think of them as your superpower so that you can stay low and keep moving forward no matter what challenges you face or what odds are against you. Learn from failure. So many of the world's most successful people had journeys that challenged them; it's called "character building" for a reason. The beauty of humanity is that it's rich and diverse, so we shouldn't compare ourselves to others or feel sorry for ourselves.

Bad things happen to everyone; you are not in a class of your own. No one said life is going to be bubblegum and roses every day. People are going to get sick. People are going to die. You're going to get fired. You're going to get depressed. You're going to gain weight. You're going to lose friends. Someone will screw you over. You are going to make mistakes. You are going to disappoint someone. That's life, so you can't regret it. It's actually what helps you learn and grow.

I could have regretted so much of what has happened to me, but I didn't. Instead, I looked inward to use these situations to propel me forward. Setbacks disappointed me, but they didn't stall or derail me. One time, I got fired from a job I absolutely loved because I asked for a raise. When the HR person offered a salary that I thought was not fair, I said something under my breath that she heard so she fired me. I mean it was my fault; my reaction was terrible and once I put my foot in my mouth there was no going back. I thought my life was over. I couldn't breathe; it was like a gut punch and it was also massively embarrassing. But I

RULE #7 LIVE WITH NO REGRETS

don't have any regrets because I learned how to approach a conversation about my salary. And I learned very quickly how horrible that made me feel and I never wanted to feel that way again. After leaving that dream job, I got the biggest gift ever. Months later, the former boss of the company that fired me offered to start a company with me and put me in charge of it. The role was better than the one I got fired from!

When I left Google, I went back to my own communications company, and while I said I would never join another company full time, I was approached to apply for a really big role at Facebook. It was larger than the remit I had at Google; it included the Middle East, Turkey, and *all* of Africa. But when I went through the interview process, I came up short on all the questions related to the African market. I was devastated. How could I be so stupid that I didn't anticipate those questions? I called my sister in tears.

"Everything's over. I'll never work in tech again," I told her.

"Clearly you didn't prepare enough," she said.

She was right. I didn't do my homework. This taught me that every time you go to an interview—and business meetings too—you have to prepare. You've got to study. I couldn't just rely on my track record at Google. In business, you need to anticipate what the other side needs (sounds like value creation, right?). From that day forward, I was going to rely on myself to be prepared. And because I relied on myself to learn from my failures and tough times, I don't regret any of them. P.S.: Not getting that job at Facebook turned out to be great for me. Within weeks, I got a call to consult for the prime minister of the UAE and the ruler of Dubai in his executive office, which paved the way for so many business opportunities and relationships that I am still building on many years later.

If you rely on yourself and lean in to your strengths, you can and will achieve anything.

You can get through difficult moments. And you can do hard things. In contrast, if you live with regret, you are not focusing on the future and moving forward. What might seem like a big career setback could end up being a major blessing in disguise that is setting you up for something bigger and better.

I'm sure some people would look at one of the saddest situations for me with regret, but as I've mentioned, that word never crossed my mind. When I was 14-years old, my life changed forever. My mom started limping, losing her balance, and slurring her speech. After countless appointments—specialists, labs, second opinions—she was diagnosed with Multiple Sclerosis, a debilitating neurological disease where your brain stops sending messages to your muscles to move and you lose control over your body, your cognitive abilities, and your ability to function independently.

This was a turning point, the start of a journey that shaped who I became.

My older sister, Amany, had graduated high school and was about to go away to college. While a new chapter of her life was starting, I was dealt completely different cards. Pretty soon after her diagnosis, my mother couldn't walk without help and her hands trembled so much she couldn't use them. She was 44 years old and needed to be fed. Her favorite ritual—sitting with a piping hot cup of tea in her hands—turned into sipping tea at room temperature through a straw.

RULE #7 LIVE WITH NO REGRETS

As she continued to deteriorate, I became her nurse, hair stylist, personal chef, and entertainer. On school days, I got up at 6 A.M. so that I could get my mom out of bed, brush her hair and teeth, take her to the bathroom, feed her breakfast, give her all her meds, and set her up for the hours I was at school. This included leaving her something to eat on the edge of the coffee table and setting the TV to her favorite channel. I'd drive her to physical therapy three times a week in Minnesota's unforgiving winters; heating the car before bringing her out of the house; dressing her in a winter coat, boots, a hat, and a scarf; and carrying her down the stairs into the garage. Then I'd load the wheelchair into the trunk.

At an age when I needed parenting, I was the responsible one. Rather than going to high school parties and football games on weekends that I wanted to be a part of, I kept close to home either to take care of my mom's needs or to keep my dad company. I could tell that my mom's condition and the fact that he was losing his partner was taking a toll on my dad. So I would spend a lot of time talking to him about his day and making sure I was always home to have meals with him. I never resented it. It was my duty and I wanted to be there for both of my parents. Family first. Some might ask why we didn't have a full-time nurse or in-home nursing care; it never occurred to us to hire help. It wasn't readily available and our culture was to care of your own as long as you could.

I had been caring for my mom for 13 years. As I mentioned in Chapter 1, my dad, mom, and I moved to the Middle East when I was 27 because my dad got a job in the UAE. Five years after that move, my dad was diagnosed with ALS (Lou Gehrig's disease), which is terminal. So now both of my parents were gravely ill and I was their sole caretaker. They were in and out of hospitals and unable to eat or take themselves to the bathroom. Not only was this emotionally exhausting, but it was also financially draining. I also felt so alone at times; I was juggling it all on my own because we were in Egypt and my sister was back in Minnesota with her own family to attend to. Yes, my parents had relatives and friends who were good about coming over after work. But stopping by for a cup of tea and chitchat wasn't the same as cleaning their feeding tubes, doing their enemas, or moving their atrophied bodies every two hours because they had bedsores. Almost a year to the day that he was diagnosed, my dad called me into his bedroom.

"Go get your sister," he said. Amany was visiting with her husband and two young kids from Minnesota.

"I'm going to die today. I just feel it," he told both of us. "If I go into a coma, I don't want you to resuscitate me. I don't want my grandchildren to see me like this anymore. This isn't a way to live. I'm not who I am. Just let me go."

"No, Dad," I cried.

"Open my closet," my dad said, ignoring my protests. "I want to tell you what to do with a few things."

"Dad, we're not talking about this now. You're going to be fine."

"It's getting late," he said. "You should go to bed."

But I couldn't sleep. Two hours later, my dad went into a coma.

Eventually we got him to a hospital, where he was intubated. Despite my father's words earlier that evening, I wasn't willing to let him go. Something inside me said this wasn't his time.

I sat in a blue vinyl chair by his bed all night. The next morning, he woke up and looked at me.

RULE # 7 LIVE WITH NO REGRETS

"I wasn't going to give up on you," I said. Even with a tube down his throat, he managed to crack a smile at me, a nod to my stubbornness I guess.

Before that night he had been angry about being sick; but after he was resuscitated, he was so grateful. He wound up living another year and that was the best year of his life.

I took him on a farewell tour to the United States, where the university had a big reception for him, and there was a going away party in our hometown in Mankato. Back in Cairo, every Friday night, I had different friends come over and watch football games with him. He had the opportunity to go through all of his personal belongings and decide who he wanted to give each item to. It was an incredibly touching and personal experience that I will always remember. He had a reason and a story behind everything as he instructed us. For example, he would say, "Give this to my sister, she would love this," or "Please give this to my college mate, he will get a good laugh when you send it." He was so grateful to have the time to do it himself, and he did it with tremendous love and affection. He even instructed us on how to organize his library of music. When we went through his closet, he shared stories and anecdotes about everything. He would tell us the story behind a tie he bought for a special occasion or the last time he wore a particular Hawaiian shirt. It was a priceless experience.

My main objective was to make both my parents comfortable, but this wasn't just about the big things. In fact, it's the little things that are the big things.

I had a duty to take care of them. And I did it to the nth degree; I was not going to sacrifice anything. Taking care of my parents in the way that I did never felt like a choice. It felt like my duty, one that I was determined to do really well. Yes, I was responsible for them and their medical decisions.

But the way I saw it, I was also responsible for making the house fun by playing their favorite music, having our dog Maggie sit with them, and making sure my dad always had one of his two favorite blankets on the bed: either the University of Michigan or University of Illinois. I was trying to make what they were going through positive and give them as much as I could of the life they had before.

For example, during the holy month of Ramadan, one tradition is to break your fast with an apricot drink called *qamar el-din*. My dad couldn't swallow, so I took the apricot juice and poured it into an ice-cube tray. I was going to make sure he could taste Ramadan, just differently. I placed the apricot ice cube in his mouth and he sucked on it slowly with a big smile. He was gleefully able to experience the flavor of Ramadan and feel a part of the annual tradition.

It's the small things that are the big things and those are the things you can't regret.

When my dad died in the hospital almost a year to the day after he'd called me into his bedroom, I could accept it. Why? Because I'd had an extra year with him, and he had an extra inning of life.

The day that he died I felt assured. It was the right time.

Still, my dad's death hit me really, really, really hard. Because my mom was sick for so long and she couldn't speak or express herself, I was really close with my dad. Unlike my mom, who was incapacitated—which was devastating—my dad was mentally with it until the end.

With ALS, your brain is 100 percent functional, so even when my dad couldn't talk, we had little boards with letters that he'd point to. On the other hand, my mom would go months without speaking a word. She could raise her eyebrows and react to things around her but it took a lot of work to get her to talk. And if she did it was one word—the same word every time: *Maha*. The *only* person who could

RULE # 7 LIVE WITH NO REGRETS

truly get a reaction out of her was me. On a good day, I would sing her one of her two favorite songs, "Ala Kad El Shoq" or "Asmar Ya Asmarany" by Abdel Halim Hafez, and she would light up like a Christmas tree and get a twinkle in her eye. I would keep singing the verse and pause so she could sing along. Sometimes my persistence paid off and she would say a verse. I spent hours pampering her with things like painting her nails and doing her hair. I would say, "Hello my name is Maha and I will be your stylist for today. Today's special is a fancy braid." I would do anything to bring fun into her life.

The night we got back from my dad's funeral, I was journaling when I paused and said out loud, "Dad, if you're with me, I need a sign. I just want to know that you're still taking care of me."

It sounds crazy, but a moment later, the lights flickered on and off. He was trying to tell me that he was okay. He may have been. But I wasn't.

The next day, I went outside. One guy was sweeping the street and another was buying oranges from the corner market stand. It was confusing to see all these moments of normalcy when everything in my world was in slow motion. How was life going on as usual? My world was shattered.

Fifteen months after my dad died, my mother passed away. With both of my parents gone and all the nurses, visitors, and other staff out of the house, I was alone.

I was used to having people around me 24/7, even when I got up in the middle of the night to go to the bathroom. After my parents died, the silence was deafening; and the loneliness was a sensation I'd never imagined.

Shortly after we buried my mother, I was getting dressed for work when I caught my reflection in the mirror. *What am I doing?* I thought. *What is my life now?* At 37 years old, my whole identity was as the caretaker, the responsible one, the hero of the family. I was constantly praised for being such a good daughter. But now, for the first time in my life, I was free to do anything I wanted and yet I was frozen. My life was a blank canvas. I could travel. I could sleep in. I had no one to worry about and no responsibilities. But who was I without those responsibilities? Who was I if I wasn't a caregiver?

I thought about going back to the States, but I wasn't ready for any more change. I couldn't even think about selling the house, moving and finding a new job. So for a very dark 18-month period, I stood still. Rather than doing anything new or drastic, I worked harder than ever at my job, desperately needing to cling to something familiar every day. I was afraid that I was too fragile to do anything outside of that.

Looking back, I see that it made me self-reliant. Yet it is also because of this duty and family first that I became a value creator. This became an underlying theme in my life that started at home but then became part of my work and every aspect of my life. My upbringing and relationship with my parents were the seeds of bringing value to others in meaningful ways, big and small. This made a huge impact for them and for me.

As you can see, I didn't just cakewalk into the life and business that I have today. I had to deal with a lot of real-life adversity—things that you're probably dealing with too. But the truth is this: if you rely on yourself and lean in to your strengths, you can and will achieve anything. During more than two decades of caring for my ill parents, I could have felt sorry for myself and mourned all that I missed out on. However, those thoughts didn't cross my mind; that's not how I viewed things. The hand I was dealt has given me a truly unique edge that has no doubt contributed to my success. It's not something I wanted or wished for, but I wouldn't have it any other way.

RULE #7 LIVE WITH NO REGRETS

I learned that when caring for someone, it's important to approach each day as a new opportunity to find a way to succeed, while also balancing your needs with theirs. It's akin to the announcement they make on airplanes: "Put your oxygen mask on before assisting others." You must rely on yourself to make the best choices and decisions each day. Be patient and avoid overwhelming yourself; give yourself the grace to do what you can with what you have at that moment. Hasty actions lead to poor decisions, so trust yourself to do the right thing, one step at a time. Above all, live with no regrets. Don't second-guess or overthink things. Accept that this is your story, and the lessons and reflections will come in due time.

The goal for you is to take your struggles and turn them into strengths. Not only is this healing, but it can propel you to do great things.

Living with No Regrets in 7 Principles

This book is based on seven rules of self-reliance, and I want to end with another list of 7; this time they are principles for living with no regrets.

1. Accept this is your journey. The ultimate way to rely on yourself is not to judge yourself for the negative things that happen to you or your business. I want you to find a way to accept them, embrace them, and when you can, celebrate them. When my parents got sick, a lot of people told me to put them in a nursing home. But that never crossed my mind and at the time I didn't even feel any stress or anxiety about what we were going through. I just thought, *This is our journey. We need to deal with it. Just stay low and keep moving.*

2. Learn how to deal with adversity. Life is messy. You have heard that before, right? Everyone faces challenges and adversity. EVERYONE! So learn how to deal with it and—like a muscle—train yourself. You learn how to deal with it by having self-awareness of how you operate under stress, pressure, or disappointment. Do you need to go for a walk, or take some deep breaths? Or do you need to get help from experts to solve a work problem? In business, we can regret a lot of things, like missing opportunities, spending money on the wrong thing or having a marketing campaign go wrong. Learn how to deal with it and prepare yourself for scenarios that might come your way. I've faced numerous setbacks, but you know what I do? I repeat to myself, "Everything is going to be okay," and I take deep breaths. Because everything will be okay. Push through the challenges and stay focused—there will be a surplus waiting for you on the other side. I promise.

3. Stop dwelling. We are only on this Earth for a limited time. Don't spend energy and time dwelling on the past or overthinking something that has happened to you that you cannot control or change. In one year or five years from now, will this be important to you? Usually it's bigger in our minds and hearts than reality. When you rely on yourself, you don't have the bandwidth to carry unnecessary baggage everywhere you go, so open your time, energy, and heart to things that truly matter and make you happy.

4. Be intentional. Make choices and take actions that align with your values and goals so that you can look back on your life with a sense of satisfaction and fulfillment rather than regret. This is true in business and your personal life. Once you know what your intentions are, set your goals and priorities to align with them. They might change with time, but if you aim to stick to your intentions, you truly have the best opportunity to live them. People say put your intentions into the universe, manifest your dreams by defining them. These ideas work and keep you aligned to

RULE # 7 LIVE WITH NO REGRETS

your purpose and meaning so you can make decisions that reflect your priorities and things you care about. It's easy to live with no regrets when you know what your values are and you work hard to stick to them *intentionally*.

5. Learn from failure. You will make mistakes and experience failure—something that is almost always part of being a human, let alone an entrepreneur. You may make a bad hire, spend money on something that isn't worthwhile or get treated badly by a client. What is important is that you learn from it. I got fired from a job, and I never made the same mistake twice. Failure hurts. It's embarrassing. Failure sets us back emotionally and mentally. But failure is the greatest lesson. From failure comes creativity, resilience, innovation, character, compassion, and perspective. I could write a whole chapter on how it can help you live a life of no regret. This is not to discount the meaning of failure, but I want you to look at it differently. Pause and ask yourself what you can learn from your failures. I have a sign next to my bed that I see every day when I get up; it says, "Don't be afraid to fail, be afraid not to try," said by the GOAT himself, NBA great Michael Jordan.

6. Turn your struggles into strengths. Use life's lessons to build yourself and reflect upon them: don't bury them or ignore them. I turned my struggles into my strengths. I had all the odds against me and I found that my superpower was being a value creator at a time when nobody was creating value for me.

7. Take accountability. Rely on yourself for your successes and failures. Instead of blaming others by pointing fingers, take ownership and accountability for yourself and your life. You are the driver.. We can't blame anyone for the decisions we make or the way we show up in the world. Living with no regrets means you step up and take accountability for your actions.

When a Failure Isn't a Failure

Alexis Ohanian is a tech entrepreneur and investor who successfully co-founded and invested in many companies, including Reddit, Daily Harvest, and Instacart, to name just a few. But these companies might not be here if Ohanian hadn't failed first.

In 2005, Ohanian and a co-founder presented one of the most esteemed tech start-up accelerators, Y Combinator, with an idea for an app to order food. Y Combinator rejected the app on the spot. In fact, they told Ohanian and his partner that they hated their idea. (This was several years before smartphones hit the market, so yes, he was ahead of his time.) He and his co-founder were devastated. Dejected, they went back to the drawing board trying to think of another business proposal. Eventually, they came up with the idea for Reddit, a social news website and forum, and presented it to Y Combinator again. They loved it and today Reddit has 850 million monthly active users and was sold to Condé Nast for $210 million (this was in 2006). What Ohanian called a giant fail setback, he now calls the thing that changed his life.

RULE # 7 LIVE WITH NO REGRETS

> Don't be afraid to fail, be afraid not to try.
>
> — Michael Jordan

RULE #7
LIVE WITH NO REGRETS

You understand that the most fulfilling life is one where you truly live with no regret.

RULE # 7 LIVE WITH NO REGRETS

Cheat Sheet

- **Be intentional:** Make choices and take actions that align with your values and goals so that you can look back on your life with a sense of satisfaction and fulfillment rather than regret.
- **Align to your purpose and meaning:** Make decisions that reflect your priorities and things you care about.
- **Learn from failure:** You will make mistakes and experience failure. What is important is that you learn from it.
- **Turn your struggles into strengths:** Use life's lessons to build yourself and reflect upon them; don't bury them or ignore them.
- **Take accountability:** Rely on yourself for your successes and failures. Instead of pointing fingers, point thumbs and take ownership and accountability for yourself.

Reflection Exercises

1. Time to dig deep. What do you regret and why?

2. What were some struggles you faced and thought everything was over? Now explain how you turned these struggles into strengths.

3. Share a lesson about failure you learned. What is the backstory?

4. What are you grateful for?

5. How much time a day or a week do you spend journaling or reflecting?

6. Share a story of a time when you taught a valuable lesson to someone else.

FINAL WORD

An entrepreneur is someone who jumps off a cliff and builds a plane on the way down.

— REID HOFFMAN

In a world of constant change, be forward thinking and forward looking. In this final chapter, I want to leave you with what I believe are the five most important principles that will shape you profoundly. And why, you need to invest in these core areas.

Artificial Intelligence and Generative AI

You didn't think I would get through a whole book and not talk about AI, did you?

The impact of AI on business and employees is profound and will accelerate the growth and development of both. Get ahead by learning to embrace a culture of experimentation. Experiment with AI because you can't benefit from its features or functionality until you understand it. Find out what it can do for you personally, what it can do for your business and how it can drive efficiency and improve profitability by reducing costs.

The biggest challenge that AI has right now is what people value the most: *trust*.

Paul Leonardi, a professor at University of California, Santa Barbara said that if there were one universal law of technology that existed, it would be this: people use digital tools in ways you can't fully anticipate or control. He is right: it's the lack of control and uncertainty where this AI thing is going that makes us nervous.

I want to put this into context for you. It took Facebook four and a half years to reach 100 million users and it took Instagram two and a half years to reach 100 million users. It took ChatGPT, one of the most popular LLMs (large language models) on the market today, only *two months* to reach 100 million users. Wow.

Leonardi said that the faster a technology spreads, the less time users have to learn it from one another and mimic patterns of use.

The fact that the technology continues to be "generative" means that the experience you have today is a completely different one than you had last week. The term *generative* refers to "AI's ability to generate new content, data, or information that is not directly copied or replicated from existing examples." Generative AI models are designed to create original and contextually relevant content, such as text, images, audio, and even video, based on patterns and knowledge learned from large datasets and user inputs and content. AI tools are enabled to continuously change by themselves, and each time you provide new information or data, the technology and its capabilities grow. The time to learn about AI is now, before you're left behind.

Be Mission and Purpose Driven

Business leaders are facing increasingly blurry lines when it comes to how to navigate social and geopolitical issues in the workplace and the marketplace. This is exacerbated by social media, where there is a call from consumers and employees to know "where you stand" to prove your moral and ethical values. But where are the boundaries and how should you weigh in? In the United States, we see what happens when companies are caught in vulnerable positions related to social issues. When the war

FINAL WORD

broke out between Hamas and Israel, companies felt pressured to e-mail their employees and take a public stance on social media.

Today, companies need to be equipped with how to be effective communicators. Their responsibilities go beyond having to know how to communicate their brand ideas or marketing campaigns. They also need to be masterminds of complex cultural minefields, geopolitical issues, and crisis management.

The first hurdle they need to overcome is how to win over their own employees before consumers. It's the employees who are revolting and the ramifications on relationships and trust have far-reaching implications for a company's reputation and bottom line. This is why it's so critical to have a very strong mission and purpose that guides you and your team. Rely on your values when your back is up against the wall to propel you forward, and then repeat these values in good times and in bad.

People care about supporting businesses that have a mission and a strong purpose. Consumers make purchasing decisions with more than their wallets; they are using their conscience to drive their actions. Employees don't want to work for businesses that care about profit over people, are doing harm to the environment, or have unethical practices and policies. We see this behavior unfold decade to decade, generation to generation.

Fasten your seatbelt because here comes Generation Alpha. Gen Alpha is people born around 2010, and they are set to become the largest generation ever, with more than 2 billion members by 2025. This generation has created a new consumer segment focused on both millennial parents and their Gen Alpha children. Gen Alpha is socially aware and cares deeply about global issues such as climate change, poverty, and mental health. Gen Alpha cares about strong mental health, a career they love, financial stability, comfort to be themselves, and emotional confidence. They are the most racially diverse generation, thanks to their millennial parents.

Gen Alpha's future careers will include jobs that don't exist yet, making education and technology crucial. They value financial literacy and prioritize brands that align with their values. They are all about being accountable, mission focused, and purpose driven and are loud and proud about it. Brands and businesses should focus on appealing to the combined cohort of millennial parents and Gen Alpha, as this group will have the greatest spending power in history. They are dubbed "honey badgers" because they are brave and defy authority. And because they are growing up in the "great screen age" they are getting more schooled and will progress faster because growing up with AR (augmented reality) and AI will shape how they learn, work, socialize and shop.

Is your business ready for Generation Alpha? Cement your purpose and mission; that's a great place to start.

Recreation, Wellness, Well-Being, and Play

Never have we had to spend more time and effort to relax. To do nothing takes work. A product of an always-on world, today entrepreneurs, employees and even consumers are exhausted. Thanks to the virtual, hybrid, back-to-the-office whiplash there is growing tension between the workforce and the workplace, which is having a massive impact on the bottom line. This is why recreation, wellness, well-being, and play have become so important today and will be even more important in the future. Workplace stress, screen fatigue, and political disruption are all weighing on us.

Recreation matters; taking time to play is not only good for your body but your mental health too. Taking breaks at work, prioritizing sports, and fitness, and even traveling and exploration are proven by scientists to be the key to longevity and business success. They also lead to greater job satisfaction, improved productivity, and overall happiness. When you trust your employees by giving them freedom and flexibility to complete their tasks, it empowers them and leads to employee retention. At my company, I am relentlessly focused on results and outcomes, not how many hours my team members spend at their desks. I couldn't honestly tell you what time they start or end their days; I don't micromanage with "office hours." Instead, I focus on what we spend our time doing with each other and for our clients.

The role of the office has been completely redefined as a place for collaboration and nuances. If you're going to make your team members come to the office, then have a purpose to make it effective. So many experts have written about how work is not someplace you go, it's something you do. How hybrid teams function are being studied, and gone are the days of "management by wandering around," a term coined by management expert Tom Peters. More than 40 percent of the workforce in the United States is hybrid. Today, managers need to be agile and optimize for the productivity of their staff and their lives. They must understand how important having a flexible work environment is for their performance and well-being. Stanford economics professor Nicholas Bloom published a study that said workers put a high value on having a flexible workplace and that working remotely is equivalent to an 8 percent pay raise to them! That's incredible.

People want to have more time to do things they enjoy and reduce their stress. This is why they love saving time by doing meal prep and saving money by embracing the DIY movement. From gardening to home improvement to bread-making, DIY is a bursting phenomenon. Did you know the do-it-yourself market is expected to reach $1.287 billion by 2028? That's self-reliance in action by the numbers. The reason? It was definitely sparked by the pandemic, when everyone had to rely on themselves for services they may have outsourced, but it's also fueled by the desire for self-satisfaction, environmental awareness, wanting to belong to a community and boosting one's own skill development. It also gives your brain a boost: doing skills with hand-eye coordination can actually grow your brain.

So schedule some fun, plan recreational activities and prioritize your wellness and well-being. Not only will you be healthier, but your business will be too.

Though I want to be completely honest, you can't have it all.

It's a fact of life that we must make trade-offs, sacrificing one thing to reap the benefits of another. For example, if you want to launch a new product, you may have to forgo extra expenses like a team off-site so that money can go to your marketing campaigns. If you want to be at your daughter's spring concert, you may have to sacrifice the opportunity to present at an important business meeting and be okay with someone managing it differently than you would have. Trade-offs are part of life as an entrepreneur.

You'll find yourself weighing decisions and balancing options because you're not going to be able to do everything. Sometimes both choices are difficult to make. The classic dilemma entrepreneurs face is the trade-off between growth and profitability. Pursuing growth requires you to invest and potentially run at a loss in the short term to acquire customers or expand product lines. Should you sacrifice profitability and is the company financially stable enough to do that? Some entrepreneurs prioritize profit margins over growth because trying to do both can be a challenge, especially if there are limited resources within the company.

FINAL WORD

> Never underestimate the power of a compelling narrative.

Entrepreneurs need to make tough decisions on where to spend resources, deploying the right pricing strategies and determining the threshold for risk they can absorb.

Hello, Frictionless World

We live in a real-time world. We want our information in real time. We can share a thought and broadcast it to the world in real time, and we can connect with anyone anywhere in the world in real time. And sometimes this means we want technology or people to get out of the way because we want frictionless experiences. A frictionless experience is where any obstacle or inconvenience is removed to make an experience easier and faster.

When you go over to your friend's house and want to "share password" with a click of a button instead of having to re-enter it, that's a frictionless experience. A one-click shopping experience perfected by Amazon is a frictionless experience. Those self service kiosks at the airport where you can print your boarding pass, luggage tag and be on your way—yep, a frictionless experience.

Entrepreneurs need to think about how to cater to consumers' growing desire for frictionless experiences. Shoppable trends are one to pay attention to. Coresight Research estimates the livestream shopping market at $512 billion. The trend involves a seller broadcasting live video of themselves showing and explaining products while viewers ask questions and make purchases in real time. Facebook and Instagram allow you to buy products directly from Amazon using their platforms—during live streams and from feeds, stories, or posts—instead of having to leave the app to log into Amazon. That's frictionless and real time at work!

Meet PingPod, a pay-and-play venue where you go to play Ping-Pong (table tennis) anytime you want. You book a table

FINAL WORD

> Storytelling is the essential human activity. The harder the situation, the more essential it is.
>
> — Tim O'Brien

with your app, scan your phone to unlock your pod and start playing. You don't interact with anyone. Nobody is working the front desk, and you don't have to waste time checking in. Because they don't have hourly workers or team members on-site, they offer low prices and the business has incredible margins. They only pay for security services (remote cameras monitoring the pods) and cleaning crews. And we are seeing this concept play out in other verticals. Have you heard of *Picklemall*? Entrepreneurs are converting unused mall space into indoor pickleball courts. Not only can you pay and play using an app, but once you arrive and check in with your app, it also triggers the court cameras to capture your gameplay footage in real time, tracking your performance, and helping to improve your game. Now that's an experience.

Entrepreneurs need to be ready to take advantage of a real-time, frictionless world. And be strategic about which industries need it. Consumers rejected Amazon Go where you walk out of the store without dealing with cashier kiosks because consumers didn't want the Amazon experience in person. Think about that.

> Communication is the single most powerful tool that connects us.

Be Very Good at Storytelling and Crafting Narratives

You will never survive as a brand or business if you are not good at storytelling.

The art of effective communication is hard to execute if you don't understand how consumers behave and communicate. People want connection: they connect with stories and relate to stories. Stories are what move us and create opportunities to engage and act. When was the last time you took an action based on a bad story? Never, right? But think of a time a story moved you or inspired you. If you do one thing after today, take a hard look at how good you are at telling stories and know that it doesn't have to be expensive or tedious to create a compelling narrative.

Narratives are a vital aspect of human communication and culture.

Brands that invest in effective storytelling will win because they understand what makes or breaks a brand. It's important to tell stories authentically and consistently; these are the key foundations for effective communications. In a world saturated with marketing messages, consumers seek brands they can trust and relate to. Convey your idea or "story" in simple terms by making it easy to digest and understand. Think short, emphatic, simple. Craft clear, compelling, and consistent stories. The way you tell your story depends on what your objective is. Are you trying to inspire, educate, inform, dispel, influence, engage, or build support. Customize your approach based on what you are trying to achieve.

Do something that makes you proud of yourself. Look at what problem you solve or what value you're bringing to others by your kindness and your intentions. Ask yourself "what if": What if you did this instead of that? Open your imagination to find a way to do the right thing or do a better thing. Examine your impact on employees, customers, friends, colleagues, partners, and *the planet*. And most of all use these tools to rely on yourself.

Tim O'Brien, who has won acclaim for his books about the Vietnam War, put it this way: "Storytelling is the essential human activity. The harder the situation, the more essential it is." And he is right. The problem is people don't realize how much effort you have to put into repeating your story. Tell it to everyone and share it more than you think you should. Repetition is the key to understanding. Think of how a jingle for an ad works—the more you hear it the more it sinks in! With communications it's harder because you don't have a song or a tagline; instead, you have a narrative. But a narrative is the hardest thing for companies to define for themselves.

A good narrative is a message that is written in plain, clear language that is short and breaks through. Narratives are a vital aspect of human communication and culture. You often hear of people fighting to get their "narrative" out front because a good narrative has the power to influence, persuade, shape identity and express emotions or experiences. It has the power to engage and impact audiences emotionally and intellectually. Being good at crafting or building a strong narrative is essential if you're going to be an effective communicator or storyteller.

Never underestimate the power of a compelling narrative. Your narrative can transform your company, your customers, or your colleagues if you care deeply to touch others with meaning and purpose. For your story to be credible and well received, you have to believe it yourself and live it with conviction. Because at the end of the day, the most important story you tell is the story you tell yourself. Make it a magnificent one.

FINAL WORD

> The most important story you tell is the story you tell yourself.

JOIN MY COMMUNITY!

If you would love to join my community and connect with me, visit **mahaabouelenein.com**.

I also have a Facebook group called **7 Rules**—please join us. There you can get free checklists, additional playbooks, merch, and more.

I offer workshops, coaching, and professional communications services through my company with my awesome team. Please visit digitalandsavvy.com for more information.

You can subscribe to my podcast *Savvy Talk*, which is available on all podcast players, and follow me across social media at:

- LinkedIn: **Maha Abouelenein**
- Instagram: **@mahagaber**
- TikTok: **@maha.gaber**
- X (Twitter): **@mahagaber**
- YouTube: **@digitalandsavvy**

INDEX

A

Abouelenein, Amy, ii, 31, 103, 262, 264, 296
Abouelenein, Gaber, 43, 149
Abouelenein, Maha
  AmCham, role of, 1–2
  Associated Press, role of, 52
  business started by, 121
  career and self-reliance, experience of, xix, 12
  CBS Evening News with Katie Couric, role of, 179-181
  Dubai Future Foundation, role of, 93-94
  early life and career of, 66-71, 105-106, 251-252, 260-261
  Egyptian government, role of, 1, 31. *See also* Egypt
  family of, 30-32, 42-47, 65-67, 147-149, 262-269. *See also individual names of family members*
  General Mills, role of, 29, 32, 90-92
  Google, role of, xvi, 13, 55, 73, 126-127, 154, 178-184, 261
  NBA, role of, 87-88
  Netflix, role of, 55-56, 73
  Orascom Technology Solutions, role of, 32-39, 117
  Promoseven Weber Shandwick, role of, 52-55
  Savvy Talk podcast, 171, 290, 298
  social media handles of, 220, 290
  "sprints" (Obama administration), role of, 98-101
  UAE government, role of, 261
  VeeCon, role of, 196, 200-202
accountability and accountability partners, 131, 143, 218-219, 271
adaptability and agility
  audience, knowing and adapting to, 70-71, 217
  goals, adapting, 17
  as self-reliance characteristic, 20
advance work, 10, 88
adversity, 269
Advision, 121
Alexander, F. M., xi
allyship, 162-163
Amazon, 284, 286
American Chamber of Commerce (AmCham), 1-2, 155
American University of Sharjah, 30
anticipation of needs, 104-107

apologize-pause-rebuild steps, 189
Arab Spring (Egypt), xvi, 181-184
artificial intelligence (AI), 151, 277-278
Associated Press, 52
audience
  knowing and adapting to, 66, 216-217
  writing for, 7
authenticity, 209
awareness, 213

B

Bastian, Ed, 203
Be a Long-Term Player (Rule #6), 229-256. *See also* networking
  for business success, 229-231
  cheat sheet for, 254
  defined, 230, 253, 255
  networking and, 239-252
  reflection exercises, 256
  relationship building and, 134, 217, 235-241
  reputational risk vs. financial reward and, 234
  short-term sacrifice for, 231-232
  valuing people over profit, 232-234
Be a Value Creator. *See* Value Creation (Rule #2)
behavior
  consistency of, 95-96, 209-210
  learning and, 163-164
Bezos, Jeff, 206
Biden, Joe, 100, 122
Big Machine Records, 119
big picture. *See* Stay Low, Keep Moving (Rule #1)
Blinken, Tony, 100
Boston Consulting Group, 167
boundaries, creating, 170
Branson, Richard, 208
Braun, Scooter, 119
Brilliant Minds, 241
Bryant, Kobe, 229
Buffett, Warren, 40
Burj Khalifa (Top of the Burj), 190-191
Burleson, Nate, 248-249
Business and Philanthropy Climate Forum (United Nations), 15

C

cancel culture, 187-190
Careem, 190-191

CBS Evening News with Katie Couric, 179–181
Chanel, Coco, 29
ChatGPT, 153, 278
Chopra, Deepak, i, 93–95, 231
Clarkson, Kelly, 119
Clear with Computers (CWC), 105–106
Climate Change Conference (COP28), 15
Clinton, Hillary, 122
"closing space," 95
communication. *See also* Reputation as Currency (Rule #5)
   internal communication, 191–195
   listening and importance to, 82
   photography and, 89, 200, 245
   skills needed for, 135
   storytelling, 214, 236, 286–288
consistency of behavior, 95–96, 209–210, 249
content, sharing, 250
Couric, Katie, 125, 179–181
COVID pandemic
   NBA and, 160–161
   travel trends and, 203–204
   workplace changes and, 17, 212, 282
creator economy. *See* Don't Be a Waiter (Rule #3)
credentials, showcasing, 214, 218
crisis communication
   apologize-pause-rebuild steps, 189
   examples of, 54, 177–184, 190–191, 198–202
   preparation for, 195–196
   recovery from crisis, 202–205
   response to crises, 198–202
Crush It! (Vaynerchuk), 72–73
culture (workplace), 74–75
curiosity, 130–131, 149–150

D

Dao, David, 198–199
decision-making, as self-reliance characteristic, 21–22
Delta Airlines, 203–204
Democratic National Convention (DNC, 2008), 122–126
De Simone, Alex, 75
direct messaging (DM), 244
disruption, 159. *See also* Unlearn, Relearn, Invest in Yourself (Rule #4)
Don't Be a Waiter (Rule #3), 115–145. *See also* investment, core areas for
   cheat sheet for, 143
   creating as choice, 122–130
   creating vs. waiting, 115–121

   creator economy growth, xi–xii
   defined, 143, 144
   reflection exercises, 145
   transitioning from waiter to creator, 130–135
Doorknock Mission to the United States (American Chamber of Commerce), 2
dreams, pursuing, 118, 132–134
Driscoll, Mark, 29
Drucker, Peter, 152
Dubai Future Foundation, 93–95
dwelling on past, 270

E

Easterly, Jen, 100
Egypt
   American Chamber of Commerce (AmCham), 1–2, 155
   author's move to, 30–39
   business culture of, 34, 69–71
   Obama's state visit to, 126
   prime minister's office of, 2–12, 231
   Rise Up (tech event), 74
   uprising (2011), 126, 177–184
empathy, 198
entrepreneurship. *See also* Don't Be a Waiter (Rule #3); investment, core areas for
   building value for yourself, 128
   core areas of investment for, 277–289
   creator economy growth, xi–xii
   growth of, xi–xii
   personal brand for side hustle, 221–222
execution, for Value Creation, 85–86
"Executive Lectures" (Minnesota State University, Mankato), 103

F

Facebook, 81, 177–179, 184, 220, 261, 278, 284, 290
failure. *See also* Live with No Regrets (Rule #7)
   fear of, 17, 129
   learning from, 271
Federal Reserve System, 165
financial issues
   doing work for free and, 78, 84, 237–238
   financial literacy and improvement, 165–171
   reputational risk vs. financial reward, 234
   valuing people over profit, 232–234

INDEX

first time experiences, creating, 92–95
Fitzgerald, Richard, 40–41, 41, 47
Floyd, George, 162
focus, 39–47
Franklin, Benjamin, 1
frictionless experience, 284–286
FTX, 186

G

Gaber Abouelenein Scholarship, 149
Gandhi, Mahatma, 147
GaryVee, 72, 230–232. *See also* Vaynerchuk, Gary
General Mills, 29, 32, 90–92
Generation Alpha (Gen Alpha), 279–280
gig economy, 167–168
goals, adaptation of, 17
Goldman Sachs, xi
Gold-Onwude, Ros, 88
Google, 13–14, 55, 73, 126–127, 154, 178–184, 261
Gordon, Jeff, 92
Green room, networking in, 245
growth. *See also* Unlearn, Relearn, Invest in Yourself (Rule #4)
  growth mindset as self-reliance characteristic, 23–24
  small opportunities as leading to bigger opportunities, 47

H

Hashad, Hatem, 121
Higgins, Matt, 155–158, 230, 237–238
hiring
  direct messaging for recruiting, 249
  gig economy and, 167–168
  of professional help, 170
  Value Creators, 111. *See also* Value Creation (Rule #2)
Hoffman, Reid, 277
Holmes, Elizabeth, 186

I

Iger, Bob, 152, 245
imposter syndrome, 22–23, 163
informed, staying, 217
initiative, as self-reliance characteristic, 19–20
innovation, 152. *See also* investment, core areas for; Unlearn, Relearn, Invest in Yourself (Rule #4)
Instagram, 278, 284
intentionality, 270–271
internal communication, 191–195
introverts, networking by, 246

investment, core areas for, 277–289
  artificial intelligence (AI), 277–278
  frictionless experience, 284–286
  investing in yourself, 151–153. *See also* Unlearn, Relearn, Invest in Yourself (Rule #4)
  mission and purpose, 278–280
  recreation, wellness, well-being, and play, 280–284
  storytelling, 286–289
IT Cosmetics, 120

J

Jordan, Michael, 134, 271

K

Kennedy, John F., 191
Kerry, John, 100
Kerry, Teresa Heinz, 126
KFC, 199
Khosrowshahi, Dara, 106
King, Gayle, 87
knowledge. *See* Unlearn, Relearn, Invest in Yourself (Rule #4)
The Kris Fade's Show (Virgin Radio), 81
Kwik, Jim, 150

L

Lauder, Estée, 115
learning. *See* Unlearn, Relearn, Invest in Yourself (Rule #4)
Lee, Spike, 88
"Leh Beydary Keda" (Ruby), 43
Leonardi, Paul, 277–278
Leslie, Jack, 53, 55
Lima, Jamie Kern, 120
Limitless (Kwik), 150
Lincoln, Abraham, 177
LINKdotNET, 33
listening, 82. *See also* communication
Live with No Regrets (Rule #7), 259–276
  cheat sheet for, 275
  defined, 274
  principles of, 269–271
  reflection exercises, 276
  setbacks, learning from, 272
  setbacks as normal, xvii, 259–269
Lovin Dubai, 40, 41
Lovin Dublin, 40

M

Mankato State University, 30
Martin, Mark, 91
McKinsey & Company, 167
McNulty, Kevin, ii, 91

meditation, advantages of, 17-18
micro-aggression, 162
Middle East. *See* Egypt; United Arab Emirates
Minnesota State University, Mankato, 103, 148-149
mission, 278-280
Mohammed, Sheikh, 208
Mohan, Neal, 88-89
Momentum, 27
Monaco, Lisa, 100
Moussa, Seham ("Susie"), 147
Mubarak, Hosni, 3, 179, 181
Museum of the Future, 93
Musk, Elon, 209

N

narrative. *See* storytelling
NASA, 191
NASCAR (National Association for Stock Car Auto Racing), 29, 32, 90-92, 298
National Basketball Association, National Basketball Players Association (NBPA), 87, 134, 160
National Basketball Association (NBA), 87-89, 133-134, 160-161
Nazif, Ahmed, 4
needs, anticipation of, 104
negotiation, 169-170
Netflix, 55-56, 73, 204-205
networking
  author's experience with, 251-252
  creating opportunities for others, 86-89, 217-218
  at events, 243-245
  expanding opportunities for, 163, 213
  for introverts, 246
  for learning, 155-158
  for relationship building, 134, 217, 235-242
  on social media, 243-245. *See also* social media
  superconnectors and, 242
Nike, 134
No Ego (Wakeman), 73
non-disclosure agreements (NDA), 48

O

Obama, Barack, 98-100, 122-126
Obama, Michelle, 125-126
O'Brien, Tim, 285, 288
Ohanian, Alexis, 272
online learning, 154-155

online reputation, protecting, 216-217. *See also* Reputation as Currency (Rule #5)
options, exploring, 134-135, 213-214
Orascom Technology Solutions, 32-39, 117
"Overrated vs. Underrated" (Vaynerchuk), 133

P

participation, 216
personal brand. *See also* Reputation as Currency (Rule #5)
  benefits of, 213-214
  building, 30, 205-206
  Crush It! (Vaynerchuk) on, 72-73
  defined, 206-209
  importance of, 212-213, 226
  offline, building, 214, 217-219
  online, building, 214
  personal vs. professional information of, 219-222
  protecting online reputation and offline, 216-217
  qualities of, 209-210
photography
  networking with selfies, 245
  opportunities for, 89
  verifying, 200-201
Picasso, Pablo, 63
Picklemall, 286
PingPod, 286
pivoting, flexibility for, 52-56. *See also* Stay Low, Keep Moving (Rule #1)
play, 280-284
positioning, 65-71
pricing, of products/services, 168-169
professional help, hiring, 170
Promoseven Weber Shandwick, 52-56
purpose, 210, 278-280

R

Radio Row (Super Bowl), 132-133
Rand, Ayn, 165
Reagan, Ronald, 18
recognition, stealth mode vs., 48-50
recreation, 280-284
relationship building. *See also* Value Creation (Rule #2)
  doing work for free/investing time, 77-79, 237-238
  networking for, 134, 217, 235-242. *See also* networking
  relationship maintenance and, 249-250

INDEX

trust for, 184–187, 235
relearning, 161–164
Reputation as Currency (Rule #5), 177–227
  cancel culture and, 187–190
  cheat sheet for, 224–225
  crisis communication and, 177–184, 195–205
  defined, 223
  internal communication and, 191–195
  personal brand and, 205–214, 217–222, 226
  protecting online reputation, 216–217
  reflection exercises, 227
  reputation building, 226
  reputational risk vs. financial reward, 234
  reputation management, 134, 190–191
  trust and, 184–187, 235
research and analysis, 135
rewards, 51–52
Rise Up (tech event), 74
Rohn, Jim, 157
Roush Racing, 91
Ruby (Egyptian singer), 43

S

Sabri, Sherif, 43
Saeed, Khaled, 177
Savvy Talk podcast (Abouelenein), 171, 290, 298
Sawiris, Naguib, 32–39
Sawiris, Nassif, 32
Sawiris, Samih, 32
The Secret (book), 118
"secret sauce" (positioning yourself), 65–71, 132
selfies, networking with, 245
self-reliance, 1–26. *See also* Be a Long-Term Player (Rule #6); Don't Be a Waiter (Rule #3); Live with No Regrets (Rule #7); Reputation as Currency (Rule #5); Stay Low, Keep Moving (Rule #1); Unlearn, Relearn, Invest in Yourself (Rule #4); Value Creation (Rule #2)
  author's experience with. *See* Abouelenein, Maha
  characteristics of, 19–24
  defined, xv, 12–19, 25–26
  detachment and, 51
  importance of, xi
  self-awareness for, 14–19

self-confidence and self-worth for, 19, 129
selling your vision, 101–102
September 11, 2001 terrorist attacks, 54
setbacks. *See* Live with No Regrets (Rule #7)
7 Rules (Facebook group), 290
7 Rules of Self-Reliance. *See also individual rules*
  #1: Stay Low, Keep Moving, 29–60
  #2: Value Creation, 63–112
  #3: Don't Be a Waiter, 115–145
  #4: Unlearn, Relearn, Invest in Yourself, 147–175
  #5: Reputation as Currency, 177–227
  #6: Be a Long-Term Player, 229–256
  #7: Live with No Regrets, 259–276
Sharing the Mic campaign, 162
Sharjah Entrepreneurship Festival (UAE), 80
Sheehan, Michael, 124
Silver, Adam, 87
Sinek, Simon, 241
sleep, need for, 18
smiling, importance of, 105–106
social media. *See also* individual names of social media companies
  author's presence on, 219–220, 290
  direct messaging (DM), 248–249
  focus and, 42
  networking on, 243, 244, 248–2502
  speaking opportunities, 244–245
Spielberg, Steven, 126
"sprints" (Obama administration), 98–101
Starbucks, 189
Stay Low, Keep Moving (Rule #1), 29–60
  cheat sheet for, 58
  defined, 57, 59
  focus for, 39–47
  opportunities to learn with, 30–39
  origin of term, 29–30
  pivoting and flexibility for, 52–56
  reflection exercises, 60
  rewards of, 51–52
  small opportunities as leading to bigger opportunities, 47
  stealth mode for, 48–50
stealth mode, 48–50
storytelling, 214, 236, 286–288
strategic thinking, 134
strength
  recognizing, 89–92
  from struggles, 271
  10X your strengths, 131–132
Super Bowl, 132–133
superconnectors, 242

Survey of Household Economics and Decisionmaking (SHED, Federal Reserve System), 165-166
Swift, Taylor, 119-120

T

technology, investing in yourself and, 151-153. *See also* investment, core areas for
10X your strengths, 131-132
Thatcher, Margaret, 18
Theranos, 186
Top of the Burj (Burj Khalifa), 190-191
transaction thinking, 242
Trump, Donald, 209
Trup, Brandon, xiv
trust, 184-187, 235. *See also* relationship building
20 percent time (Google policy), 13-14

U

Uber, 106
United Airlines, 198-199
United Arab Emirates (UAE)
American University of Sharjah Sharjah, 30
author's work for, 261
Dubai, conducting business in, 102
Dubai Future Foundation, 93-94
Sharjah Entrepreneurship Festival, 80
Top of the Burj, 190-191
United Nations, Climate Change Conference (COP28), 15-16
United States Agency for International Development (USAID), 2
Unlearn, Relearn, Invest in Yourself (Rule #4), 147-175
cheat sheet for, 173
defined, 172
for financial literacy and improvement, 165-171
investing in yourself, importance of, 151-153
knowledge, sharing, 96
learning methods for, 153-158
learning on/from job, 164-165
learning opportunities, recognizing, 30-39
lifelong learning for, 147-151, 174
reflection exercises, 175
relearning, 161-164
unlearning, 158-164
U.S. Bank Stadium, 200-201
U.S. Census Bureau, xii

V

Value Creation (Rule #2), 63-112
cheat sheet for, 109
creating value for others, xvii, 12, 86-89
creating value for yourself, 128, 153-158. *See also* Unlearn, Relearn, Invest in Yourself (Rule #4)
defined, 108, 110
delivery of, 71-85
execution for, 85-86
first time experiences for, 92-95
hiring Value Creators, 111
importance of, 63-65
positioning yourself for, 65-71
principles of, 95-104
reflection exercises, 112
strength recognition for, 89-92
Vaynerchuk, Gary (GaryVee), i, 70, 72-73, 75-85, 88-89, 133-134
VaynerMedia, 75
VeeCon, 196, 200-202
VeeFriends, 200
vigilance, 217
Virgin Radio, 81
visibility, 213
vision, selling, 101-102

W

waiting vs. creating. *See* Don't Be a Waiter (Rule #3)
Wakeman, Cy, 73-75
"We Are All Khaled Said" (Facebook page), 177-179
Weber Shandwick, 52-56, 75
wellness and well-being, 280-284
West, Kanye, 188
Williams, Brian, 180
Williams, Serena, 259
Winfrey, Oprah, 120, 124, 184, 208
women, financial circumstances of, 165-167
work-life balance, remote/hybrid working and effect on, xii-xiii
World Economic Forum, 7-10

Y

Y Combinator, 272
Yousef, Bassem, xvi
YouTube, 88, 133, 154

Z

Zaki, Osama, 147
Zara, 189

ACKNOWLEDGMENTS

As I sit to pen these acknowledgments for my first book, I am filled with a deep sense of gratitude toward a group of exceptional individuals whose support and belief in my journey have been the guiding stars in this endeavor.

First and foremost, to my Editor, Melody Guy. You are the first person who believed in me and guided me throughout this entire journey. My gratitude is immeasurable! The entire team at Hay House is a dream team—thank you, Lizzi, Nusrah, Lindsay, Diane, John, Ellen Jo, Riley, Pip, and Arya-Mehr. I am so lucky to have you as my publisher—TRULY!

My heartfelt thanks to Camila, whose insightful feedback was invaluable. Camila, your keen eye and ability to delve into the intricacies of every story and detail encouraged me to look twice—and then some—at every aspect of my writing. Your contributions have been instrumental in refining this manuscript into what it is today.

To Jackie Hawkins, who managed me, the book, every deadline, and every single detail to bring it to market with me. I am eternally grateful for your calm touch, proactive approach, and all-around incredible value to me and this process. You made everything better—and MORE FUN!

A big thank you to Dan Rovzar, who led the book sales strategy with finesse. To Roman Miranda, Carissa Estreller, and Spenz Serrano: you built an incredible marketing engine! Special thanks to Siddarth Astir for sharing his experience, insights, and much-needed advice—and for picking up the phone every time I called for help. And to Lillian Sotelo for the eye-catching book cover design!

I am grateful to Nena Madonia for her belief not only in the potential of this book but also in me as an author. A special thank you goes to Michele Bender, who supported the book proposal and helped me lift the project off the ground, allowing me to write the book with passion and fervor in every line.

To my team at Digital and Savvy: your support and understanding have been vital in this journey. Your ability to step in when needed, cover for me, and maintain excellence in our projects allowed me the space and peace of mind to focus on bringing this book to life—and to drive all the press and events with heart.

Last but certainly not least, my deepest appreciation goes to my family. Your patience and love have been my anchor. Balancing work and this passion project meant putting so much on hold, and your understanding during this time has meant the world to me. This book is not just a reflection of my efforts but also a testament to the sacrifices and support you have all generously provided. To my sister Amy: you are my role model, my guiding compass, my best friend—and I cannot imagine myself without you. In closing, this book is as much yours as it is mine—a collective labor of love and dedication. To each of you, I am eternally grateful. Stay low, keep moving!

ABOUT THE AUTHOR

Maha Abouelenein is a strategic communication expert and entrepreneur with more than three decades of experience. As the CEO and founder of Digital and Savvy, a global communications consulting firm with offices in the United States and United Arab Emirates, Maha has been instrumental in orchestrating transformations in communication strategies for clients that include global corporate giants, high-growth start-ups, sports organizations, top governments, CEOs, and high net-worth individuals.

With a reputation for delivering results, Maha possesses a unique blend of creative, strategic, and analytical prowess, enabling her to guide projects from inception to execution. Maha is about relationships, including building, nurturing, and serving them. She is an advocate of value creation and the pursuit of cultural relevance as the cornerstones for effective storytelling and communications.

Raised and educated in the United States by Egyptian parents, Maha is at home in both the Western and Arab worlds, offering a global perspective that translates in her work. She serves as a bridge between cultures, providing invaluable support to companies and high-profile executives seeking to navigate business opportunities into the Middle East market including the UAE, Saudi Arabia, and Egypt. She is active in the tech, sports, entertainment, and gaming industries. Maha is an advisor to LockChain.io and sits on the global board of directors of the Associated Press.

She handled communications for some of world's largest tech companies in the Middle East—from Google and Netflix to Udacity and Careem (Uber Middle East) and more. She helped PR giant Weber Shandwick cement their presence in the Middle East, opening 18 offices in the region and leading the Cairo operation. She supported the largest IPO and the largest acquisition in Egypt's history at Orascom Telecom. She also supported promotions and sports marketing programs and strategic partnerships for the Olympics, NASCAR, ATP Tennis, women's hockey, and the NFL at consumer product giant General Mills before becoming an entrepreneur.

A sought-after strategist and speaker, Maha takes the stage to share her expertise on personal branding, reputation management, modern communications, and the transformational power of storytelling. She was honored as one of the most influential women in Dubai, named one of the most impactful Egyptians, and nominated as of one of Forbes Power Women of the Middle East. In the U.S., she was named by *PR News* as one of the Game Changers in the PR industry and one of Minnesota's Leading Women in Business by the *Minneapolis/St. Paul Journal*.

Maha is the host of the *Savvy Talk* podcast, where she engages in thought-provoking conversations with industry leaders. Maha passionately advocates for the power of storytelling and self-reliance in the modern age, emphasizing personal branding as a transformative pathway to leadership. Maha is a dual citizen, an avid tennis player, and resides in Wayzata, Minnesota, with her dog Coco.

We hope you enjoyed this Hay House book. If you'd like to receive our online catalogue featuring additional information on Hay House books and products, please contact:

Hay House UK Ltd
1st Floor, Crawford Corner,
91–93 Baker Street, London W1U 6QQ
Tel: +44 (0)20 3927 7290; www.hayhouse.co.uk

Published in the United States of America by:
Hay House LLC
PO Box 5100, Carlsbad, CA 92018-5100
Tel: (760) 431-7695 or (800) 654-5126
www.hayhouse.com

Published in Australia by:
Hay House Australia Publishing Pty Ltd
18/36 Ralph St., Alexandria NSW 2015
Tel: +61 (02) 9669 4299
www.hayhouse.com.au

Published in India by:
Hay House Publishers (India) Pvt Ltd
Muskaan Complex, Plot No. 3,
B-2, Vasant Kunj, New Delhi 110 070
Tel: +91 11 41761620
www.hayhouse.co.in

Let Your Soul Grow

Experience life-changing transformation – one video at a time – with guidance from the world's leading experts.

www.healyourlifeplus.com

CONNECT WITH
HAY HOUSE
ONLINE

hayhouse.co.uk   @hayhouse

@hayhouseuk   @hayhouseuk.bsky.social

@hayhouseuk   @HayHousePresents

Find out all about our latest books & card decks • Be the first to know about exclusive discounts • Interact with our authors in live broadcasts • Celebrate the cycle of the seasons with us • Watch free videos from your favourite authors • Connect with like-minded souls

'The gateways to wisdom and knowledge are always open.'

Louise Hay